STOP MAKING SENSE

PSYCHOANALYSIS AND POPULAR CULTURE SERIES

Series Editors: Caroline Bainbridge and Candida Yates

Consulting Editor: Brett Kahr

Other titles in the Psychoanalysis and Popular Culture Series:

Television and Psychoanalysis: Psycho-Cultural Perspectives
  edited by Caroline Bainbridge, Ivan Ward, and Candida Yates

The Inner World of Doctor Who: Psychoanalytic Reflections in Time and Space
  by Iain MacRury and Michael Rustin

The Psychodynamics of Social Networking: Connected-up Instantaneous Culture and the Self
  by Aaron Balick

STOP MAKING SENSE

Music from the Perspective of the Real

Scott Wilson

Routledge
Taylor & Francis Group

LONDON AND NEW YORK

First published 2015 by Karnac Books Ltd.

Published 2018 by Routledge
2 Park Square, Milton Park, Abingdon, Oxon OX14 4RN
711 Third Avenue, New York, NY 10017, USA

Routledge is an imprint of the Taylor & Francis Group, an informa business

British Library Cataloguing in Publication Data

A C.I.P. for this book is available from the British Library

ISBN 9781782201984 (pbk)

Edited, designed and produced by The Studio Publishing Services Ltd
www.publishingservicesuk.co.uk
e-mail: studio@publishingservicesuk.co.uk

CONTENTS

for Petra

ACKNOWLEDGEMENTS

I should like to acknowledge a number of people who have read or commented or enabled in some way the production of this book and its various chapters: Caroline Bainbridge, Marie Hélène Brousse, Edia Connole, Suzanne Dow, Sam Goodman, Paul Hegarty, Eleni Ikoniadou, Petra Jackson, Nicola Masciandaro, Graham Matthews, Svitlana Matviyenko, Michael O'Rourke, Simon O'Sullivan, Richard Rushton, Karin Sellberg, Ron Tweedy, Hager Weslati, Ann Wilbourn, Véronique Voruz, Colin Wright, Natalie Wülfing, and Candida Yates.

Some material in this book has appeared before in other publications. Parts of Chapter Five first appeared in "Amusia, noise and the drive: towards a theory of the audio unconscious", in Goddard, Halligan, and Hegarty (Eds.), *Reverberations: The Philosophy, Aesthetics and Politics of Noise*. London: Continuum Press, 2012, pp. 16–25. It is reprinted with permission from Bloomsbury Press, plc. Chapter Fourteen appeared as "The Braindance of the Hikikomori: towards a return to speculative psychoanalysis", *Paragraph*, (2010) 33(3), Edinburgh University Press, pp. 392–409 and appears with permission from Edinburgh University Press. Material from Chapters Thirteen and Fourteen appear in "Violence and love: in which Yoko Ono encourages Slavoj Žižek to Give Peace a Chance" in Goodman and Matthews (Eds.), *Violence and the Limits of Representation*. London: Palgrave, and appears with permission from Palgrave.

ABOUT THE AUTHOR

Scott Wilson is Professor of Media and Psychoanalysis at the London Graduate School, Kingston University, London. His books include *The Order of Joy: Beyond the Cultural Politics of Enjoyment* (SUNY Press, 2008); *Great Satan's Rage: American Negativity and Rap/Metal in the Age of Supercapitalism* (Manchester University Press, 2008); and *Melancology: Black Metal and Ecology* (Zero Books, 2014). He is the editor, with Michael Dillon, of the *Journal for Cultural Research* (Taylor & Francis).

The application of psychoanalytic ideas and theories to culture has a long tradition and this is especially the case with cultural artefacts that might be considered "classical" in some way. For Sigmund Freud, the works of William Shakespeare and Johann Wolfgang von Goethe were as instrumental as those of culturally renowned poets and philosophers of classical civilisation in helping to formulate the key ideas underpinning psychoanalysis as a psychological method. In the academic fields of the humanities and social sciences, the application of psychoanalysis as a means of illuminating the complexities of identity and subjectivity is now well established. However, despite these developments, there is relatively little work that attempts to grapple with popular culture in its manifold forms, some of which, nevertheless, reveal important insights into the vicissitudes of the human condition.

The "Psychoanalysis and Popular Culture" book series builds on the work done since 2009 by the Media and the Inner World research network, which was generously funded by the UK's Arts and Humanities Research Council. It aims to offer spaces to consider the relationship between psychoanalysis in all its forms and popular culture that is ever more emotionalised in the contemporary age.

In contrast to many scholarly applications of psychoanalysis, which often focus solely on "textual analysis", this series sets out to explore the creative tension of thinking about cultural experience and its processes with attention to observations from the clinical and scholarly fields of observation. What can academic studies drawing on psychoanalysis learn from the clinical perspective and how might the critical insights afforded by scholarly work cast new light on clinical experience? The series provides space for a dialogue between these different groups with a view to creating fresh perspectives on the values and pitfalls of a psychoanalytic approach to ideas of selfhood, society, and popular culture. In particular, the series strives to develop a psycho-cultural approach to such questions by drawing attention to the usefulness of post-Freudian and object relations perspectives for examining the importance of emotional relationships and experience.

Stop Making Sense: Music from the Perspective of the Real makes an invaluable contribution to this project. Drawing on a Lacanian paradigm of psychoanalysis, the author, Scott Wilson, articulates a compelling new theory of music as an art form that prompts unique modes of social bonding that can be understood as emanating not from the register of the imaginary, but, rather, from that of the real. In this way, Wilson argues, music can be understood as playing a mediating function for the subject, one that allows the subject to transcend the restrictive boundaries of sense-making in order to glimpse something of the often agonising intimacy of subjectivity and relatedness. For Wilson, Lacan's excursions into the real provide a tool with which to excavate the sonic reality that underpins the subject's modalities of being. The author offers a witty and erudite *tour de force* in this work, which encompasses such diverse themes as neoliberalism, delusion, psychosis, love, agony, and ecstasy. All of this is brought to life for the reader in a series of playful and compelling readings of the work of musical artists including The Beatles, Brian Eno, Yoko Ono, Hank Williams, Phil Collins, and Johann Sebastian Bach. The book makes a timely and engaging contribution to the series, showing the ways in which music in all its forms operates in exchange with the unconscious registers of experience.

Caroline Bainbridge and Candida Yates
Series Editors

The obscure origins of this book lie in a parlour game that was devised a few years ago as a response to boredom with the music played at dinner parties. While enjoying the hospitality of a friend, a number of guests declared that they could no longer bear the music she was playing. While the host agreed that she was also tired of her collection, she was, nevertheless, affronted. Flicking back raven hair, she issued a challenge that met with counter-challenges that thus gave rise to a game of devilish intersubjectivity. The aim of this game would be to inflict the maximum pain on all the other players with the choice of a song. Each member would choose a song in a competition to discover, by democratic means, which was the most unbearable. The constraint, however, would be that one had to confess, on one's honour, to loving the song in question. There would be two rounds, and voting would take place after each round, the awfulness of each song being ranked on a scale of 1–10. At the same time, contestants would attempt to identify the owner of each track of shame.

I cannot remember all the entries, but on this particular night a Hawkwind track complete with a ten-minute drum solo contested Neil Diamond's "I Am, I Said" alongside a Boredoms track that consisted of two and a half minutes of belching. None of these could match the winner, however, Nick Cave's "A Box for Black Paul", which narrowly defeated "Guitar Man" by David Gates and Bread. Nine minutes of tuneless doom-laden, howling pretension was stoutly defended by its advocate as "post-parodic genius".

The second round raised the stakes by introducing an example of 1970s German pop, Merle Haggard, Courtney Love, and some more Japanese noise that met with howls of derision. Way too entertaining. Profound, intense groans of agony, however, were produced by Judy Tzuke's "Stay With Me Till Dawn". Indeed, this looked the likely winner until the final track was played: "The Carpet Crawlers" by Genesis. It took some time for people to recover from their own carpet crawling, biting, and gnashing of teeth. But when they did, there was no question which song would win, by a unanimous vote.

Ahh, Phil Collins . . . of whom more will be heard later.

* * *

This book offers a new theory of music as a form of social bond analogous to, but quite distinct from, language as it is understood according to the Lacanian orientation in psychoanalysis. Located in a mediating position between the subject and the real, music is here regarded as a form of social bond analogous to, but quite distinct from, the language of speech, operating "outside sense". In so doing, the book contributes to work on psychoanalysis, music, and sound studies even as it takes issue with the central premise informing that work. For the tradition represented by Mladan Dolar, *A Voice and Nothing More* (2006), David Schwarz, *Listening Subjects* (1997), and Kaja Silverman, *The Acoustic Mirror* (1988), the role of sound is reduced to voice and voice, somewhat paradoxically, to the Imaginary register, thereby subordinating sound to vision.

The book has three parts: a first part that explains its theoretical and methodological underpinnings that are based in a reading of subjects and symptoms, and second and third parts focusing on contemporary examples that look at how music has become both a powerful locus of discontent and a form of orientation in an age of "ordinary psychosis" (Jacques-Alain Miller), figured by the conjunction of avant-garde music, techno-science, and economic rationality that has rendered the conventional distinction between music and noise arbitrary.

I take music to have three essential elements: it is an organised, particulate system of sounds that is related both to noise and the voice. In the book, I show how the relation between these three elements operates in various ways broadly analogous to the clinical structures that provide the basis of psychoanalytic diagnosis. As is well known, these structures are all, in the Lacanian clinic, an effect of language and an unconscious that is structured like a language, following certain principles of structural linguistics derived from Saussure and Roman Jakobson concerning the signifier and the function of metaphor and metonymy. In his elucidation of these functions, Lacan famously had recourse to the condition of aphasia. Here, I appropriate the neurological condition of amusia, where music as a specific form (both mathematical and social/cultural) is perceived as an agonising noise. Accordingly, I coin the term *a*musia where the "*a*" marks the point of the intimate exteriority of dissonance with the social bond that the cultural form of music instantiates from the position of the real that is outside sense. The "*a*" denotes the noise not just left over from the cut in sound produced by music, but also the point of singular enunciation and discordance with one's own sonic reality. Throughout, this notion of *a*musia is developed in relation to three well-known figures who have not only inverted the traditional distinction between music and noise evident in amusia, but have deterritorialised it from the concerns of an individual perception or symptom. The electronic ambient sounds of Brian Eno, the operatic screams of Yoko Ono, and the formidable noise-music of Merzbow operate at the *a*musical limits of music.

The book argues that music can be the vehicle of a specifically audio unconscious through the offices of dissonance and repetition, offering different modalities of being, or of regulating *jouissance*, particularly in the cases of psychosis and autism. Indeed, the clearest evidence for the approximate symbolic dimension of music is found in psychosis, where music can both sustain a relation to reality, and provide a reasonably stable basis for delusion in the face of the abyss opened out by foreclosure from the paternal signifier. This is evident in the case of Judge Schreber himself, but here I consider two other examples: the cases of the mathematician John F. Nash Jr, subject of the film *A Beautiful Mind* (Howard, 2001) and author of the "Nash equilibrium" that provided the basis for the social justification of neoliberal economics, and Mark Chapman, the first American to assassinate someone on the basis of his music. Both Nash and Chapman were, in their different ways, affected by various series of screams associated with The Beatles. They have this in common with many others born in the latter half of the twentieth century, of course, but the cultural dimension of music and its relation to symbolised reality through the power of delusion is discussed in this book in the context of the social transformations introduced by Anglo-American neoliberalism from the end of the 1970s. The great neoliberal experiment has, it seems, in no way been abandoned following the financial crisis of 2008, quite the contrary. For Michel Foucault, American neoliberalism is not an update of a theory of the state of nature, but a form of governance that generates a subject that bears all the hallmarks of psychosis understood in Lacanian terms. If this experiment culminated in 2008 with the spectacle of the virtual collapse of neoliberal capitalism through the negative equilibrium achieved through the paralysis of paranoid bankers unwilling to lend to each other, then this is entirely consistent with the structure outlined here. If not "ordinary psychosis", as outlined by Miller, it constitutes, nevertheless, an imperative to behave *as if* one were psychotic in Lacan's classical sense. The exemplary sociological figure that symptomatises this general condition and the effects of its acceleration by globalised telecommunication is the "hikikomori". This is the Japanese name for youths who have withdrawn from all conventional social contact, sunk in quasi-autistic *jouissance* engaged in computer-based entertainments.

This book, therefore, looks at the cultural and social role of music as an open as well as closed system where, throughout, the audio unconscious locus of *a*musical desire can be tracked, outside sense. Music is often regarded as a "language" of the real in two senses: as a particulate system of essentially meaningless notes and tones that nevertheless provide regularities offering structure and orientation, and as the language of love, a means of mediating *jouissance* or the agonies and ecstasies that result from the real of sexual difference. With reference to specific examples drawn from the different clinical categories of Lacanian psychoanalysis, this book argues that music can be an art form that is organised around this perspective of the real, bringing for those speaking beings stuck in sense an other *jouissance*—

and where *jouissance* was an other knowledge may follow—of a different form of orientation. *Stop making sense!*

Look how the floor of heaven
Is thick inlaid with patens of bright gold.
There's not the smallest orb which thou behold'st
But in his motion like an angel sings,
Still choiring to the young-eyed cherubins.
Such harmony is in immortal souls,
But whilst this muddy vesture of decay
Doth grossly close it in, we cannot hear it.

(William Shakespeare, *The Merchant of Venice*)

Introduction: Fear of music

> "I was walking along a path with two friends—the sun was setting—suddenly the sky turned blood red—I paused, feeling exhausted, and leaned on the fence—there was blood and tongues of fire above the blue-black fjord and the city—my friends walked on, and I stood there trembling with anxiety—and I sensed an infinite scream passing through nature"
>
> (Edvard Munch, *Journal*, Nice, 22 January 1892)

Whether it was the volcanic eruption that burst from Krakatoa to leave a blood-red sky from 1883–1884, the scream of nature red in tooth and claw, or the dying agonies of God, the strange figure in Edvard Munch's famous painting presses its hands against its ears in horror and agony. *The Scream* is not just a single image created in 1893, of course, but a series of images produced between 1893 and 1910. It is a series of repetitions of the same image of profound dissonance with one's sonic environment. One of the most resonant images of the twentieth century and beyond, *The Scream* reverberates in aspects of culture from the exalted to the disposable. Among many other things, it is a powerful statement that the heavens no longer resound with the music of the spheres, but are rent by a primal scream that fulminates from the dawn of time. While in this muddy vesture of decay we cannot hear the harmony of immortal souls, and neither do we believe in them any more; we do sense an inhuman voice: a scream passing through nature, and the more we cover our ears against its background radiation, the more loudly it echoes throughout inner and outer space like cosmic tinnitus.

Munch was almost the exact contemporary of Sigmund Freud and his anguished figure could easily have been the father of psychoanalysis himself, since reportedly, "when exposed to music while out on the town in Vienna or Munich [Freud's] automatic response was to immediately place his hands over his ears to block out the sound" (Diamond, 2012, p. 1). Freud, it seems, suffered from a form of melaphobia, the fear or hatred of music. As we shall see in Chapter Two, Freud's displeasure with music was associated with ignorance: "a turn of mind in me rebels against being moved by a thing without knowing why I am thus affected and what it is affects me" (Freud, 1914b, p. 211). Freud's distress concerned the fact that music does not make sense, and yet affects or moves him without him knowing why. This lack of knowledge Freud has in common, ironically, with many musical geniuses, those who attest to knowing nothing about the source of their inspiration or quite why a particular phrase or series of notes brings joy or sorrow. This apparently senseless "other knowledge" conventionally associated with music transcends the particular *savoir-faire*, or know-how, it takes to make it, just as it transcends the musical ignorance that nevertheless hears and is affected by it in pleasure or pain, or often a combination of both. It is this relation between the non-sense of music and its powerful affectivity (for better or worse) that is the subject of this book. It is in this dynamic relation, which operates alongside language in the context of a world of speaking beings, that we can discern the movements of a specifically audio unconscious.

In his book *Against Understanding: Commentary and Critique in a Lacanian Key* (2014), Bruce Fink underscores the essential idea that "the primary goal of psychoanalysis . . . is not understanding but change" (p. 5). The process of understanding, making sense, formulating conclusions, all too quickly "reduces the unfamiliar to the familiar, transforms the radically other into the same" (Fink, 2014, p. i). Understanding always refers to that which one already knows and is, thus, a locus of fantasy. At the same time, it is precisely the senseless that provides the source of all possible understanding. As Jacques-Alain Miller avers, "one is never taught by anything other than that which one doesn't understand. One is never taught by anything other than by nonsense" (Miller, 2013a, p. 18). For psychoanalysis, the important thing is to move the subject to speech and the affectivity of music is precisely something that both broaches speech and its limits, an enigmatic form that points to the conjunction of speech and the unconscious desire that exceeds it, that seeks to go beyond words. For Freud, there was something fearful about music that indicated a repressed desire. The melophobia that made Freud clasp his hands to his ears in the presence of music, the sonic experience of fear and desire about which he professed his ignorance, will be discussed in more detail in Chapter Two. For now, it might be worth considering the significance, if any, of the experience of music as an object of phobia by way of an introduction to the main themes of this book.

The founding text in the psychoanalytic clinic of phobia is Freud's case study on Little Hans, following the example of which a particular phobia always contains for psychoanalysis a certain utility and value in that it crystallises in an object indefinite fears or anxieties. When it occurs very early in life, such crystallisation supports the process of individuation that senses mortal danger from the very universe that has given rise to it. As Freud suggested in the case of Little Hans, phobia is an effect of the question that being raises for the subject "from where he was before the subject came into the world" (Lacan, 2006, p. 432). For the infant, this place is, of course, the mother's body, a site of dependency but also, perhaps, potential re-engulfment. There are plenty of animal mothers who eat their young, after all. Anxiety may occur the moment the discontinuity sensed by an infant apprehends the vulnerability of its existence in the felt presence of a voracious outside. For Jacques Lacan, a phobia is an imaginary object that supplements through substitution the relative failure of the paternal function to place a symbolic limit on maternal demand. Phobia is sometimes regarded as an effect of a lack of boundaries; the phobic object, therefore, has a paradoxical nature in that it is an object of fear that also operates as a kind of boundary, a form of protection.

One can only speculate why music may function in this way. Apparently audible in the womb, along with, and in contradistinction to, the mother's voice, music is often associated with the "oceanic" feeling that Freud suggests provides "the source of religious energy", since it derives from the pleasurable residue of an infantile sense of "limitlessness and a bond with the universe" (Freud, 1930a, pp. 64–65). Confessing that he is incapable of discovering such a feeling in himself (p. 72), Freud further notes that such a feeling is in fact the expression of a strong need for protection. "The derivation of religious needs [derives] from the infant's helplessness and longing for the father" and the protection he represents (p. 72). For Lacan, and those who follow the Lacanian orientation in psychoanalysis, the father or paternal function associated with his name is there to provide a boundary to such a feeling of limitlessness which, when it comes up against non-pleasurable objects and excitations, can rapidly become a locus of manifold fears. Operating precisely like a phobic object, the God of Solomon and the Old Testament is the crystallisation of such fears. In Seminar III, Lacan pays tribute to the inventors of a God through which these innumerable fears are replaced "by the fear of a unique being who has no other means of manifesting his power than what is feared behind those innumerable fears" (Lacan, 1993, p. 267).

From creaking floors to things that go bump in the night, sound, as David Toop explores in *Sinister Resonance* (2010), has a singular capacity to evoke fear even as music has charms to soothe the savage breast, in the well-known phrase of William Congreve. The most minimal definition of music holds that it is a particular organisation of sound, the principle of order providing, no doubt, the reassurance of form that a sudden eruption of noise disorientates. Another element is, of course, song and the musical element of the maternal voice that provides the basis, through imitation, for the speech of the infant. Perhaps melophobia has to do with this double or triple nature of music, the sense of the noise that evokes fear, on the one hand, the association with the materiality of voice, especially in its plaintive mode as a vehicle of longing, demand, and desire, and, on the other, with the precision of mathematical form. All are essential here precisely because, in Lacanian terms, they are exterior to the linguistic signifier and, thus, the name-of-the-father. That is to say, in the fear of music there is the threatening sound of the outside, the memory of the terrifying proximity of maternal demand, and the melophobic protection of a heterogeneous form in the absence of the paternal signifier.

The threefold nature of music

There are two apparently contrary Greek myths concerning the origin of music. The most familiar myth, from Homer, accounts for the invention of the lyre by Hermes when he discovers that a turtle shell can produce sound. With this discovery that given materials of the universe have pleasing sonic properties, comes ultimately the whole post-Pythagorean notion that music is a kind of sonic maths and, as such, is consistent with the laws of the universe revealed by mathematics. The contrary myth, from Pindar's Twelfth Pythian Ode, concerns Pallas Athena who, upon hearing of Perseus's slaying of Medusa, attempts to connect with "the sorrowful lamentations" of her sisters, and "framed the full-sounded harmony of the reeds that she might imitate with instruments the deep groans proceeding from Euryale's fell cheeks" (Pindar, "Pythians Ode XII: to Midas of Agragas", in West, 1964). The Medusa's head, with her snakes for hair, used subsequently as an escutcheon of terror, has long been associated with fear and, since Freud, castration, female genitalia, and desire (Freud, 1963, pp. 202–203). Music is here established in relation to fear, desire, and death, providing form and vehicle for an enunciation that groans in mourning, railing at the senselessness of death, the reeds giving voice to inexpressible sorrow. Thus, Athena passes on the invention of the flute to mortals for the entertainment of the people, even though music never quite escapes the melancholy tenor of its origins, "Whatso of bliss is among men, ne'er does it appear unmingled with woes" (Pindar, Ode XII, in West, 1964). In its ability to give an ordered expression to the otherwise inexpressible pain of mourning, to give form to the formlessness of feminine *jouissance*, structure to non-sense, the musical "reed" operates as a kind of phallus that would suggest its utility as an object of phobia in Lacanian terms. But not just phobia; as we shall see, all the main diagnostic categories in psychoanalysis can be discerned in particular arrangements of music, voice, and noise.

In general, however, in its rare discussions of music, Lacanian psychoanalysis emphasises voice. Along with the gaze, voice as an example of *objet petit a* is one of the key Lacanian contributions to the psychoanalytic theory of object relations. Like *The Scream*, Lacanian psychoanalysis usually hears only the voice of demand or suffering rather than music as a symbolic form that, moreover, many believe bears in its mathematical properties the formula for the real. Music is generally of interest to psychoanalysis where it is regarded as "a voice and nothing more" (Dolar, 2006), that is, stripped of any aesthetic qualities or semblance of meaning that might be attributed to it. But in this, psychoanalysis is no different from the history of western philosophy. If epistemology privileges sight and light (insight, concept, *theoria*, enlightenment, and so on), ontology privileges voice; it is "phonocentric", in the vocabulary of Jacques Derrida. "There has only ever been one ontological proposition", wrote Gilles Deleuze, famously: "Being is univocal" (Deleuze, 1997, p. 35). From Parmenides to Heidegger, Duns Scotus to Deleuze himself, "it is the same voice that is taken up, in an echo which itself forms the whole deployment of the univocal" (p. 35). In this book, I am suggesting that music be regarded as quite distinct from language, even speech, though not entirely from enunciation. Speech and music are separate even when they may be brought together in the same site of enunciation or in the same object, as in a song. Indeed, music can take the place of, or enable, the development of speech, as in some cases of autism and aphasia. In this book, it is essential that music not be regarded as a subcategory of language. It is not a pre- or proto-language; it is not the pure materiality of language, the excess of language, or *lalangue*.

Lalangue and the real unconscious

However, in so far as musical form derives from the tradition of song, it can be said to emerge alongside, but distinct from, speech. In her book *Lacan—The Unconscious Reinvented* (2014), Colette Soler iterates the usual psychoanalytic positioning of music as a pre-symbolic effect of maternal voice, but with a significant difference of central importance to the argument of this book. Soler argues that later in his career, Lacan revises his initial understanding of the unconscious as structured like a language to a notion of the "Real unconscious" that is an effect of *lalangue*. *Lalangue* refers both to *"langue"*, the reservoir of virtual signifiers necessarily prior to any actual articulation of speech, or *"parole"*, and "lallation", from the Latin *lallare*, which refers to the act of singing "la, la'" (as in a lullaby, for example) to infants who might imitate them in preparation for speech (or, indeed, song). As the example of singing indicates, "langue" as "an inconsistent multiplicity of differential elements that do not fix meaning" (Soler, 2014, p. 10) can equally refer to those elements of sound that become organised as notes and tones in pieces of music as they can refer to phonemes and words. Soler argues that in the later Lacan there is in the production of the unconscious a "move from the causal incidence of language to *lalangue*" (p. 32) This means that while the unconscious is an effect of a system of differences, those differential elements do not have to be words. Moreover, their resonance can be all the more affective (and effective in the unconscious) through their repetition, the repetition of an initial dissonance—Soler cites Lacan's "example of the slap that . . . runs from one generation to the next" (p. 32). Soler's first point, then, is that "the unconscious is a direct effect of these elements" that operate purely at the level of sound rather than language (p. 32). Second, the sonorous nature of these repetitive sounds of lallation "do not exclude the function of the Other" through which the subject is symbolised as a subject even though they are without syntax or sense:

> La, la, la, like one precedes any two in the chain. For this reason, the enigmatic ones in the song of what is heard have a direct effect when they are linked to the enigma of sex. Lacan hammered it home often enough that there is no pre-verbal for the one who speaks, but that there is pre-language in the sense of syntax. The song—or better still, the "melody"—of the parents is not the message of the Other and exceeds it, just as the unconscious as *lalangue* exceeds the unconscious as language. (Soler, 2014, p. 33)

It is interesting here how Soler's words exceed the message of Lacan in the sense that she moves from the "song" of the Other to its "melody", a sequence of notes that is formally independent from any voice that might sing it. The verbal is exceeded here relative to music as a symbolic form, along with the parents that the melody passes through, and the unconscious as language. No doubt this is why Soler is keen to "limit the responsibility of parents to their children" in the effect that the melody of the Other produces in the unconscious because of the contingent nature of the "encounter [*tuché*] in the way one hears", the radical singularity of the dissonant or traumatic encounter with the real that, while "missed", is iterated in the automaton of unconscious repetition that, as an effect of pure sound, is articulated just as well—if not better—in music as in language. In this way, the lallation of *lalangue* produces the Real unconscious as opposed to the one structured like a language. "*Lalangue* is not Symbolic but Real. Real, because it is made of ones outside the chain and thus outside meaning (the signifier becomes real when it is outside the chain), and of ones which are enigmatically fused with *jouissance*" (Soler, 2014, p. 35). But in this move from the symbolic to the real unconscious, we can surely take a path through music where the "ones" resonate outside sense more (or just as) sonorously than with words. Indeed, the symbolic form of music, of a particular melody or refrain, is closer to the Real in this respect, a way through which the kernel of a particular musical or "amusical" symptom or symbolic formation can be perceived from the perspective of the real and, thereby, point the way to its resolution (Soler, 2014, p. 36).

So, while it is important to distinguish music itself from *lalangue* and the site of the maternal voice and body, there is no question that the imaginary effects of music are immense. Music cannot be entirely reduced to the imaginary register as the mirror of reflected meaning or significance that makes sense to the ego, but, at the same time, music is a profound locus of delusion—not least in the idea that it has special powers of speech. Indeed, the heterogeneity of music and voice is evident in the desire that music speak, that it say what words cannot say. Conventionally, music is attributed with a special, imaginary power of speech, that it is able to address the question of existence in a way that escapes language. That this is indeed a delusion does not dispel the desire for musical speech, but, further, in a way that is neither reducible to the imaginary nor the residue or substrate of speech and language, music as a specific form and structure generates effects of an audio or real unconscious. As such, it must be distinguished from speech even though it is no doubt the case that music only has significance—only has *meaning*—for speaking beings in so far as it is misperceived as speech. But music that resonates from the perspective of the real says nothing and has no meaning, any more than mathematics. The correspondences that are found in mathematics and music seem to suggest that they must mean something, but they do not. "To extract a natural law is to extract a meaningless formula", says Lacan, similarly a refrain. Formulae consist of "pure signifiers", and "the idea that such a signifier might signify something . . . means that God is present in natural phenomena and speaks to us in his language" (Lacan, 1993, p. 184). Since music has no propositional content, no reference to anything other than itself, no predication, it actually makes no sense to say it is either meaningful or meaningless, since "music does not even have the *possibility* of being meaningful" in a linguistic sense (see Patel, 2008, p. 304). It is, therefore, outside the opposition that might make the term "meaningless" meaningful as an effect of linguistic difference. Music has no relation to meaning, not even a negative relation. Music is not a code; it cannot be decoded.

It is a different question with the psychoanalytic notion of voice, however, which is also held distinct from language and from meaningful speech. Miller (2007) defines the category of voice "as everything in the signifier that does not partake in the effect of signification", and "precisely that which cannot be said" (pp. 141, 145). To the degree to which music can be regarded as an "unspeakable object", it can be subsumed into the category of voice. However, music as an object has a specific form that can be related to, and distinguished from, both formlessness and noise. I take music to have three essential elements: music, noise, and voice.

First, in its most minimal definition as a particular arrangement or organisation of sound, music makes a "cut" in sound that is related to the dissonant noise to which it refers, retrospectively, as its formless origin, and the noise that falls out or remains excluded from the specific sonic arrangement. Second, then, some notion of noise, of non-music, is essential to music even though any sound and, therefore, any noise can be music. Noise cannot be simply opposed to music as in the sense of disorganised sound; there is no noise as such in this respect, merely difference—or, rather, dissonance. Moreover, if we are to believe Pythagoras and his followers, there is no disorganised sound since, in so far as it is comprised of laws, the whole universe is music. Indeed, as we know from John Cage, any temporal framing, echo, or iteration immediately provides the minimal form of organisation necessary for the perception of music. Yet, precisely because music here is defined as an effect of repetition that either confirms the regularity necessary to determine the existence of mathematical laws, or provides the merest basis of sonic reflection necessary to perceive organization, such repetition must be preceded by some initial, no doubt mythical, irruption of pure dissonance that is missed, hidden behind the noise that heralds the drive to come that will be captured by the awareness of sound and its resonance. This primordial dissonance, therefore, inhabits music as its real orientation prior to the voice that similarly inhabits the discourse of the Other for Lacan. As Miller confirms, this

> voice inhabits language, it haunts it. It is enough to speak for the menace to emerge that what cannot be said could come to light. If we speak that much, if we organize symposiums, if we chat, if we sing and listen to singers, if we play music and listen to it, Lacan's thesis implies that it is in order to silence what warrants to be called the voice as object little *a*. (Miller, 2007, p. 145)

Lucidly, Miller defines the Lacanian category of voice in contradistinction to language, speech, and, indeed, music even as he implies its necessity to all. With regard to music, this voice emanates from a site of enunciation that articulates the subject's own inherent senselessness, noise, or dissonance to that of the universe. Yet, following this notion of voice as object *a*, it is possible to produce a new term, "*amusia*", appropriated from the condition of melophobia, where the "*a*" marks the point of the intimate exteriority of dissonance to the repetition that articulates music. The "*a*" denotes the noise not just left over from the cut in sound produced by music, but the point of singular enunciation and discordance with one's own sonic reality.

The perspective of the real

We know very well from Lacan's seminal chapter in Seminar 11, *The Four Fundamental Concepts of Psychoanalysis*, that the encounter with the real is always missed and that it is located beyond the repetition that it nevertheless inaugurates: "the real is that which always hides behind the automaton" (Lacan, 1986, pp. 53–54). At the same time, it seems, in the history of psychoanalysis the automaton is always *heralded* by sound, some startling or traumatic sound that awakens the dream of life and sets in motion the battery of signifiers that articulate the drive. For Freud, it was the "shell shock" that caused the traumatic neuroses of soldiers otherwise uninjured from the battles of the war in Europe from 1914–1918 that provided the context for his reflections on "repetition compulsion", the "death drive" and the trauma that is eventually mastered by symbolisation in *Beyond the Pleasure Principle* (Freud, 1920g). Lacan uses the example of some mysterious "knocking" that kicks off and forms the representational basis of his own

dream that he suggests, poised between perception and consciousness, was attempting to keep him asleep. He then connects this
facet of his own dream to the dream of the burning child, another
dream "made up entirely of noise" that is predicated on "a noise
made to recall [the dreamer] to the real", but which merely hints at
another reality beyond it, inherent to the dream of sound and meaning. Lacan could not be clearer here: noise is not the real, even though
it is through noise that the real makes itself felt and which forms the
basis of the drive that will be articulated in the chain of sounds that
form language—and, indeed, music.

> The real may be represented by the accident, the noise, the small
> element of reality, which is evidence that we are not dreaming. But,
> on the other hand, this reality is not so small, for what wakes us is the
> other reality hidden behind the lack of that which takes the place of
> representation – this, says Freud is the *Trieb*. But . . . if, for the lack of
> representation, it is not there, what is this *Trieb*? We may have to
> consider it as being only *Trieb* to come. (Lacan, 1986, p. 60)

It is only at this point, with the arrival of the drive heralded by the
noise that masks the insistent silence of the real that any "perspective"
may be organised in the sense of depth of either sound or vision.
Perspective is an attribute of the drive and its aim. Accordingly, the
sense of perspective is orientated around the particular noise in which
the real insists in both the site of its enunciation, on the one hand, and
the particular mode of organisation perceived in its repetition, on the
other. The real is not noise, then, which logically means it must be
silence, which, moreover, as both art and science attest, is impossible.
For Lacan, the real is not noise, not least because noise always heralds
the *Vorstellung*, the chain of representations that encircle and seek to
make sense of it retrospectively. This also implies that in its initial
eruption, noise is outside sense, and, as such, brings us into proximity with the real of which one is also a part. As Miller writes concerning the inherent delusion of discourse relative to the real, "what we
call the real is something that cannot be made sense of. And that is
why we use the category of the real. So beware of making sense"
(Miller, 2009, p. 159).

In this book, I show how the relation between these three
elements—music, noise and the voice—operate differently in various ways related to different perspectives of the real that echo in a

supplementary way, that is to say, with a difference, the clinical structures that provide the basis of psychoanalytic diagnosis. These structures are all, in the Lacanian clinic, at least in its initial instantiation, an effect of language and an unconscious that is structured like a language following certain principles of structural linguistics derived from Saussure and Roman Jakobson concerning the signifier and the function of metaphor and metonymy. Music, as we have argued, emerges like language for speaking beings from *lalangue* to produce an audio or real unconscious that operates through the offices of dissonance and repetition, as a particulate system of sounds, that is heterogeneous but also supplementary to language, offering different modalities of sublimation and *jouissance*, for example, in the cases of psychosis and autism.

Stop Making Sense: Music from the Perspective of the Real is an attempt to elucidate the idea of an audio or real unconscious that passes through the Other offering an approximate, yet different, relation to the symbolic order. While the question of meaning arises most forcefully in relation to the formal power of music, it is in the symbolic distinction between music and noise, a distinction that is relational, cultural, and highly subjective, that establishes the extimate relation between the subject and the structure of meaning and affect that organises it. Here, it might be useful to note that this book does not give any special, technical significance to the term "affect" that has been appropriated by sound studies from philosophy (see, for example, Thompson & Biddle, 2013). However, in so far as this interest in affect concerns what music and sound "does" rather than what it "means", and relates to "the fluctuations of feeling that shape the experiential in ways that may impact upon but nevertheless evade conscious knowing", this book is broadly in sympathy with the project (Thompson & Biddle, 2013, p. 6). The reference in this book, however, is to psychoanalysis, not to philosophy, and the former has a whole vocabularly of affects that the single term, abstracted by philosophy, misses, it seems to me. Certainly, the locus of affect generated by the force and structure of music produces unconscious effects, impulses of and from a desire for an Other knowledge outside sense.

Indeed, the production of an audio unconscious in which music has a privileged role can be translated quite straightforwardly in the terms well known from the early Lacan. As we have suggested, the perception of music as a particular organisation of sound depends upon a symbolic distinction between music and non-music. The privileging of one order of sound as music condemns the rest as noise. This is an operation equivalent, in Lacanian terms, to symbolic castration, an operation that would erect a particular formation of music to phallic proportions. Music becomes phallic, therefore, in two essential ways. First, it consists entirely in meaningless tones and notes, analogous to pure signifiers. Second, through the cut of this essential division that gives shape and form to the raw materiality of sound, music becomes the very sign or symbol of the symbolic order as a whole, just as, correlatively, music is often seen in its organisation as homologous to social order. The notion of amusia is essential here because it is the ambivalent space within which the distinction turns, since music is perceived as noise, pure dissonance, but on the prior understanding that it is music. Music is perceived as painful noise, singing as screaming, in a way that clearly perceives, symptomatically, the symbolic violence of music and, by extension, the social order that is continuous with it.

Music, the ability to play it and recognise it, musical *savoir-faire* and technical know-how, are, of course, culturally constrained and now and again bump up against the dissonant sounds and alien techniques of foreign cultures that speak foreign languages. Since it is heterogeneous to language, music can provide a very interesting point of connection between distinct cultures, both positively and negatively. In what is known as the west, over the years, the strange music of other cultures has been read as a sign of ethnic authenticity or *jouissance* that has been used as the basis of love or hatred, but always in relation to an ignorance that is unshakable. The delusion that music contains some semblance of meaning establishes a relation to the question of meaning, thereby turning it into an object of passion—love, hatred, or ignorance.

Natura musicans and the non-sense of the real

Since Edvard Munch sensed the infinite scream passing through nature in 1893, the understanding of music has become transformed. In the wake of Luigi Russolo, Edgard Varèse, Olivier Messiaen, Pierre Shaeffer, John Cage, and Karl-Heinz Stockhausen, among many others, music has become regarded as an open system encompassing nature and machines in which the distinction between music and noise is shifting, difficult, if not impossible, to define. There is also "noise-music", the existence of which formally abolishes the term noise that gives the genre its name. Supremely, the old idea of *natura musicans* has been revived, in which music permeates, even constitutes, the whole world. This is a world that consists of an assemblage of musical milieus from the co-evolutionary symbioses of multicellular beings to the unimaginable subatomic domain of super strings, the secret vibrations supposedly constitutive of all matter, including dark and anti-matter. The failure of the symbolic order to maintain clear distinctions, definitions, and boundaries has been suggested as one possible cause of the apparent increase not just in cases of phobia and other neuroses, but also in psychosis, to the extent that, in 1999, Jacques-Alain Miller offered the new clinical category of "ordinary psychosis" that problematises the hitherto fundamental binary distinction between neurosis and psychosis articulated by the Name-of-the-Father (see Miller, 2009). While ordinary psychosis can be seen as an effect of the lack of definitions—that is to say, the lack of the lack introduced by clear-cut definitions—music becomes full with noise when it lacks similar definition and is rendered continuous with the general ambient environment.

In a recent essay in which he reflects on the "responsibility" he has taken throughout his career in "answering" for what is "essential" in Lacan's teaching, Miller isolates a key phrase from Lacan's last seminar that "gives an orientation" to the understanding of the late Lacan and, indeed, retrospectively to the *oeuvre* as a whole.

> What is, in fact the point that attracts thought [in the late Lacan] . . . One writes a song, a light-hearted ditty or a grand symphony. But for anyone who gets involved in thinking, in communicating something of this thought, a chord is struck, the opening chord. And in this "Everyone is mad, that is, delusional" I hear the chord, the root chord. (Miller, 2013b, p. 19)

It is interesting and appropriate that Miller should deploy the metaphor of music here in order to convey the idea that, in his later seminars, Lacan regarded meaning itself not simply as a semblance, but language as a whole, the chain of signification, as a locus of delusion in the impression it gives of being able to make sense of the real.

In the grand musical arrangement or orchestration of his work there is but the *one* chord—the *one* of the la la la of *lalangue* that reorientates Lacan's work from the perspective of the real. This not simply that language ultimately makes no more sense than music, but provides in the manner of music the support and impetus for multiple delusions. To the degree that all speaking beings remain under this impression that language can make sense, "*tout le monde est fou, c'est-à-dire, délirant*" ("everyone is mad, that is to say, delusional"—see also Miller, 2009, p. 159). However, the one chord, or chord-of-the-one, that Miller describes resonating throughout Lacan's teaching generally provides the basis for a reorientation of his thought and discourse in a musical direction for those following the Lacanian orientation in psychoanalysis. The chord itself, of course, is "unorientable" (p. 19); since it is drawn from a multiplicity of differential elements exterior to language, the chord has the power of orientation that is itself unorientable, that is to say, has no place in any system of signification. Music is, thus, the only thing that is not delusional, precisely to the degree to which it is acknowledged that it makes no sense, since it comprises meaningless notes and phrases that yet have the power to orientate and enjoin thought.

It is precisely this chord—the one found by Miller in his musical analysis of Lacan's *oeuvre*—that orientates this book in its attempt to show how music, including voice and noise—provides a principle of orientation from the perspective of the real in various clinical structures evident in culture, society, and politics affected by music. In this musical reorientation of Lacanian discourse, the name-of-the-father is no longer the definitive organising principle that determines the various diagnostic categories, but is just one symptom among others. As Guéguen argues,

> the Name-of-the-Father works as a *function* (in the mathematical sense) and not as a signifier of a totality. It can thus be upheld through many devices, many values ascribed to the variable: it becomes one among many other ways of ensuring a strong hold on what we call reality [and] a shared social bond. (Guéguen, 2013, p. 72)

Music can operate as just such a function in this mathematical, that is to say, symbolic way even in the default of language and, indeed, even in the default of mathematics. Indeed, the clearest evidence for the approximate symbolic dimension of music is found in psychosis, where music can both sustain a relation to external reality and provide a reasonably stable basis for delusional reality in face of the abyss opened out by the failure of language and foreclosure from the Name-of-the-Father. This book looks at the cultural and social role of music as an open as well as closed system in an era of generalised psychosis, as it functions as a melophobic supplement to language. Music, as an alternative particulate system, comes to supplement the symbolic order of language based on the name-of-the-father the moment it is impeached and displaced by the conjunction of artistic and economic freedom. This is especially evident in the generalisation of *avant-garde* musical processes and their integration into commercially successful pop and rock music. In what follows, I look at how music takes on the double function of precipitating this condition, but also plotting a path through it. There is no question that what Lacan calls the imaginary register takes on greater prominence relative to the symbolic order, but this allows forms of music greater affective and effective force.

Throughout the book, clamorous modes of being are defined with regard to a threefold definition of music where music is the principle of organisation of sound that implies as its defining other not disorganised sound, but the heterogeneous noise of dissonance in relation to a particular mode of repetition and voice, the "extimate" point of enunciation that haunts all music and discourse. Amusia involves the splitting of music and noise in such a way that on the basis of music we hear a noise that turns voice into a rending scream that passes through the order of things; as a result "I" become noise relative to the social formation symbolised by musical form. Melophobia concerns the impossible unity of music and noise in the terrified perception of a formless form that protects the subject from the maternal voice as devouring envelope; as a result, "I" am a block of affect that precipitates a flight (*phobos*, the conjunction of fear and flight) of becoming music. Autism involves the splitting of music and voice so that music protects the subject from the voice of enunciation and subsumes all noise such that music provides the architecture of a rim that can articulate the inside and the outside of the subject; in this way, music "speaks" for me in the absence of voice. In psychosis, there is no noise but the unity of voice and music, so that music provides the structure for a plurality of voices; the schizophrenic "we" are held together and counterpointed in the structure of music. For the *a*musical pervert, the phallic "cut" of music is disavowed and noise fetishised to the point of becoming everything, pure voice where voice is entirely subsumed, Tetsuo-style, into a general cacophony of noise that returns *jouissance* to a world desertified by mathematical order; "I" am voice as thick, non-symbolisable, non-fungible, unassimilable, yet undisplaceable, noise.

There various musical modalities of being and *jouissance* are discussed in the context of a critique of neoliberalism and the structure of general psychosis that it installs. This condition has been accelerated by the regime of digital telecommunications since the early 1990s, which has seen the emergence of various new symptoms that are all, as Soler argues (2014), related to the autistic *jouissance* to which we have been confined, alone together, as Turkle has noted (2010), with our gadgets and networked computers. Alongside examples of general psychosis and ordinary autism, three figures are given special consideration in the book as artists who have not only inverted the traditional distinction between music and noise evident in *a*musia, but have deterritorialised it from the concerns of an individual perception or symptom. The electronic ambient sounds of Brian Eno, the operatic screams of Yoko Ono, and the formidable noise-music of Merzbow operate in the midst of the crisis of symbolic indefinition at the *a*musical limits of music. These figures sustain, and are sustained by, a practice that is, the book argues, symptomatic of the age. But further, through the specific modality of dissonance immanent to their practice, Ono, Akita, and Eno disclose and, in some ways, compensate for the maladies of western society exacerbated by the strategies of neoliberal governance.

PART I
AMUSIA

Music and the love of the master

ORSINO, DUKE OF ILLYRIA:

If music be the food of love, play on,
Give me excess of it that, surfeiting,
The appetite may sicken and so die.
                    (Shakespeare, *Twelfth Night*)

The demand is predicated, significantly, on a conditional that locates the master in the position of uncertainty, ignorance. *If* music be food, and *if* music be the food of love, play on. The master does not know, but in the "existential impasse" of his solitude (Kojève), he wants to feel; he wants love. It is the unnamed musicians who know, that is, how to play. Located in the position of knowing, the musicians are nevertheless slaves in the sense that their play is work; it is doubtful that music is for them primarily the food of love, simply rather the means to earn food. The end of their work is the master's enjoyment, which here he seeks in love that he hopes may be nourished by music. And the master demands to be stuffed with it, filled to the brim, overflowing. The master's enjoyment is swollen with music, locus here of excess, so that it becomes all, it becomes One, albeit the lonely one,

3

wanting love and death. In his solitude, consumption is the sole manner of the master's risking of death, but only to the degree to which it is captured by the music that inflates it to the limit. For Orsino, music becomes the vehicle of an oral drive whose trajectory, captured by the locus of sound, tends, like all the drives, towards death. This is the destiny of music itself: to rise and descend, to play and die, to sound and fall silent.

While the master may possess his musicians and demand they play, he cannot possess the music itself; it is not a product. In its evanescence, music is sovereign. "Simultaneously more and less a lordship than lordship, sovereignty is totally other" (Derrida, 1985, p. 256). Moreover, it is as an effect of this sovereign alterity that the slave-musicians become for a moment the masters of the master's mood, in an interminable overturning—evoked by the Duke's ennui at the Twelfth Night of Christmas festivity—that can only expend itself in death. There is no dialectic here, just a process of repetition that turns on some Other thing that is nothing but a sound. Not a signifier, even less the signifier of the master, but an operation or function of a sovereign principle that sutures *jouissance* to a rhythm and a refrain that rises and falls . . .

CHAPTER ONE

The Marriage of Figaro and Freudian melophobia

In spite of the sentiments of Cleopatra and Duke Orsino, music is not just the food of love; it also feeds hatred and ignorance. Vladimir Nabokov could envisage no worse torture than a piano sonata, Ulysses S. Grant would recognise no song other than Yankee Doodle Dandy, Charles Darwin's elaboration of his theory evolved all music away, and Che Guevara's irrhythmia danced a *shoro* to a tango beat. These instances are offered by popular neuroscientists such as Oliver Sacks, Daniel Levitin, and others as examples of varying degrees of amusia. There are a number of types of amusia, both congenital and acquired, all denoting in different ways a radical tone-deafness usually attributed to some genetic defect or brain damage.

Not all of these examples of amusia, however, appear to have anything obviously to do with physical impairment. Oliver Sacks mentions William and Henry James who both, curiously, in their very different oeuvres, maintain almost complete silence on the topic of music, speculating that perhaps they failed to develop any interest or facility because they grew up in a house without music. Yet another famous example cited by Sacks is that of Sigmund Freud, though it would be difficult to attribute lack of exposure to music as the cause since he lived in Vienna, one of the great cities of music. Sacks mentions that Freud's nephew, Harry, claimed that Freud "despised music", though he is himself sceptical. However, Freud certainly "made a point of proclaiming his ignorance in musical matters and admitted that he could not carry a tune" (Gay, 1988, p. 168). He mentions his musical deficiency and consequent lack of interest famously in the opening paragraphs of his essay *The Moses of Michelangelo*. Freud confesses that his pleasure in art, particularly literature and sculpture, resides in the intellectual challenge they pose to interpretation, rather than in the sensuous appreciation of aesthetic qualities. Freud is interested in uncovering meaning and effects. Since he can make no sense of music, it gives him no pleasure, or, rather, some turn of his mind "rebels" against being affected, presumably in an unpleasant way, without knowing the reason why (Freud, 1914b, p. 211). Such a repression clearly suggests that music, for Freud, has a significant unconscious force.

When, on occasion, his family would brook no rebellion and he consented to be dragged to an opera, mostly Mozart, he would spend his time thinking about "his patients or his theories" (Sacks, 2007, p. 292). Perhaps it was this unconscious connection between Mozart and Freud's theoretical self-reflections that emerges in one of the few references to music in *The Interpretation of Dreams* (1900a), where "he virtually boasted about his tone deafness" (Gay, 1988, p. 168). This occurs in the preamble to the "Count Thun" dream, where Freud describes his previous day's activities that provide the source and part of the material of the dream he subsequently analyses. Freud is waiting at Westbahnhof station for a train to take him to his holiday home at Bellevue, but is held up by the arrival of Count Thun on his way to see the Emperor. Angry at both the arrogant demeanour of Thun and the fact that he and the other would-be travellers are being made to wait until Thun has departed, Freud passes the time by fuming and looking out for anyone else who might come along and claim "the patronage of the great" and get their own compartment allocated to them. If this happens, Freud contends he will

> kick up a fuss, that is, demand equality of treatment. Meantime I am singing to myself something which I then recognize as an aria from *The Marriage of Figaro*:
>
> *Will der Herr Graf ein Tänzelein wagen, Tänzelein wagen,*
> *Soll er's nur sagen,*
> *Ich spiel ihm eins auf.*

(If milord Count should want to go dancing/He'll pay the piper, I'll call the tune.)

(I doubt if anyone else would have recognised the melody.) (Freud, 1900a, p. 210)

In the midst of the confusion caused by Thun's arrival, and anxiety about catching his train and getting an appropriate berth (particularly one with a toilet facility), Freud finds himself humming a little refrain, apparently in a territorialising response to the confusion about territory, rights, and rivalry. But it is a tuneless refrain; he doubts anyone else would recognise it; indeed, he doesn't recognise it himself initially. If "the role of the refrain . . . is territorial" just in the way that a bird "sings to mark its territory" (Deleuze & Guattari, 1988, p. 312), what is the function of a tuneless refrain? A song to mark one's disharmony with the world, perhaps, or, further, a song that announces its own internal dissonance, its discordance with itself even as it provides a means of marking a territory and situating oneself uncomfortably within it. "Meantime I am singing to myself something", something of which Freud is initially unaware and which has come unbidden from the unconscious. He recognises it when he perceives it as a form of speech, as an aria from *The Marriage of Figaro*, Mozart's opera from Beaumarchais's comedy that he had recently seen in Paris. The famous refrain keeps him company, even as it expresses, in disharmony with itself, an unspoken rebellious defiance.

In his tuneless singing that betrays an unconscious identification with Figaro's resentment and anticipated revenge at the expense of "milord" the libidinal Count, Freud's recourse is to the sovereign principle of music itself, the "tune" rather than the piper who plays it. Music and the means to summon a different tune is also the means to revolt. Freud adheres to the sense of the libretto as his melophobia enacts the resistance to the power of tunefulness generally. In his retelling of the event, Freud acknowledges that the unconscious humming of the aria brought with it "all kinds of impudent and revolutionary thoughts", associating the libertine count of Beaumarchais's comedy with Count Thun, the Prime Minister of Austria. He recalls the journalists who ridicule him, punning on his name in calling him Count Nichtsthun (*Thun* = do, *Nichtsthun* = do-nothing). But, at the same time, Freud reproaches himself, deciding that rather than Figaro, it is the Count himself and his enjoyment that is the point of identification and even sympathy. "Truly I don't envy him; he is now on his way to a difficult visit to the Emperor, and *I* am really Count *Nichtsthun*: I am going on holiday" (p. 212). Freud's discordance with himself, his well-known work ethic conflicting with his desire for enjoyment (he says he has "all sorts of enjoyable plans for my holiday"), is played out in the oscillating identifications with Figaro and the two Counts.

Upon Thun's departure, Freud eventually gets to his train and manages to find a first class carriage, but is irritated to discover that, as he suspected, it has no access to a lavatory. Freud's urinary difficulties have become legendary and the relative absence of public conveniences has often been attributed as the reason for his dislike of America. In the Count Thun dream, this point of inconvenience and frustration becomes significant when, asleep and dreaming later in the carriage, he wakes up with the urge to urinate. Freud proceeds to describe the dream and give what has seemed to others an extremely "circumstantial" interpretation in which the aria disappears from both the dream and the analysis (Gay, p. 111). Instead, the initial resentment felt at Thun combined with the experience of urinary deprivation provides the source material for a "Rabelaisian" revolt in which "Freud imagines himself as a giant who can mobilise his prodigious powers of pissing and farting against the over-polite aristocracy" (Robertson, 1999, p. xxvii). Characteristically, Freud does not stop there and the gargantuan narcissism of this rebellion is related further back to an instance in his childhood. At the age of seven or eight, Freud "invaded his parents' bedroom out of sexual curiosity, and then urinated in his excitement" (Gay, p. 23), only to be castigated by his father to the effect that he would never amount to anything. He would be a "do-nothing".

In a footnote to *Civilisation and Its Discontents* later developed into a short paper on "The acquisition of and control of fire", Freud speculatively connects the acquisition and control of fire to the renunciation of "the homosexually-tinged desire to put it out with a stream of urine" (Freud, 1932a, p. 187). He further applies this speculation to an interpretation of the myth of Prometheus, who purloined fire from the Greek Gods by hiding it in "a hollow stick, a fennel-stalk" (p. 188). Freud typically regards the fennel stalk or reed as "a penis symbol", a tube in which the unconscious connection and reversal between urine and fire takes place, ultimately associating fire with sexual desire and excitation. "When we ourselves speak of the 'devouring fire' of love and of 'licking' flames – thus comparing the flame to a tongue – we have not moved so far away from the mode of thinking of one of our primitive ancestors" (Freud, 1932a, p. 190). The reed, or fennel-stalk, is also the same object that Athena puts to her lips when she decides to mourn the death and decapitation of Medusa, wishing, in the words of Pindar, "to imitate with instruments the deep groans proceeding from Euryale's fell cheeks". Perhaps, in Freud's identification with the music of the piper's pipe in *Figaro* that may fan or deflate the Count's ardour according to who calls the tune, we can see the "homosexually-tinged" anxiety informing Freud's melophobia and his passion for ignorance concerning the enjoyment brought by music.

It seems a little surprising that this Oedipal scene in his parents' bedroom, according to Freud the real source of the anxiety and wish underlying the dream, does not take Freud straight back to Figaro and his outrage and excitement at Count Almaviva's intention to claim *droit du seigneur* on the night of his wedding with Susanna. Paternal rivalry and ambivalence is staged in the aria in the terms of a metaphorical challenge to dance in which Figaro will devise the Count's exposure and downfall. Paternal authority is challenged by cunning to a duel for mastery and the right to enjoy the body of his wife. Given that these are the very stakes that Freud eventually finds, after much circumlocution, latent in the manifest content of the dream (Freud, 1900a, p. 216), it is perhaps strange that so little attention is paid to the aria by the interpretation or, indeed, the dream itself. The one reference to *Figaro* in the dream interpretation comes in a parenthesis and concerns the musical phrase "(. . . *Isabelita, no Ilores que se marchitan las flores*" [Little Isabel, do not weep because the flowers wither]. The Spanish comes from *Figaro*) (Freud, 1900a, pp. 213–214). This is related to the Count Thun figure in the dream who scorns the flower of Germany and sticks in his "buttonhole something that again must be a flower". Surprisingly, given the conflation of the two Counts in Freud's humming of the aria, this scornful plucking and sporting of the rose is not taken by Freud as a reference to defloration. Instead, it is related to Shakespeare's *3 Henry VI*, the Wars of the Roses, and the white carnation of Austria's anti-Semites and the red of their opponents, the Social Democrats. It is not so much the presence of the political dimension that is surprising in this Freudian analysis, it is the absence of the sexual one, unless we take "flower" to be another "symbol of the penis" and their wars a form of erotic combat.

If dreams are the royal road to the unconscious, this dream, in which many have suggested "there are complexities upon complexities" (Gay, p. 23), reveals that road can be quite a circuitous one with many detours and blind alleys. When it begins to sing, however tunelessly, the unconscious takes a more direct route. Perhaps this is significant, given that Freud's melphobia clearly suggests that music has, for him, a—albeit repressed—phallic dimension. Consequently, there are further complexities to negotiate when this musical route is followed.

It is well known that *The Interpretation of Dreams* was being written at a time when Freud's confidence in his intimate friendship with his correspondent, Wilhelm Fliess, was starting to falter. The interpretation of the dream of Irma's injection that famously opens the book and provides the model for dream interpretation can appear a tangled web of insight, evasion, and self-censorship. While Freud interprets the dream as a wish to be exculpated as the source of Irma's suffering, tantalisingly, Freud himself confesses that there are elements of the dream's interpretation that he prefers not to reveal. He then offers a challenge to readers "to try being franker than I have been", a challenge they have been keen to take up (for a thorough survey and analysis of the dream and its critical reception, see Botting, 1999). For the biographer, the censorship concerns Fliess's surgical incompetence with regard to one of Freud's patients, Emma Eckstein, whose nose Fliess operated on only to neglect to remove a piece of gauze that subsequently caused serious nosebleeds. Initially assuming there was no physical cause, Freud diagnosed the bleeding as a symptom of hysteria, only for Fliess's neglect to become apparent later. Eckstein is accepted as one of the figures forming part of the composite dream character, Irma. "Freud's reading constitutes a massive displacement", writes Peter Gay, "the doctor whose conscientiousness he wished to establish with this dream was far less himself than Fliess" (1988, p. 83). The biographical charge is that Freud knew this, recognised it in the dream, but omitted it from the published interpretation, thereby giving an essentially false significance even though its meaning as a wish-fulfilment is retained. The affection for Fliess must have been intense indeed if it could compromise the interpretation of the dream that Freud offers as the dream of dreams, the key to his whole method. This was the dream for which, Freud wrote to Fliess, he might be remembered with a marble tablet on the wall of Bellevue, commemorating that "Here revealed itself, on July 24 1895, the secret of the dream to Dr. Sigm. Freud". Other than this rhetorical flight, Freud failed to discuss the dream or its significance in his correspondence with Fliess, since the dream discloses the anxiety that Freud is both the victim and accomplice of Fliess's incompetence. As Lacan suggests, Irma is a festival of condensations, but of all the figures superimposed on to the image of this woman, not least of them is Freud himself. For Lacan, Freud's horrendous discovery, in Irma's throat, is the image of the formlessness of his own hideous *jouissance*, the revelation of the interior of the body, that *"you are this − You are this, which is so far from you, this which is the ultimate formlessness"* (Lacan, 1988, p. 155). The body that Fliess opens to the *jouissance* of his fumbling scalpel is his own as much as it is Irma's—or Emma Eckstein's. The intensity of Freud's relationship with Fliess (he calls him his "daemon" at this time), an intensity that gives the dream such a horrifyingly condensed complexity, Freud recognised later as having its source in what he considered to be the latent homosexuality shared by both men. The intimate friendship was also an amorous rivalry that eventually broke up in acrimony and "paranoiac" recriminations (see Gay, 1988, pp. 274–276).

Freud took years to shake off the painful memory of Fliess, and continued to see versions of him everywhere in his subsequent friends and acquaintances. Intriguingly, as he wrote to one of them, Sandor Ferenczi, of his difficulties with another, Carl Jung, these primal memories could be summoned by music. In 1912, Gay records, he wrote

> "I have just come from 'Don Giovanni' . . . In the second act, during the Don's festive supper, the hired band plays the snatch of an aria from Mozart's *The Marriage of Figaro* and Leporello remarks, 'That music seems very familiar to me'." Freud himself found "a good application to the current situation. Yes, this music, too, seems very familiar to me. I had experienced all this already before 1906" – that is, with Fliess in the last angry years of their friendship: "the same objections, the same prophecies, the same proclamations that I have now been got rid of." (Gay, 1988, p. 277)

Lacan says nothing of music, and neither does he regard Freud's relationship with Fliess as having anything other than marginal significance in his reading of Freud's Irma dream. While denying, somewhat disingenuously, that he is revising Freud's interpretation of his own dream, and that it is "out of the question to analyse dead authors", he avoids the temptation to supplement the interpretation at the point Freud breaks off. Rather, Lacan considers the whole of the dream and its interpretation from the point of view of its addressee. The dream, Lacan argues, is addressed to future analysts; its purpose is to teach them something about the logic of dreams and the workings of the unconscious. This pedagogical effect resides as much in what is shown or demonstrated as in what is said.

What is shown is that Freud's ego disintegrates from the moment of the horrifying vision of the opened, voiceless throat. It splinters into a number of comical alter egos while Freud's discourse disintegrates into a series of ellipses punctuated by the names of chemical formulae: "a propyl preparation, propylene . . . propionic acid . . . trimethylamine (I see its formula before me printed in bold type)" (see Lacan, 1988, p. 170). For Lacan, the agency of the dream is, at this point, taken over by the subject of the unconscious, whose place is marked by the signifier of the phallus. This phallic signifier is "trimethylamine", a chemical formula, a word that, in the context of the treatment of Irma, makes no sense. It functions as a pure signifier, devoid of meaning, though its phallic dimension is suggested since it is "a decomposition product of sperm" (Lacan, 1988, p. 158). In Freud's own analysis, the word is linked directly to Fliess (the only time he alludes to his friend in the interpretation, significantly at its climax), who, in his research on sexual chemistry, believed "trimethylamine to be one of the products of sexual metabolism. So this substance leads me to sexuality, that factor to which I attribute the greatest significance in the origin of the nervous afflictions I want to cure" (Freud, 1990, p. 116). It leads Freud right to the heart of the matter of dreams and, perhaps, right to the heart of the matter of this particular dream with regard to the sexual chemistry between Fliess and himself. But this is not the conclusion drawn by Lacan, for whom the dream is not about sex but about death.

The trimethylamine phallus, especially when considered purely in the form of its formulaic denotation, signifies nothing, for Lacan, but "the nature of the symbolic". It is in the nature of the symbolic to be nothing other than symbol, symbols referring to other symbols, in relation to which the ego fades. This is what occurs in Freud's dream and its interpretation, the meaning of which is that the ego wishes to efface itself from the credit of having discovered the secret of the dream and created psychoanalysis. *"The creator is someone greater than I. It is my unconscious. It is this voice which speaks in me, beyond me"* (Lacan, 1988, p. 171). His self-effacement is a function, Lacan argues, of what Freud will later call the death drive that emerges in relation to the symbol in the form of "this speech which is in the subject without being the speech of the subject" (p. 171).

> In the dream of Irma's injection, it is just when the world of the dreamer is plunged into the greatest imaginary chaos that discourse enters into play, discourse as such, independently of its meaning, since it is a senseless discourse. It then seems that the subject decomposes and disappears. In this dream there is the recognition of the fundamentally acephalic character of the subject, beyond a given point. This point is designated by the N of the trimethylamine formula. That's where the *I* of the subject is at that moment. (Lacan, 1988, p. 170)

"Propyl . . . propylene . . . propionic . . . trimethylamine . . ."[1] This senseless discourse that stutters and *plays* with pure signifiers, the letters or notes of scientific formulae, is *musical*. Like musical notes, they may be pure or empty signifiers, but they still have rhythm and tonality. When the resistance of Freud's rebellious intellect gives way, he becomes, as we have seen with *The Marriage of Figaro*, comically musical, and this music leads him directly to the amorous excitement of sexual rivalry, here, in the context of his intense transferential relation with Fliess. Once signification has been stripped of all meaning, once the ego has dissolved, become invested with the death drive in relation to the mechanism of the symbolic, the machine of differentiation itself as denoted by the letter, there is still the musicality of spacing that it opens up, the rhythmic beat of a blank, the force of which remains in excess of language as pure machine. And it is in this rhythmic excess that the trace of life is sustained, dancing over the implacable silence of the death drive.

For Lacan, the unconscious is a "senseless discourse" that is, nevertheless, rigorously "structured like a language". Music as a mode of organised sound signifies nothing, has no referent other than itself and yet is a mode of symbolisation. As a symbolically designated form, in performance and on record, music is regarded as a form of communication, although what it communicates is never certain. Is music, as such, structured like a language—a language that is not one, like the unconscious? It seems that music bears an uncanny relation to the Lacanian notion of the unconscious, a relation that needs to be considered next along with the relation between rhythm and the drive that is disclosed by the *a*musical symptom of arhythmia.

CHAPTER TWO

Dance and "condansation": Che Guevara's *a*-rhythmia

Condansation

Cabrera Alvarez's biography of Che Guevara describes a local dance at which the future revolutionary is required to attend with a friend, Alberto Granados. As the evening unfolds, Guevara motions to his amigo and asks him to look out for him because at a certain point he's going to have to attempt to dance: "Runt, listen well, I'm going to dance, but you know . . .". Granados knows perfectly well that his comrade "is incapable of distinguishing a military march from a *milonga*", and Guevara asks Granados to give him a little kick when the band strikes up a tango. Alvarez continues the story:

> More or less every other piece played by the improvised band is a tango, but for some reason they suddenly play a Brazilian *shoro* enti- tled "Delicado". Granados remembers the song was popular at the time his friend began to court Chichina, and wishing to remind him of that time, taps him with his foot. Ernesto takes a young woman out to dance. The tempo of the *shoro* is quick but he doesn't hear it. He dances to the beat of a tango, marking out his steps with mathemati- cal precision. (Alvarez, 1987, p. 77)

Years later, when reflecting on guerrilla tactics, Guevara writes,

> characteristic of this war of mobility is the so-called minuet, named from the analogy with the dance: the guerrilla bands encircle an enemy position, an advancing column, for example; they encircle it completely from the four points of the compass, with five or six men in each place, far enough away to avoid being encircled themselves; the fight is started at any one of the points, and the army moves toward it; the guerrilla band then retreats, always maintaining visual contact, and initiates its attack from another point. The army will repeat its action and the guerrilla band, the same. (Guevara, 1961, p. 6)

In this way, he continues, the enemy column becomes trapped, expending energy and ammunition as its soldiers are picked off at regular intervals, while the guerrilla force remains in a relatively secure situation.

Here are two examples of Ernesto "Che" Guevara dancing. The first illustrates the relatively unknown fact of his irrhythmia, his inability to perceive and synchronise to a regular beat or recognise different rhythms and dance steps. In a social and, indeed, libidinal setting, this inability is a handicap and Guevara seeks to overcome it through a practiced reduction of music and dance to its mathematical principles. Such an exercise (and its failure) illustrates both the proximity between music and maths and its difference. Clearly, and this is the whole point of the anecdote, he makes a bit of a fool of himself; he's exposed, awkward, literally out of step with his community.

In the second anecdote, from Guevara's textbook *Guerrilla Warfare* (1961), he uses the metaphor of a dance, a minuet, to describe the successful prosecution of guerrilla warfare. Why, given his singular difficulties on the dance floor, would Guevara have chosen, of all things, a dance as a figure for his own expertise? Perhaps to show that, on the contrary, he can indeed dance, both in theory and in practice, in a theatre of war. But here, of course, only one partner in the minuet is dancing—the guerrilla pack. The army does not know, at least initially, that it is in a dance until it realises that it is being *danced* to death. The rhythm of dance here is a subtle form of immobilising, fatal violence. Perhaps, since he cannot experience the pleasure and satisfaction of rhythm, this is what dancing is to Che Guevara.

It is characteristic of the unconscious that it knows. But this knowledge is the effect of a repression such that the subject of the unconscious does not know that it knows, knowledge emerging variously in dreams, parapraxes, negation, and other acts of speech. The unconscious that thus emerges also tells us something about the form of repression. Here, music is a form of repressive violence that "subjectifies" in a particular way. Like language, music operates symbolically to individuate but not through the attribution of a name. Rather it can individuate—or perhaps differentiates or separates is a better word—through abjection. In an aside to his commentary on James Joyce in Seminar 23, Jacques Lacan comments on this peculiarity of music and dance. "Il y a quelque chose dont on est tout à fait surpris que ça ne serve pas plus le corps comme tel – c'est la danse. Ça permettrait d'écrire un peu différemment le terme de *condansation*" [There is something about which one is quite surprised that it does not serve the body more, the body as such: it is dance. It allows us to write a little differently the term *condansation* (Lacan, 2005, p. 154, translated for this edition)]. Lacan's pun on the Freudian notion of condensation suggests that a certain rhythm (like a single idea, metaphor, or symptom) can be considered to bear several associative chains in which the body and psyche can become entangled. As Lacan suggests, the dance does not serve the body. While the body, for Lacan, is often circumscribed by body-image, here the dance does indeed not return to Guevara a satisfying reflection. But Lacan also says the "body as such" (*le corps comme tel*), implying, perhaps, a more profound discordance between the body and dance in a kind of double resistance. Surprisingly, Lacan says, dance does not serve the body as much as one might think, even as the body is led by the dance and struggles to keep time with the music. In relation to music's organised system of sound, Guevara is out of time, reduced even at the dance to the status of the disorganised noise that he actually perceives and struggles to control mathematically. Accordingly, this accentuates his difference and awkwardness as he becomes isolated on the dance floor, comically alone (with his amused or bemused partner) surrounded by the others. If we were to think of Guevara's irrhythmia in terms of a psychoanalytic symptom (thereby renaming it *a*-rhythmia), we could say that here an unconscious drive resists the satisfactions of sublimation offered by the dance, perhaps, given Guevara's politics, because they symbolise—which is to say they are a "condensation" of the satisfactions of—a community that is complicit in its own repression. As Lacan writes in Seminar 11, between these two terms – drive and satisfaction – there is set up an extreme antinomy that reminds us that the use of the function of the drive has for me no other purpose than to put in question what is meant as satisfaction. (Lacan, 1976, p. 166)

For Guevara, the repressed returns in the forests of Cuba, where another violent rhythm is imposed on Batista's troops. The drive discloses that it knows very well how to dance and to deploy its force in a satisfying way, unleashing on its enemies the *jouissance* of death. But what sort of drive is it? The drives that Freud associated with the various erogenous zones (oral, anal, genital) that Lacan supplemented with the scopic and invocatory drives are ultimately supplanted by the life and death drives (*Eros* and *Thanatos*) on which Freud speculated in *Beyond the Pleasure Principle*. The example of Che Guevara would suggest that both drives are "condensed" on to the rhythm of the dance with the result that the repression of Eros returns in the death drive, differently regulated, in a play of stealth and gunfire, silence and dissonance, projected on to the enemy.

Structured like a language

"[I]t suffices to listen to poetry . . . for a polyphony to be heard and for it to become clear that all discourse is aligned along the several staves of a musical score" (Lacan, 2006, p. 419). This statement from the *Écrits* underscores that if anything is like a language without being one, it is music. Lacan's conception of the unconscious as structured like a language (or even *lalangue*) is unlike the general understanding of the idea of the unconscious associated with Freud since there is nothing subterranean, infernal, or primordial about it. Lacan is quite emphatic about what the unconscious is not: it is not "a species defining the circle of that part of the psychical reality which does not have the attribute (or the virtue) of consciousness" (Lacan, 2006, p. 703). This includes the sensory (or extra-sensory) domain, habit, the phenomenon of the split personality; it is not the locus of genius, telepathy, second-sight; it is not an archive of learned or integrated reserves of memory; it is not the soup of passions that occasionally rise up and get the better of us; it is not a locus of instinct or heredity ground either in the archaic, the primordial, the evolutionary past, or genetic code (2006, p. 703). Lacan's conception of the unconscious is, on the one hand, very thin, but, on the other, universal for a particular type of speaking being. What is the unconscious, then, for Lacan? "The unconscious *is* a concept founded on the trail [*trace*] left by that which operates to constitute the subject" (2006, p. 703). Since it is language, or the differential elements of *lalangue* that constitutes the subject, the unconscious as an effect of language is, therefore, structured in a similar way. This is not just the privileged language of dreams, but language *per se*, and, as such, "the presence of the unconscious . . . can be found in every discourse, in its enunciation" (p. 707).

However, Lacan's idea of language is quite a specific one, derived from a rethinking of Saussure that perceives a radical separation between signifier and signified. Indeed, language, as an assemblage of sounds and symbols, is nothing but a chain of signifiers in which meaning, the signified, is never really anything other than a semblance, an apparition. Yet, although the signifier is devoid of a signified, this very poverty becomes the support for signifying excess, as in the case of poetry. Not just poetry, all discourse is polyphonic, so that sound both precedes and generates a plurality of possible meanings, layers of semblance. The analytic model, therefore, for listening to speech is music, since "all discourse is aligned along the several staves of a musical score" (Lacan, 2006, p. 419). The unconscious, it seems, is structured like a language, but only in so far as that language is arranged as if it were a piece of music; it is precisely because of this that the unconscious can exercise its agency in so far as drives and the primary processes Freud calls displacement and condensation "can connect 'empty signifiers' to psychosomatic functionings, or can at least link them in a sequence of metaphors and metonymies" (Kristeva, 1984, p. 22). Analysing the discourse of the unconscious does not therefore seek out 'the effect of meaning that is operative in interpretation, but rather the articulation in the symptom of signifiers (without any meaning at all) that have gotten caught up in it" (Lacan, 2006, p. 714). Evidently, in its purest form, psychoanalysis would be more akin to reading a piece of music than literary criticism.

However, there is potentially a serious problem in this emphasis on the musicality of the unconscious, and that is whether or not music could be said to constitute a subject. Since "a subject intervenes only in as much as there are, in this world, signifiers that mean nothing and must be deciphered" (Lacan, 2006, p. 712), the question remains whether a form that makes no propositions, has no concepts or images, can constitute a subject in the apparent absence of any power of representation. Certainly, a melody or a musical score can be regarded as "signifiers that mean nothing", but do they demand to be deciphered? Steven Spielberg seemed to think that music is something that can demand interpretation because, in his film *Close Encounters of the Third Kind* (1977), which stages first contact between humans and aliens, it is precisely with a simple five note tune that the latter announce themselves and the former regard as a phrase to be deciphered.[2] The utterance of the five note phrase successfully establishes, for the humans, the aliens as subjects of an utterance. These space creatures are, of course, entirely fictional and perhaps the use of music as an alien language simply reinforces its status as supplementary or indeed as solely an imaginary language. For Lacan, "the unconscious is purely an effect of human language", although he does not rule out other species of animal should they come to posses at least some degree of human language, (2006, p. 707) or be subjected to it in the form, no doubt, of domestication. The conventional human–animal divide, therefore, remains essential for Lacan, not just in his understanding of the unconscious, but also in the distinction between imaginary and symbolic registers. Just as all the creatures of the world apart from the human ones are designated with the term "animal" and confined to the imaginary, that is also supposed to be the sole location of music.

It is an interesting curiosity of music that it can be intensely enjoyed by people who know nothing about it. Yet, it is not controversial to say that, in the last instance, even the *savoir-faire* or "know-how" of musicians cannot account for the profound enjoyment offered by music. Does not this enjoyment also imply an unconscious "knowledge" that exceeds musical know-how? An enjoyment that one experiences but knows nothing about would, in Lacanian terms, locate music in the realm of the *jouissance* of the Other, a mysterious realm that lies in excess of the phallic signifier and the phallocratic symbolic order, but also, therefore, strictly speaking, beyond the field of the unconscious.

No doubt it is for this reason that music has such a marginal place for psychoanalysts, especially those following Lacan (see Régnault, 2012). As we have seen, music is related back to the pre-linguistic sphere of maternal dependency. Kristeva, for example, characteristically celebrates the radical potential of "pre-linguistic musicality" even as she relegates it, as an effect of "poetic language", to a more primitive or secondary position in relation to literature; music is regarded by Kristeva as a predominantly "semiotic" form rather than a symbolic one. The semiotic describes a state of transition from the pre-oedipal fragmented body that is, nevertheless, "always already invested with semiosis" and the post-oedipal subject with "his always symbolic and/or syntactic language" (Kristeva, 1984, p. 22). Similarly, for French and American Lacanians Anzieu (1974), Rosolato (1974), Silverman (1988), and Schwarz (1997), music is subsumed within the pre-symbolic imaginary register as an "acoustic mirror" that is an effect of the maternal voice. Located in the semiotic, in the pre-linguistic echolalias that enclose the infant in the maternal space of the acoustic mirror, music occupies a position in psychoanalysis in relation to language that is consistent with the Western philosophical and scientific tradition. Music is always either "a deficient means of articulation, or . . . a privileged one" (Bowie, 1990, p. 176). For philosophy, music is an empty formalism preoccupied solely with the emotions rather than the intellect (Kant) or, on the contrary, music can say the unsayable and open up a mode of communication beyond the limits of mere words (Nietzsche). For neuroscience, music is regarded as valuable because it promotes cognitive development, and for evolutionary biology, music is perhaps precisely the "activity that prepared our pre-human ancestors for speech communication" (Levitin, 2006, p. 260) or, on the contrary, it is a decadent by-product of language with no evolutionary significance whatsoever (Pinker, 1997). Until quite recently, neuroscience formalised this oppositional logic in the brain and music was located, along with art, on the right hemisphere, or feminine side, of the brain that supposedly dominates the left-hand side of the body, in opposition to the more masculine side of the brain that processes language and mathematics and dominates the right-hand side of things.

This "phallic" oppositional logic of masculine and feminine, reason and emotion, art and language, excess and deficiency, immaturity and maturity Lacanian psychoanalysis diagnoses very well, but need not necessarily reproduce as it seems to do with music where it is located in the imaginary realm along with animals and women, or feminine *jouissance*. Neuroscience, at least, has, it seems, now developed a more complex view. Far from being limited to one half of the brain, "music listening, performance, and composition engage nearly every area of the brain that we have so far identified, and involve nearly every neural subsystem" (Levitin, 2006, p. 9). As the new neuroscience acknowledges (Antonio Damasio, Joseph LeDoux, V. S. Ramachandran, and Francisco Varela), the internal world of the brain is not a sealed-off, hard-wired automatism; the external world is inseparable from the structure of neurological processes of self-modification. The brain is now seen as essentially plastic; cultural forms such as language, art, and music can produce and modify activation vectors in the brain (see Ansermet & Magistretti, 2007; Johnston & Malabou, 2013; Malabou, 2000). Furthermore, these dimensions, while interconnected, are modular or functionally heterogeneous, if supplementary. For example, most people with congenital amusia, people who are "profoundly disabled in musical perception . . . are virtually normal in their speech perceptions and patterns" (Sacks, 2007, p. 104). At the same time, those people rendered totally speechless by severe expressive aphasia can often still sing, so that music and song can provide a therapeutic means of reconnecting or reinventing language circuits (see Sacks, 2007, p. 214).

While it is essential that psychoanalytic notions such as the unconscious retain their heterogeneous position with regard to scientific understandings of the brain, this "does not mean that they are without any relation" (Ansermet & Magistretti, 2007, p. 12). While psychoanalysis is concerned with the question of meaning (and its absence) rather than biological function, language is not the only force that broaches that question. Other forms bearing information in the sense of particulate systems can structure and direct drives. Moreover, as Ansermet and Magistretti suggest, it is at the level of affect that the (non)relation between the two heterogeneous orders might be activated (pp. 12–13). As a locus of affect that articulates semblances of meaning grounded in feeling and emotion, displacing *jouissance* along a series of non-sensical sounds, music can be said to occupy that zone of (non)relation between the two heterogeneous orders of neuroscience and psychoanalysis. The unconscious, if there is one, or even more than one, might consist in multiple traces of competing drives or forces, a network of antagonisms both creative and repressive, human and nonhuman, organic and inorganic, verbal, visual, and aural. As such, these antagonisms would both establish and undermine a shifting "subject" that is always ultimately posited as a question—a "who?"—that is internally and externally divided into an assemblage of qualities and quantities of force.

Alongside language, then, music is a form that can individuate, produce a sense of subjectivity and a subject whose traces can be tracked through a specifically audio unconscious through its ability to generate excess intensities of affect that are connected to other associations and memories. Music is not supplementary or a primitive form of language, it is not a pre-linguistic substrate of language; it is a distinct form with its own force. It is a form of differentiation the force of which leaves its own unconscious traces quite distinct from the traces left by language. These traces do, however, continually cross over and interconnect. The "letter" of music, the minimal unit of differentiation, is evident not just in the tone that is heard and the note that symbolises it, but also in the timbre that reverberates from the specific and singular machine of enunciation. It is multi-dimensional and addresses the brain and the psyche in a way that is different to language. However, where music intersects language and the symbolic order generally, the crucial point of differentiation that constitutes a subject of music clearly concerns the difference between music and non-music: noise. It is not simply that music, as an organisation of, and differentiation from, noise, presupposes a "listening" subject through the production of the difference. Rather, it is on the threshold of the dissonance that sustains the noise immanent to music as its modality of excess that a subject is constituted as a locus of restriction, antagonism, repression, resistance, and transformation.

Amusia

In his development of the notion of an unconscious structured like a language, Lacan famously had recourse to the scientific—that is to say, both linguistic and neurological—condition of aphasia. In the elucidation of a specifically audio unconscious, the condition of amusia takes on a special significance. Amusia is an example of associative agnosia "in which perception seems adequate to allow recognition, and yet recognition cannot take place"; it involves "a normal percept stripped of its meaning" (Farah, 2004, p. 2). Agnosias such as amusia and prosopagnosia (the inability to recognise faces) are useful for neuroscience in ascertaining the contingent and modular (evolutionary) nature of perceptual apparatuses and neural "knowledge" systems that abstract and pattern the object-stuff of perception. At the limit, the loss of certain phenomenal qualities might imply the emergence of new forms, and, indeed, new forms of knowledge.

Judging by the cases of amusia collected in Oliver Sacks's book *Musicophilia* (2007), the condition, which varies enormously, never concerns simply a case of deafness or indifference to music. Amusia does not describe a world of silence or, indeed, of the absence of music so much as the presence of noise. Music, or aspects of it, is perceived as noise. Sometimes, the condition affects melody, sometimes harmony, producing a "dysharmonia". Sometimes, it affects rhythm but not metre, sometimes the reverse. Even in the more extreme instances, it remains the case that music is not absent, but experienced as an overwhelming dissonant negativity. In a classic case from the neurological literature, Hécaen and Albert described one man, apparently a former singer, who "complained of hearing a 'screeching car' whenever he heard music" (cited in Sacks, 2007, p. 101). For Vladimir Nabokov, music was agony and he complained of feeling "flayed alive" when he heard orchestral music. The condition of amusia, therefore, describes not so much the absence of music, but the presence of noise that causes subjective fragmentation where things fall apart.

Che Guevara, as we have seen, found it impossible to synchronise to a specific beat, an inability which he had in common with his compatriot Eva Peron, neither of whom could dance, not even the tango. For Guevara, this inability seems also to have supported a hatred of American popular music, particularly jazz and rock and roll. Of course, it is possible to find other examples of socialist antipathy to the regular groove of American popular music, most notably Theodor Adorno, but even a musician and composer like Stockhausen seems to have had an irrational—which is to say excessive—dislike for popular music on the basis of its regular beat. One of the interesting things about this resistance to rhythm concerns its "a-naturality". While for Stockhausen it was the unnaturalness of the beat's "military" regularity and uniformity that he found objectionable, for others the ability to synchronise well to a beat always denotes a proximity to nature. Rhythm is conventionally predicated upon naturalness. Some people have "natural" rhythm they say, while others, most notably white men, cannot dance. Such a deficiency is conventionally compensated, in this well known racist exchange of qualities, by a higher degree of civilisation, represented no doubt by classical music. Even if one does not normally dance to classical music, however (there are, of course, exceptions), it certainly has rhythm, even though such rhythms convey music that it is conventionally assumed serve the intellect rather than the body.

This well-known attitude to rhythm and dance is curious given their ubiquity across cultures and, furthermore, the current sugges-tion from neuroscience that the ability to spontaneously (that is, instinctually) synchronise to a beat is both natural—in the sense of being evolved—and also specific to the human species. "Beat percep-tion" apparently opens up the world as a specifically human spatial–temporal domain because, according to Anil Patel, it

> is anticipatory rather than reactive . . . beat perception is a complex phenomenon that likely has sophisticated cognitive and neural under-pinnings. Specifically, it involves a mental model of time in which periodic temporal expectancies play a key role. This may be one reason why it is unique to humans. (Patel, 2008, p. 102)

As we can see, this is evident from Che Guevara's guerrilla dance, where the ability to predict movement, predicated upon the rhythm of anticipated beats is essential, as is the spacing that this movement also implies. Yet, rhythm profoundly defeats his own body and motor co-ordination. But there can be no distinction between the beat instinct (if there is one) and the social formation that encapsulates it and to which it can perhaps be condensed. Such a "beat instinct" is, there-fore, much closer to what psychoanalysis calls a drive than a biologi-cal instinct, not just because it is apparently one of those special traits, like the acquisition of language, awareness of death, and so on, that supposedly differentiate human beings from other animals, but because it is always already bound up with a social formation—indeed, like language or rituals of mourning.

The dance drive

Such a "dance drive" would be this inextricable link between an "instinct" (if instincts still exist in science) and a social formation that is condensed (or "condansed") into the form of a particular beat or rhythm that segments and propels it but to which it is not identical. The dance drive of the audio unconscious is *a*-rhythmic even as it is produced by rhythm; like Che Guevara, it always misses the beat towards which it aims. Freud, as Lacan notes, was insistent that the drive does not have rhythm. Lacan offers this commentary in Seminar 11:

> In the drive, there is no question of kinetic energy [no *Stosskraft*, shock force or life force]; it is not a question of something that will be regulated with movement. The discharge in question is of a different nature, and is on a different plane. The constancy of the thrust forbids any assimilation of the drive to a biological function, which always has a rhythm. The first thing Freud says about the drive is, if I may put it this way, that it has no day or night, no spring or autumn, no rise and fall. It is a constant force. All the same, one must take account of the texts and of experience. (Lacan, 1976, p. 165)

The last sentence is important here, and wariness is necessary when confronted with assertions about how, in contradistinction with the drive, rhythm is once again folded into the circadian domain of the natural and the biological. As neuroscience contends, beats are as a-natural as the human being itself. Neither biological nor entirely cultural, but on "a different plane to both", the drive is artificial and yet exerts a "constant force" that is at the same time not a "life force", or what Freud called *Lebenstriebe*. For Lacan, however, because the drive is an effect of the cut introduced by language and the signifier, "every drive is virtually a death drive" (Lacan, 2006, p. 848). Furthermore, while Lacan does not mention it in his paper on the unconscious, the drive is also profoundly silent, a state that doubly denotes the drive as artificial and always and only ever a death drive. Death, of course, only has psychic reality; there is no death in the physical universe, just the transformation of matter and energy. Even so, the scientific analogy that Lacan suggests for the drive in the *Écrits* comes from electromagnetic theory and, in particular, Stokes's theorem, which allows him "to situate the reason for the constancy of the drive's pressure" (Lacan, 2006, p. 847). Stokes's theorem establishes the notion of a flux, or curl flux, through an orificial circuit. The drive establishes a kind of field or lamella (another metaphor) based on a closed rim (Lacan, 2006, p. 847) (Figure 2.1).

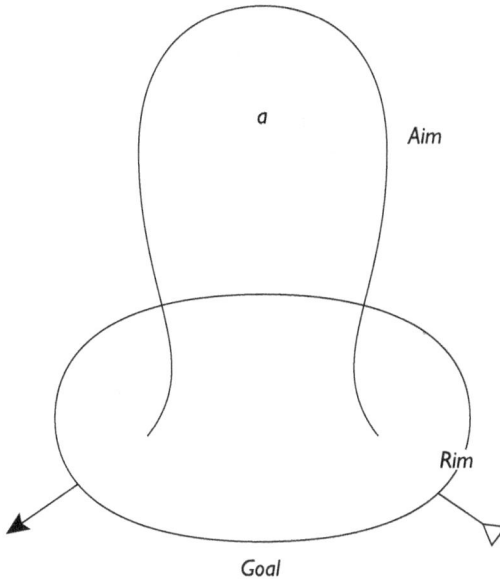

Figure 2.1.   The vector of the drive (Lacan, 1976, p. 178).

To return to the forests of Cuba, we can see how Guevara and his guerrillas establish a similar kind of field through encircling Batista's troops in the form, Guevara suggests, of a minuet that describes a similar circular structure above which rises the vector of force of the combatants or "dancers".

The drive discloses that it knows very well how to dance through dancing a minuet that describes a circle or rim characteristic of an erogenous zone, the erotic value of which, in the forests of Cuba, is defined by the *jouissance* of death. This example of Che Guevara would suggest that both life and death drives are "condansed" on to the rhythm of the dance with the result that the repression of Eros returns in the death drive, differently regulated. If there is a drive distinct to rhythm, that is to say, an instinct that is always already differentiated by, and sublimated into, particulate systems that are "condansations" of social formations, it is a drive that is paradoxically antinomic to the libidinal satisfactions it affords. There is, it could be suggested, internal to rhythm, a dissonance that is never entirely dissipated through repetition: on the contrary. As the condition of amusia suggests, noise is not exterior to music; they are the same. It is here that the *a* of *a*musia and *a*-rhythmia insists in the violent discordance and dissonance that places in question the satisfactions offered by civilisation and its forms of sonic power and organisation. This occurs precisely when these satisfactions break down and become unbearable as the violence inherent to the form is disclosed. "When we look at it [satisfaction] more closely", Lacan writes, "we see that something new comes into play – the category of the impossible" (1976, p. 166). Perhaps Guevara's *a*-rhythmia demonstrates the drive's heterogeneity to the human beat instinct, disclosing an unconscious desire for the impossible that is sublimated into revolutionary action. Cuban socialism becomes the beneficiary of this drive, but ultimately it aims at something more profound, pitching demand to the level of the impossible, to some Other Thing that might ground an alternative social order. The heterogeneity of the drive and its relation to the impossible is also disclosed through the form it takes as a kind of surrealist montage when Batista's Cuban army met the dancing guerrillas of Guevara's revolutionary forces in a fatal rim, the electromagnetic field of a minuet.

Groundhog Day: the earworm and the love song

In a typically vulgar speculation from his biography *My Shit Life So Far* (2010), that even for him is excessively disgusting, misanthropic Scottish comedian Frankie Boyle supposes that "in Groundhog Day, Bill Murray would probably have raped and killed Andie MacDowell quite a few times, really gone to town. I can see why they left that out of the movie" (Boyle, 2010, p. 114).[3] Boyle further reflects, romantically, that Bill Murray's equally misanthropic weatherman's "real triumph" is that his violence does not diminish his love for Andie MacDowell's character, even after he has used her corpse. The humour here, if there is any, resides not only in the deflationry recognition that excessive object sublimation is not at all incompatible with psychopathic perversion, but also in the way that this is set off against the banalities of Hollywood romance.

In fact, this juxtaposition between banality and violence both structures and punctuates the film and occurs through its use of music and the pop love song. The violence of Bill Murray's character, Phil Connors, is not visited on MacDowell, but it is visited on himself (he attempts to commit suicide several times, and even succeeds in doing so) throughout the film and on the alarm radio that wakes him every day, that is, of course, the same day that threatens eternally to recur, to the tinny sounds of Sonny and Cher's "I Got You Babe". However, there is nothing Nietzschean about *Groundhog Day*: on the contrary. Indeed, neither is there much romance, since the latter serves as the cynical premise for a parable about self-improvement and re-training (Connors learns French, the piano, and ice sculpture in his efforts to impress MacDowell's character, Rita). In the process, Murray's bad, grumpy weatherman becomes a Good Person and a better worker. But let us, for the moment, take Frankie Boyle's reading and suppose that there is actually love at stake in the film and that, moreover, its repetition motif is a metaphor for love that is conditioned, in *Groundhog Day* as everywhere else, by the popular love song.

This song of love, a famous duet, greets Connors at dawn, as 5.59 flicks over to 6 a.m., every time Groundhog Day begins again. The love that according to Frankie Boyle will redeem Murray's character is an accursed thing that heralds each new day as the same day, the same scene and situation, the same misery. Cue the smashing of the alarm radio as if it were Andie MacDowell, imagined source of his amorous frustration and self-loathing, as if it were love itself, some agonising, unbearable, whining noise, the very embodiment of evil's banality as the singers hold each others' little hands and boast that there is no hill or mountain that can match the scale of their love. Love is a "tormented circling" (Agamben, 1993, p. 81) that is figured, in *Groundhog Day*, by a musical "earworm" that traps the amorous subject "in a sort of loop, a tight neural circuit from which it [can] not escape" (Sacks, 2007, p. 45). For Agamben, this circling takes place around "an image painted or reflected in the deepest self" (1993, p. 81)—as if there were anything in this idea of profundity other than an infinite reflexivity.

Perhaps this is the difference between the music of love and its image. The latter assumes Narcissus as love's primary scene, its model for all future loves and identifications, while the former evokes love's pure contingency as an external force, blind Cupid's arrow that sounds even (or especially) in the night of howling winds. As Barthes notes in *A Lover's Discourse* (1978), the first thing we love is a scene. "For love at first sight requires the very sign of its suddenness . . . the scene consecrates the object I am going to love" (Barthes, 1978, p. 192). The fact that the visual object is always an effect of a prior *mise en scène* that determines the field of visibility is noted by Sacks in *Musicophilia* (2007) even as he contrasts this with the aural register. While listening is no doubt a selective process, the form of what is heard is always "preserved with remarkable accuracy" (p. 41). For Sacks, "it is this fidelity—this almost defenceless engraving of music on the brain—which plays a crucial part in predisposing us to certain excesses or pathologies . . . even in relatively unmusical people" (Sacks, 2007, p. 47). Music comes unbidden: whether you like it or not, you cannot shut your ears, and it makes you mad. This amorous music is an affliction; a diabolical possession it enters and "subverts" the brain, "forcing it to fire repetitively and autonomously (as may happen with a tic or seizure)" (Sacks, 2007, p. 41). The audioligachaeta, or earworm, can fade, but once it has entered the brain, like love the heart, "a heightened sensitivity remains, so that a noise, an association, a reference" can set it off again (2007, p. 41). Their apparent universality unites the normal with the pathological, the everyday and the eternal, sanity and madness, interiority and exteriority, banality and evil . . .

Although Barthes does not, in *Lover's Discourse*, mention the popular song (or, indeed, music at all), the love song is in contemporary life one of the main vehicles of "love's obscenity" that Barthes insists "must be assumed by the amorous subject as a powerful transgression which leaves him alone and exposed" in a reversal of values (Barthes, 1978, p. 175). The necessity to embrace abjection and humiliation—not as a form of ascesis proper to courtly love, but in accordance with the stupidity of a revolting sentimentality—raises love's obscenity to an (almost Kantian) imperative where sublimation and perversion are indistinguishable and the "deepest self" is plumbed in an indefinite process of imaginary degradation and discharged as waste. Here, we can return to Frankie Boyle and the love that finds its image in a dismembered corpse: the lover as excremental remainder.

"I Got You Babe"'s disposable pop pipes on again, comparing love's profligacy with the rent, leaving the lovers without a "pot" (to piss in, no doubt), but sure of its value nevertheless, measuring love once more in the familiar exchange of money for excrement. Love, the gift of something one does not have (Lacan): in its place a disposable piece of trash that is endlessly recycled, an irritating noise that goes round and round again. In so far as it is conditioned by the audioligachaeta of the love song, contemporary love is an effect of amusia in the sense that it is an everyday, yet miraculous, experience of the impossible in which noise and music are the same. The little refrain stakes out the territory, the scene, for love's imagining, but only as a site of consumption, a different form of speculation in which the lover is an amorous slave put to work, dissipating itself on a hamster wheel of commercial activity. Oh rose thou art sick.

But Blake and the poets know that love has always been sick, capitalism merely speculates on the site of speculation already opened out by its malaise. Music feeds or provides the condition for love by transforming language into an alien form, a refrain stripped of meaning and purpose other than to provide a territory, a scene, for the speculative imagination. In the lyrical language that has been captured by music, "every term is irreplaceable and can only be repeated" (Deleuze, 1997, p. 2), yet repetition resonates in the dissonance of a singular passion that provides the difference necessary for speculation. This dissonance resonates with music's "dark secret" that is the immanent noise experienced in love's amusia. This is the noise of disaggregation with the universe, the formlessness that noisily compels love to the singular form of its destruction.

CHAPTER THREE

From symptom to synthomy

Shake, rattle, and roll

In his book *Musicophilia* (2007), Sacks' examples of amusia are all supposed to have biological causes, but they are expressed in highly subjective forms sensitive to music as a mode of subjectification, even of power and violence. They provide a clear illustration of why, as Paul Hegarty says, "noise is not an objective fact. It occurs in relation to perception" (Hegarty, 2007, p. 3). The perception of noise is both intensely subjective and also specific to "historical, geographical and cultural location" (2007, p. 3). The term amusia does not denote the absence of music, a specific cultural and social form, but its unbearable presence that is experienced as a noise indistinguishable from suffering.

In his book, Sacks describes his own temporary experience of the condition of amusia. He reports on his experience of listening to a Chopin ballade on the radio and hearing just "an unpleasant metallic reverberation, as if the ballade were being played with a hammer on sheet metal" (Sacks, 2007, p. 101). The experience recurred a few weeks later while he was playing a Chopin mazurka on his piano. This time, the noise was accompanied by zigzags in his visual field, something that he had experienced during attacks of migraine, so he assumed the amusia was "part of a migraine aura" (p. 101). He neglects to say whether or not he was suffering from a migraine at the time, and neither does he indicate whether the migraine, if there was one, had a physical source or if he thought it might be a symptom of some psychic malaise. He does not consider why it might be that Chopin set it off on both occasions even though, in other anecdotes, Sacks testifies to his highly sensitive and suggestible audio uncon-scious.[4] Although it distressed Sacks, a piece of music that included a sampled phrase of a Chopin ballade detuned to sound like metallic reverberations might be something that fans of Aphex Twin or Autechre would be keen to hear. Or, indeed, Kraftwerk, which, to the delight of Derrick May, the founder of Detroit techno, "sounded like somebody making music with hammers and nails" (Reynolds, 1998, p. 15).

In western culture, at least, it appears that noise is a source of more annoyance and distress than vision. The phrase "noise pollution" does not have an optical equivalent in spite of western society being bom-barded by visual stimuli. This pollution does not just concern aircraft or traffic noise, car alarms, vacuum cleaners, lawn mowers, ring tones, advertising jingles, inane pop music endlessly repeated on the radio, the percussive hum of personal stereos, iPods, and so on. There is, perhaps, nothing more annoying than the sound of other people. Music can be perceived as an unbearable noise when it is experienced as the expression of the Other's *jouissance*. Perhaps this also applies where the Other is the locus of the law in an institutional as well as symbolic sense, not just when its alterity is figured in signifiers of ethnicity. Since "music can organize our bodies and keep our minds in order" (Hegarty, 2007, p. 11), this musical expression of order might well, like Sartre's gaze, be experienced as nauseating, unbearable. Could something like this be behind Nabokov's problem with the chamber music that he experienced as agony? No doubt, a certain form of amusia arises as an effect of sensibilities that are as much political as musical. For Brian Eno, "classical music . . . represents old-fashioned hierarchical structures, ranking, all the levels of control. . . . I have to say that I wouldn't give a rat's ass if I never heard another piece of such music" (Eno & Kelly, 1995, p. 12).

Sacks' main example of amusia in his book is a seventy-six-year-old woman to whom he was introduced in 2006. "DL" is the daughter of a very musical family who did everything they could to teach and acculturate her into a world of melody and song, but to no avail. Sacks does not consider whether or not the woman's amusia could be in some way related to the music of family romance and a father who made her listen and play music "again and again". Neither does he comment on a school and social circle that not only failed to recognise or take seriously her condition, but also forced her to sing publicly and attend regular concerts and musicals to such an extent that, when her amusia was recognised, she lamented that an earlier diagnosis "might have saved her from a lifetime of being bored or excruciated by concerts" (Sacks, 2007, p. 106). When she was asked what music sounds like to her, Sacks writes that Mrs L always answers "If you were in my kitchen and threw all the pots and pans on the floor, that's what I hear" (p. 106). Later, Sacks adds, she noted that she was "very sensitive to high notes" and that the opera "sounded like screaming" (p. 105). Opera, of course, is quite an acquired taste and it is possible that DL's sentiments might be shared by others who have failed to acquire it.[5]

The descriptions that the subjects of amusia give in Sacks' book are often very interesting and suggestive. DL's description of thrown pots and pans is a good example. Sacks does not give enough information to pose questions concerning any personal or idiosyncratic reasons for such a description, but it inevitably suggests some cultural connotations. A kitchen's pots and pans are not normally thrown on the floor without also signifying a crisis of some kind, producing a cacophony shattering domestic order. For many women like DL, born in 1930, the order of domesticity to which they were confined, willingly or not, was shattered, at least symbolically, by the "sexual revolution" of the 1960s. This revolution was heralded in the 1950s when young women of DL's age were invited by Bill Haley and his Comets to get out of their kitchens and start rattling pots and pans in a version of the rock'n'roll classic, "Shake, Rattle and Roll" that failed to diminish the suggestive tenor of Big Joe Turner's original. For many of DL's father's generation, attuned to the classics, such a vulgar form was, of course, not perceived as music at all, but as a racket, a hideous noise that, in the generational antagonism it represented, similarly shattered the domestic order.

At the same time, pots and pans, along with a wooden spoon, are things frequently given to troublesome toddlers in order, paradoxically, "to keep them quiet". Bashing pots and pans are many people's first musical expression. Such childish banging is not necessarily simply random or experimental, equivalent to the echolalias or lallation, in imitation of the mother's voice, that precede the child's acquisition of speech. As we shall see in a subsequent chapter with regard to an autistic boy's banging of a drum in time with a school orchestra, the banging establishes a distracting relation with the Other, in so far as it slots into the rhythm established by the orchestra, or even simply creates a dissonant racket. That music can provide the basis of a social relation is evident negatively in the case of DL, or her generation at least, for whom "Shake, Rattle and Roll" provided the noise-music that precipitated the relation or non-relation of sexual, social, and generational antagonism. Rattling pots and pans in the context of sexual suggestion and the disruption of social order has long cultural roots. Charivari (or shivaree in the USA) perhaps goes back to ancient Rome, but is usually associated with medieval Europe, particularly France, from which it was introduced into Louisiana, surviving as a practice in the Southern part of the USA until at least midway into the twentieth century. The practice involves the banging together of pots and pans and other domestic instruments, depending on cultural and historical context, in order to greet a couple engaged to be married, often in an ambiguous way. The rough music of charivari might be invoked in order to protect newlyweds from evil spirits or to draw attention to something questionable or inappropriate about the marriage, or, indeed, to drive them to marriage. As a form of popular power, charivari was sometimes the source or catalyst for popular revolt, and in France it remains a term for the noise of public ridicule. Charivari, therefore, is an important example of how noise is not exterior to music but immanent to it. It might be "rough" but the banging of pots and pans in charivari *is* music, an *a*musical music that exposes its violence and power. In the unfortunate instance of Mrs DL, all music has become a charivari, apparently always summoning, through the sound of the shattering of domestic order, discordance with her own social reality that is, nevertheless, linked to cultural and historical forms. By appropriating the neurological notion of amusia for psychoanalysis, then, we produce *a*musia where the "*a*" denotes the subjective intensity of the unconscious in disharmony with the world. The "*a*" marks the point of noise, tunelessness, the pain of the pots and pans that music is to me, or my music, my sound, is to others. I am that dissonance, that shattering explosion of pots and pans.

It would be easy to dismiss the suffering that is frequently involved in the *a*musical perception of noise as a symptom, perhaps a symptom of hysteria. For Lacan, the symptom is not a call for interpretation, but a pure *jouissance* addressed to no one. A symptom is a particular way in which the subject enjoys and suffers from the unconscious. If neurological amusia is a symptom, then it is one that experiences music as a pure *jouissance*. While *jouissance* emerges in the default of speech, occupying the place vacated by the absence of meaning, with *a*musia suffering is related not just to absence but to form. Amusia establishes the subject in a negative relation to a form that it recognises through suffering, through an experience of painful noise. In *a*musia, *jouissance* is correlated to a form—music—that communicates through non-sense. It is, thus, more like Lacan's notion of the *sinthome* in which the *jouissance* specific to a subject may be embodied in an art that Lacan elaborated in an analysis of James Joyce, one of the most musical of writers, yet who sustained an ambivalent relation to music and, indeed, language (Lacan, 2005, p. 38).

Molly Bloom's chamber pot

By the end of the "Sirens" chapter of *Ulysses*, Joyce, as he indicates in his correspondence to Harriet Weaver, has had enough of music: "since I wrote Sirens, I find it impossible to listen to music of any kind" (Joyce, in Ellmann, 1981, p. 475). Joyce wrote Sirens as a form of music, attempting to deploy through language all the formal technical resources of music. "It is a fugue with all musical notations: piano, forte, rallentando and so on. A quintet occurs in it too, as in Die Meistersinger, my favourite Wagnerian opera . . ." (Ellmann, 1981, p. 473). Yet, upon completion of the chapter, Joyce finds himself exhausted and even somewhat disgusted with the various techniques, effects, and tricks that mark the *savoir-faire* of the musician and composer. Declaiming that he no longer cares for music, Joyce writes, "I, the great friend of music, can no longer listen to it. I see through all the tricks and can't enjoy it anymore" (Ellmann, 1981, p. 473). The restricted enjoyment of classical music also reaches its limit in the chapter. As with Luigi Russolo's *Art of Noises* (1913), Joyce's exhaustion through literary simulation of the tricks and techniques of western music culminates in Leopold's Bloom's joyful discovery of noise-music. "Sea, wind, leaves, thunder, waters, cows lowing, the cattle market, cocks, hens don't crow, snakes hissss. There's music every-where" (Joyce, 1982, p. 281). Here, Joyce's hatred of music as a kind of discourse, or locus of technique, knowledge, or *savoir-faire*, gives way to a joyful revelation of ambient noise-music which discloses existence: "mere fact of music shows you are". Bloom's reverie is brought to self-consciousness in the apprehension of love and sexual difference that is disclosed in song. Molly's lilt confers knowledge for Bloom, and the self-knowledge conditioned by desire. It is at this point that Joyce refers to Pindar's myth concerning the origin of music in the mourning of Medusa, although here the reference is to "Stabat Mater". "Molly *quis est homo*" summons the grief of the Mother of Christ at the foot of the cross.

The next word, "Mercadante", refers to Saverio Mercadante's *"Sinfonia sur des themes du Stabat Mater"*, whose opening salvos of funereal horns are counterposed by an oboe solo of soft mourning that immediately evokes the originary mourning song of Pallas Athene and her sorrowful reed. Bloom's desire is then jogged and Molly's memory eroticised by the sound of Blazes Boylan's footsteps—"Jog jig jogged stopped. Dandy tan shoe of dandy Boylan socks skyblue clocks came light to earth" (Joyce, 1982, p. 281). This sound, intersecting with the faint sound of chamber music, sets off another train of associations that are articulated by a pun.

> It is a kind of music I often thought when she. Acoustics that is. Tinkling. Empty vessels make most noise. Because the acoustics, the resonance changes according as the weight of the water is equal to the law of falling water. Like those rhapsodies of Liszt's, Hungarian, gipseyed. Pearls. Drops. Rain. Diddle idle addle addle oodle oodle. Hiss. Now. Maybe now. Before. (Joyce, 1982, p. 281)

Russolo's six families of noises claim a degree of completeness, but he does not mention the sound of a woman making music by making water into a chamber pot. Here, the Pythagorean myth is, of course, referenced by the "acoustics" produced by the sound of Molly's urine, defined and evoked by Bloom in mathematical terms. The question of noise-music's site of enunciation is raised, given that Molly is located at the centre, or as the substance, of both rewritten myths. Sound emerges from the hole in the throat or in the urethra, an irreducible sound that does not partake in the effect of sense or signification, the sound that denotes precisely that which cannot be said or sung and which, through the senselessness of death (Mary's moaning at the Passion of Christ) and waste (Molly's piss), connects human life with the continuity assumed for the non-discursive life of the other creatures of the world. The passage is a testament to Joyce's urinary eroticism (something which, along with his name, he shared with Freud) that is manifest in the description he gave to his favourite white wine—"the Archdeaconness's urine"—that similarly combines the sacred and the profane in a heterological musical flow, a rhythm in which presence tumbles after the always already before of repetition.

Molly's chamber pot is pulled out again at the culmination of the novel in the "Penelope" chapter. Molly takes another piss and sorts out her monthly menstruation that is "pouring out of me like the sea" (Joyce, 1982, p. 691). It is a literary critical commonplace to point, from Molly Bloom to Anna Livia Plurabelle, to Joyce's association of the feminine with streams, rivers, "sea, wind, leaves, thunder, waters". All that could be noted here is that in Molly's chamber pot resides an alternative model of music to rival the classical myths of Pindar, for whom the art of aulos resounds to the suffering (both human and suprahuman) or the sound of the turtle shell in which was discovered, in the form of a lyre, the sonic properties of the universe. In Molly's pot, music is neither subjective emotion nor Pythagorean acoustic design, but the resonant, erotic de-formation of form (human and non-human) in a ceaseless flow of expenditure, *a*musical erotic pissss.

Joysign sinthomy of psoakoonaloose

It is another critical commonplace to describe *Finnegans Wake* as a "word symphony" because sound is more evident than sense; comprising multiple puns and varieties of paronomasia from a range of European languages, the text seems pregnant with meaning, but delivers less than a semblance, offering nothing but infinite resources for interpretative delusions. In an exchange from the book, frequently said to refer to an episode in Joyce's life when he was offered a Jungian analysis, the inability to distinguish sense from sound is said to require psychoanalysis.

> Can you not distinguish the sense, prain, from the sound, bray? You
> have homosexual catheis of empathy between narcissism of the expert
> and steatopygic invertedness. Get yourself psychoanolised! O, begor,
> . . . I can psoakoonaloose myself any time I want. (Joyce, 2000; see also
> Ellmann, 1981, p. 480)

The in-distinction of sense and sound generated and perceived in the
production of paronomasia betrays, it is alleged, a structure in which
the subject is poised between transference with the "narcissism of the
expert", a hystericised subject supposed to know, and "steatopygic
invertedness". Since "inversion" is a sexological term for homosexuality, "steatopygic invertedness" could be rephrased as a big-arsed
desire (for a big arse, perhaps). Or perhaps it refers to an inverted arse,
a big arse upturned to the sky. If there is a correlation implied in the
conjunction of arse and expert, then clearly sense, the illusory effect of
narcissistic criticism and analysis, is confounded by the sound of a
great amusical fart. What is psychoanalysis supposed to make of that?
Or, indeed, linguistics and musicology, since Joyce seems to want to
turn language into music and vice versa, producing a "reading/listen-
ing" experience in which the one displaces the other as sound subverts sense only to return, momentarily, in the non-sense of laughter.

In his late seminar on Joyce, "Le sinthome" (2005), Lacan argued
that through producing a writing that was not primarily composed of
metaphors and metonymies but of puns and "equivoques", Joyce
managed to construct a "singularised" name for himself through the
destruction of the symbolic and the discourse of the Other, the unconscious supposed to be structured like a language. For Lacan, Joyce's
sinthome involves the "littering" of the letter, an inversion of the usual
relation of excess and meaning in signification where language "stops
making sense" in the context of a general signifying excess. Yet, the
non-sense of the letter retains a promise, or remnant, of sense that
sustains in the endless literary scholarship that follows in its wake:
Joyce's name. This remnant saves Joyce, then, or his text, from full
blown psychosis, according to Lacan, establishing a relation to the
Other (at least in the shape of a readership and a literary industry);
laughter erupts when fleeting, imaginary remnants of (double) meaning are (mis)recognised in the rubble of the symbolic order.

But, while Lacan is attentive to the affective, singular subversions
of language through which the sinthome, as fourth term, hooks the

symbolic on to the imaginary via the real, he is inattentive to the approximate, yet equally affective, relation of the text to music, to the idea that the sinthome is actually a sinthomy. Just as it is a common-place to emphasise the musicality of language in Joyce, so this empha-sis should also be made in contradistinction to vision. A considerable tenor in his day, Joyce was, of course, also near blind and, therefore, the field of vision (and all the discursive metaphors it gives rise to: clarity, lucidity, transparency) is not supposed to be his favoured domain. Music, therefore, might be expected to compensate for this lack of vision through substituting music's resources of imitation, counterpoint, harmony, and echo. And so it does, in the earlier work. But, by *Finnegans Wake*, music suffers as much as language, as both forms are tortured in Joyce's attempt to turn language into music and make music speak. It is a fantastic attempt to do the impossible, a great passionate revenge on music and language that demonstrates their incommensurability, even as it consigns both to the grave in a wake.

Out of his hainamoration of language and music, Joyce produces an amusical sinthomic writing comprised not so much of notes or signifiers but of joysigns (Joycean joysigns) full with the promise of *lalangue*. Soler coins a similar neologism in her discussion of the "real unconscious" that is an effect of *lalangue*:

> The singular *lalangue* which comes to the subject through the Other is not without carrying a trace of the *jouissance* of the Other. Hence the obscenity of *lalangue*, about which one could say that it marks the subject with enjoy-signs [*jouis-signes*] both enigmatic and unprogram-mable. (Soler, 2014, p. 35).

Joycean joysigns are full with a Joycean *a*musical joy that broaches an experience of non-knowledge at the extreme limit of knowledge, in which language is turned to the non-sense of music even as music is rendered cacophonous and dissolved in laughter. With Joyce, "thera-pee" involves a session—a long session—not on the couch, but in the bar. Psychoanalysis turns into psoakoonaloose with an "eatupus complex and a drinkthedregs kink", ending an evening of riotous expenditure, appropriately enough, in the gutter, its steatopygic arse in the air.

In psoakoonaloose, psychoanalysis gives way to the non-produc-tive expenditure of laughter, intoxication, and waste matter, the "litter" of the letter. Joyce "escapes" or exceeds psychoanalysis—as indeed he does in spite of Lacan's last attempts to tie him in Borromean knots—not because he avoids it or rejects it, but because, as Lacan avows, "he goes in it straight to the best one can expect from a psychoanalysis in the end" (Lacan, 1987, p. 9). Like the sinthome, the amusical sinthomy denotes a singularity, a singular *jouissance* exterior to, or foreclosed from, the symbolic order and the metaphors and metonymies of a purely linguistic unconscious. Perhaps this is why, as we shall see, even though they may be foreclosed from the name-of-the-father, psychotics can sustain an approximate relation to symbolic systems through music and indeed mathematics and numerology.

CHAPTER FOUR

The audio unconscious

Wo es war: in the echo of its dissonance may be heard the resonance of that singular clamour for being in the music of the cosmos. Or, as Reich remarked on the unfolding sound of noise-music that his art sets in train, "listening to an extremely gradual musical process opens my ears to *it*, but *it* always extends farther than I can hear" (Reich, 2002, p. 35).

It is time to recapitulate in a brief summary, if not a sonata, the structure of the audio unconscious. For convenience, in order to stress both the similarity and the difference between the audio unconscious and the unconscious supposed to be structured like a language, I propose to trace Lacan's famous schema of desire that is, appropriately, broken up like a sonata in three or four movements. Desire is an effect of speech, but here I want to demonstrate topographically, following Lacan, how desire also operates in an audio unconscious where speech is absent or misperceived and music is the privileged form. The following schema in which the structure of relations is retained even though the terms are changed appears in the chapter "The subversion of the subject and the dialectic of desire", from *Écrits* (Lacan, 2006, p. 67–70). It is Hegel's account of self-consciousness in *The Phenomenology of Mind*, of course, that provides one of the main

points of reference to Lacan's chapter on the subversion of the subject. As Derrida notes, there is something paradoxical about Lacan's
retention of the concept of the subject simply in order to subvert it.
Here, the necessity of retaining the term in relation to a domain of
audibility heterogeneous to speech is even less obvious, even as the
presence of speaking beings somewhere in the auditorium is no doubt
essential. Lacan's subject of the unconscious is defined against both
Hegel's philosophical subject of self-consciousness and the subject of
science that the latter assumes is ejected from the objectivity of its
discourse. While the latter assembles its regimes of knowledge, its
laws and formulae, this is at the cost of closing the borders to the
regime of revealed truth that might enable them to mean something
to somebody. It is this gap between truth and knowledge that psychoanalysis hopes to bridge. While Hegel's dialectic offers a model for
Lacan, it is precisely not for the latter self-knowledge that defines the
subject: on the contrary. The knowledge that defines the subject for
Lacan is the knowledge that is borne by the non-sense of the letter
whose agency directs the subject without it knowing. It is still a
subject of knowledge; it just does not know that it knows. It is the job
of psychoanalysis, therefore, to try, by means of its own dialectic of
desire, to reveal the truth of unconscious knowledge (or at least *wo
es war*) in the speech of the analysand as an effect of the process of
analysis.

Heterogeneous to speech, music also ties together knowledge, in
the form of *savoir-faire*, and a truth about which one can say little other
than one experiences it. For there to be people ignorant of the knowledge it takes to make music who can, nevertheless, become passion-
ately affected by it (in love or hatred) no doubt implies the presence
of unconscious musical knowledge, but, further, it also suggests the
opening to a truth in the affective, revelatory experience that exceeds
all knowledge, including musical knowledge. Coming from elsewhere, what it reveals (perhaps all that it reveals) or exposes is the
finitude that is shared by everyone it affects and passes through.

The graphs depicted in Figure 4.1, drawn from Lacan's chapter,
though re-noted with different terms, attempt to show where desire is
situated in relation to something or someone that is defined in relation to sound. The first graph is the "elementary cell", sometimes
known as the "quilting point", or "button-tie", that shows the stitch-
ing of a mythical drive into the signifying chain.

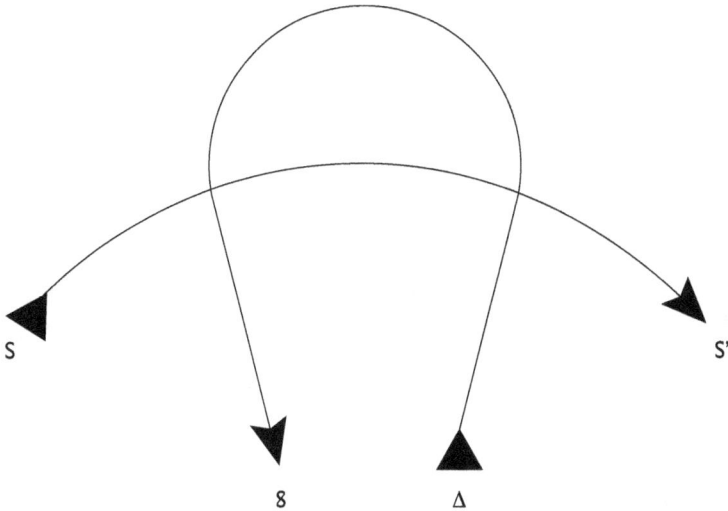

Δ⟶ 8 = the drive
S ⟶ S' = the locus of sound

Figure 4.1.   Graph 1: the elementary cell.

The myth that provides the point of reference throughout Lacan's essay is Hegel's account of self-consciousness that produces the dialectic between master and slave. However, rather than interrogating the Hegelian myth that situates the subject in relation to (absolute) knowledge, the relation here concerns the non-sense introduced by music. The myth to which I propose to refer is the scientific myth of the origin of the universe in the so-called Big Bang. The vector "S→S" describes the locus of virtual sounds that is brought into actuality through the initial big bang. The trauma of this first aural explosion is missed, however, and is only perceptible in the echo that follows, the repetition that occurs when the vertical vector re-enters the locus of sound. This establishes a point of aural perception in relation to a locus of dissonance and repetition.

Repetition establishes the rule that gives consistency to the locus of sound in two ways. First through the rhythm and spacing that establishes sound in a temporal line of different tones and beats, and second through the more profound echo of the event of dissonance that sustains, in repetition, experience and memory. In the second graph, therefore, there is no Big Other other than the locus of repetition in which repetition is the aural reinscription of dissonance. This locus and its principle of differentiation and organisation that repetition brings to sound (promising harmony, melody, and so on as well as the repetition of dissonance) provide the possibility of music.

Jacques Brel's hatred of the accordion

In Jacques Brel's famous song "Vesoul", the sound of the accordion provides the point of *a*musia that articulates the singer's ambivalent relation with Paris. In the song, the marital complaint that male desire is being pulled hither and thither by the desire of his spouse, that is itself driven by the mad dash tourism of the *bourgeoisie*, accelerates, upon the dissonant scream of the accordion, as it becomes purely the effect of a machinic oscillation, such that even the key sites of bohemian Paris become just another tourist attraction. It is a perfect musical performance of Walter Benjamin's famous essay, "Some motifs on Baudelaire", where the former suggests that the latter makes the basis of lyric poetry "the shock experience" characteristic of modernity that "has become the norm" (Benjamin, 1999, p. 158). This is music beyond the pleasure principle. At first, the relatively sedate opening of the song merely supports the highly rhythmic here-and-there of Brel's lyrics, his poetic persona being pulled along by an alter ego that is itself indistinguishable from the "fort-da" of the signifier, the names of the towns. But, upon the dissonant screech of the accordion, the music starts going like a train, becoming indistinguishable from the noise-music of urban travel. The oscillating movement accelerates, noise becoming continuous with music, in such a way that the subject of twentieth-century travel becomes wired into the shocks and rhythms of systemic motion. "D'ailleurs j'ai horreur / De tous les flons flons / De la valse musette / Et de l'accordéon". Even as the noise of travel becomes music, music itself becomes noise, particularly the unbearable wailing of the accordion, yet Brel (or his persona) demand more of it: "Chauffe! Chauffe, Marcel!" Turn it up: faster, louder, harder, in a self-flagellating racket that propels the musical locomotive, untrammelled, along the tracks of the death drive and the inevitable crash—itself systemic—that is nothing but the anorganic pulse of (re)generation, dissonance, and repetition.

At this point, Brel seems to merge into his bourgeois persona as the bohemian Parisian of Baudelaire and "Les fleurs du mal" that, as a

Belgian bourgeois, Brel desired and came to embody himself. Yet, the Paris of Baudelaire in turn becomes disclosed as yet another heritage site, just a sordid little train stop at Gare St Lazare. The noise of the accordion, clichéd signifier of Parisian romance, is abject, unbearable, the superegoic means by which the bohemian punishes himself. In television spectaculars, Brel presented the spectacle (of himself) as the bohemian poet who, even as he sneers at *la bourgeois*, becomes captured and propelled by an "auratic" logic of sound: the desire for noise, for increased shock and sensation that ultimately leaves one fatigued, emptied-out, yet again arriving at Vesoul, the most boring place in the world. Mais, je te préviens / le voyage est fini! But, no, encore!

Music, as a particular organisation of sound, offers a certain symbolic form, in its difference from the non-music that is disorganised sounds, in which can be sensed a momentary unity, harmony, or order. As such, music occupies the position of ego-ideal that hooks the imaginary on to the symbolic. The lower part of the graph that, in Lacan's original, maps the mirror stage, here describes the process of individuation [m] that is produced in the relation between music and dissonance in an experience of *a*musia. The example of Jacques Brel's "Vesoul", above, can be mapped on to the figure in the following way: the dollar sign ($) marks the point of the Belgian *petit bourgeois* Jacques that is repressed by Brel, the celebrated Parisian musician and the object of parody in the form of the alter ego, the bourgeois husband afflicted by his wife's touristic wanderlust. The extimate point of *a*musia denotes the ambivalence towards the accordion with which Brel/his persona punishes himself in his demands *"Chauffe, chauffe, Marcel!"* From the point of *a*musia, the vector goes in two directions: towards the "originary" (missed) event of dissonance that grounds the subject as an effect of its repetition, and the symbolic form "Music" in the position of ego-ideal (Figure 4.2).

Brel, as celebrated ego, is an effect of the vector $\rightarrow$ Music, where the latter denotes the music/poetry of bohemian Paris (Baudelaire's "Fleurs du mal"), the ego-ideal that provides the form and context for Brel's work and identity. The "screaming" of the accordion that marks the break in the song is, of course, the symptom of petit Jacques's discomfort with this symbolic mandate evident in the self-consciousness of the parody and, perhaps, by the fact that in the song he never makes it back to Antwerp, but is propelled along a trajectory of noise-

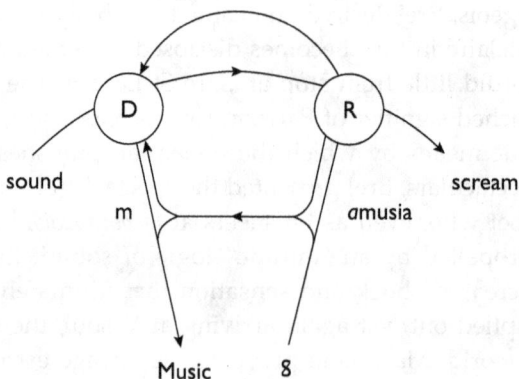

Figure 4.2. Graph 2: dissonance (D) and repetition (R).

music, the anorganic pulse of dissonance and repetition, over which he has no control.

The three delusions

In his perception and image of the locus of sound as an infinite scream passing through nature, Edvard Munch testifies that the space in which the extimacy of sound passes is voice as much as nature. Because the locus of sound passes through the voice of speaking beings, it is mis-perceived as speech, an effect of general *a*musia. The scream that passes through nature is, therefore, misperceived as an appeal. But the question arises as to whom the appeal is addressed. In speech, the appeal is a demand to the mother or father that becomes alienated as infinite desire when its specific needs are met and all that remains is the demand for love. Desire, that is always desire of the Other, remains eternally posed concerning the question of existence. *Che vuoi? What do you want of me?* Who am I? What am I for? (Figure 4.3.)

The failure of the Other to answer these questions in any adequate way means that the burden can fall on music. In its ineffability, music paradoxically suggests a locus of more profound meaning. Desire [d] emerges, in relation to music, through the delusion that it speaks, that it can convey things—feeling, emotion, truth—more than words can say. As such, it seems to promise that it can directly address the question of existence through affect and tell me, or make me feel, who I am. This essential delusion, at the end of desire, takes the various

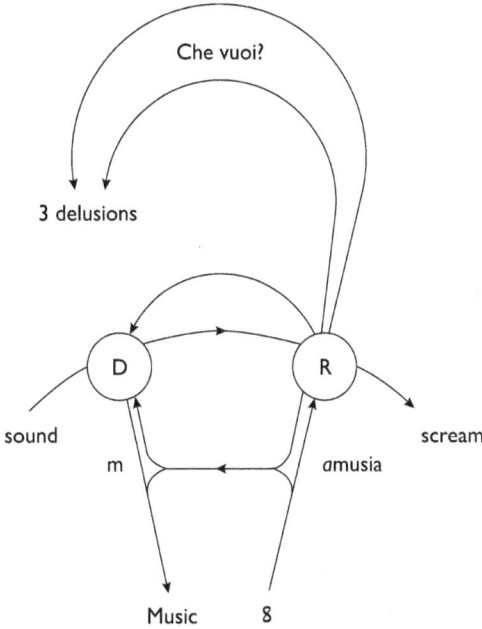

Figure 4.3.   Graph 3: the three delusions: love, hatred, and ignorance.

forms of love, hatred and ignorance (in the position of $\$\lozenge a$, the structure of fantasy). The delusion of love believes that music speaks directly to me, or, indeed, that it is only through music that I can express myself. My guitar, piano, lyre speaks of the longing of my soul that mere words cannot express. Alternatively, music speaks not to me but my rival, and I hate it. The delusions of love and hate are, of course, essentially the same, where the rival is nothing other than an alter ego. In the delusion of ignorance, music speaks neither to me nor to my rival, but purely to itself in its own language of which I am ignorant. My ignorance, however, implies it has some special access to knowledge and, consequently, to knowledge about me that I wish to know nothing about.

Audio unconscious

At the upper level of the graph, the vector that runs parallel to the locus of sound marks the place of the audio unconscious (Figure 4.4).

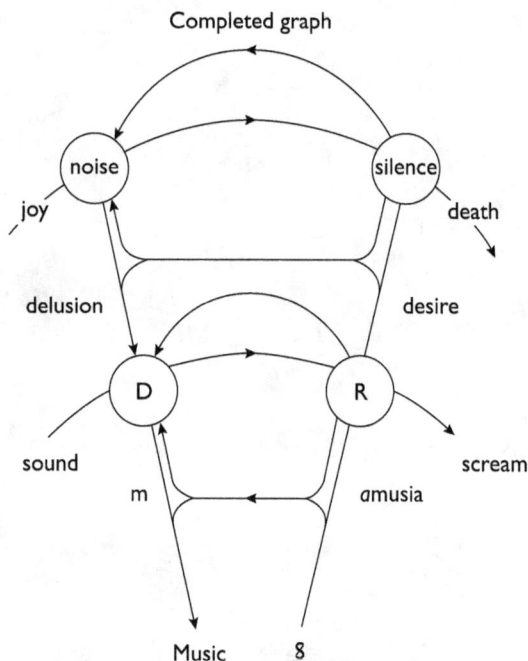

Figure 4.4. Graph 4: the audio unconscious.

The term "joy" should replace Lacan's term "*jouissance*", however, just as "death" replaces "castration". Death does not here refer to the empirical end to someone's life, but to the continuous death of someone or something that music denotes as the defining sound of a life. This does not just refer to the funeral song or desert island discs that one carries around in pleasurable anticipation of death and the celebration and commemoration of one's life; it refers to the music that, for better or worse, in joy or in agony, marks the indeterminable, endless possibility of the death of someone or something. It refers to the music that reduces us to waste, to noise that is framed by the silence of death, which returns from the past in the form of repetition in the clamour for being. It is the music of an indeterminable joy before death.

For Lacan, "the drive is what becomes of demand when the subject vanishes from it" (2006, p. 692): that is to say, the subject of language, speech. The drive is pure, speechless demand; as such, it is usually characterised as silent. While "Eros is sonorous", suggests Deleuze, "the death instinct is silent" (Deleuze, 1990, p. 241). Since, for Georges Bataille, Eros is inextricably bound to death, "Eroticism is silence" but this is because it lies at the unspeakable limit of language (Bataille, 1986, p. 246), and, as such, might well resound with the noises of animality. The place of the drive ($◊D), therefore, is denoted by silence. However, silence is impossible, as John Cage discovered when he was placed in an anechoic chamber where silence was abolished by the noise of the body that inhabited it. Consequently, when Cage staged a piece of music that consisted of a motionless pianist at a silent piano, music became whatever sounds could be perceived in the 4.33 minutes that were allotted to the performance. In the withdrawal of music as organised sound, noise-music emerged without any principle of organisation other than the pre-determined time it was given. In this noise-music, the noises of the bodies of the audience are conjoined with their ambient environment in the demand for music.

With this piece, then, Cage evoked the music of the drive, the hitherto accursed domain, for while a mouth that eats and sucks and gnaws may not speak, it is still noisy, as is the scene of a successful erotic encounter. In the absence of speech there is silence, but only for it to be filled with noise. A joyful clamour, therefore, tends towards the death that frames and determines it, the silence that is the space of its unfolding and disappearance. This noise is amusical, unlistenable, radically heterogeneous from the music of organised sound that seems to be filled with the promise of meaning. On the contrary, amusic is abject, since it consists of the noises of eating, fornicating, defecating: noises of the body. This is noise-music as waste, junk, detritus, noise as non-productive expenditure: the singular noise that I am without meaning. It is the noise of an indifferent multiplicity that discloses not just that the Other is lacking, but that there is no Other. In the place of the signifier of a lack in the Other, there is noise. There is nothing Other than the noise of joyful immanence in the clamour for being.

Hank Williams's cough

T he central conceit of Leonard Cohen's "Tower of Song" (1988), concerns a tall tower representing the pantheon of popular song in which reside all the greatest singers, alive or dead, in order of rank from top to bottom. Cohen locates himself there, but somewhere near the bottom, from where he calls to Hank Williams, a hundred floors further up, with a query concerning the extent of loneliness. Cohen receives no answer but can nevertheless hear the Country and Western singer coughing long into the night way above him.

Did Hank Williams have a cough? When he died at the age of twenty-nine, "his lungs showed evidence of edema, or accumulation of excessive fluids" as an effect of the heart disease that killed him (Williams, 1981, p. 217). The signs were there; shortly before he died he is reported to have complained, "my chest is ready to bust, I can hardly breathe" (Williams, 1981, p. 217). The heart disease was, of course, the result of alcoholism so severe that "he'd beg for whisky like a baby begs for milk" (p. 205). But, as far as I am aware, Williams was not a notorious cougher.

Leonard Cohen's enigmatic lines have been taken as an indication of his modesty; the latter has said that Williams is located a hundred floors above himself in the tower because "I know where Hank Williams stands in the history of popular song. 'Your Cheatin' Heart', songs like that, are sublime, in his own tradition, and I feel myself a very minor writer" (de Lisle, 2004). What is curious, of course, is that Hank Williams no longer sings in the tower of song where he is located because of his sublime country classics; he coughs.

Maybe Hank Williams's coughing answers the question of loneliness. This is how lonely it gets: loneliness beyond speech, beyond song, just the involuntary yet interminable sound of suffering erupting from the place where song or speech should be. For Cohen, the listener, the cough establishes and communicates some kind of presence, communicates without meaning or intention no doubt, but communicates nevertheless and keeps everyone company, keeps everyone awake, whether they like it or not. If Cohen can hear Williams's cough a hundred floors below, what must it be like just a few floors away? For God's sake Hank, take some Night Nurse. Sweet Jesus, Hank, Frank Sinatra is going insane in here. Sympathy or hostility, a relation of sorts is sustained.

But what is this dead man's cough and where does it come from? Is there a tradition of ghostly coughs or coughing ghosts? Does the cough denote a subject from whence it comes, or is it simply a cough and nothing more? Hank Williams died on New Year's Day, 1953; all that is left of him is his song, and all that is left of his song, it seems, is a cough. Perhaps this cough is the distilled remnant, the reverberating echo, of Williams's characteristic demi-yodel, that catch in the throat that he used to convey pathos in so many songs about loneliness—or being lonesome—not least in "Long Gone Lonesome Blues", "I'm so Lonesome I could Cry", and "Love Sick Blues". The latter uses the technique to such a degree that the excessive repetition of "lo-oh-ohnsome blu-oo-oos" defines for many everything that is annoying about country music. All that is left of Williams in the tower of song is this perpetual catch-in-the-throat reduced to a raw cough that expands and resonates throughout the tower in the absence of Williams himself. No one hears from Williams, he does not speak; no one sees him. A cough does not have the lexical form to designate a subject. If it refers to anything, it refers to itself in the rhythm of its eruptions, the variations in its relative thickness, volume, density, and resonance. But if a cough does not emanate from the throat of a speaking subject endowed with agency and intention, it does, nevertheless, erupt from a space divested of those qualities, at least for the period of its duration: the interior of a throat that cannot speak, act or refer to itself, but simply suffers.

What is a cough? A cough is a symptom of an underlying physical illness or some kind of manifestation, a signifier, of neurosis (see Dora, for example). Given that he has been long dead, the former can be discounted, but the psyche, neither mind nor body, inhabits the world of ghosts and spirits. Interestingly, Williams's cough, from a Lacanian orientation, could be said to occupy both of Lacan's definitions of the symptom from the perspective of the listener. On the one hand, the cough is a coded message, a response to the question "how lonely does it get?" On the other hand, the "message", if it is one, is emitted in the space of a failure to reply. Hank Williams does not answer the question, he just coughs. The coughing is not taken as a response. It says nothing; it resounds but to no one, responds to nothing, a pure dissonance that repeats. Beyond interpretation, "the symptom can only be defined as the way each subject enjoys [jouit] the unconscious, in so far as the unconscious determines him" (Lacan). Hank Williams is, of course, dead, he does not exist, but the subject of an audio unconscious ex-sists in the dissonance of the cough that repeats and resonates all night long.

Hank Williams's cough is the amusical song of the loneliness of being in which, moreover, in coughing, "he" is no longer there, just the sound of the sorrowful vehicle that coughed him up out into the world. One coughs, just as one is born, erupting from an aperture in the body, against one's will. Williams's cough that is all that is left of him even as it endlessly prevents him appearing, is the perfect cough that, precisely, has no meaning, yet persists infinitely in its suffering and its sorrow as song.

CHAPTER FIVE

From speaking beings to Talking Heads

Autism between silence and rhythm

I n his book *Big Bangs: The Story of Five Discoveries That Changed Musical History* (2001), the composer Howard Goodall offers his readers two of his most "special musical moments", one of which concerns witnessing a boy of five or six given a drum to play in a school orchestra. The child, neither smiling nor looking at the other children because he was "too autistic to focus his eyes", had to have his carer repeatedly pick up his beater for him. Nevertheless, he eventually connected and started "hitting the drum rat-tat-tat in unison with everyone else" (Goodall, 2001, p. 52). At this point Goodall noticed that the carer was in floods of tears and asked her what was wrong.

> She says, "You don't understand. I have been working with this little boy since he came here four years ago. When he imitated the rhythm of the music just then that was the first time *ever* he had responded to something another human being had done. It is his first communication with another person. I was overcome by it, that's all." (Goodall, 2001, p. 52)

Here, rhythm forms the basis of a social bond in which the sound of the beat becomes the minimal vehicle for a kind of enunciation, an assent to sound that recognises its beat in the rhythm of the Other, that is to say, the school and the musical ensemble that are articulated by the regularity of repeated sound. The carer understands the boy's beating of the stick to be a unique moment of communication, something amplified by Goodhall, who emphasises that the boy was entirely mute and unresponsive, and nothing could reach him—"not a word, not a glance, not a cuddle, not a smile, not a kiss . . ." (p. 52)— except through the connection shaped by musical rhythm.

It is generally assumed that there is a "scale" or "spectrum" of autism that ranges from the profound silence and disconnection represented by the boy in Goodall's anecdote to "high-functioning" subjects diagnosed with Asperger's syndrome. Following the Lacanian understanding of autism as a structure (rather than a spectrum), it is possible to suggest that musical rhythm functions as a rim that provides both a means of stability for the autistic subject and a mode of communication from a position "outside sense", that is, from the perspective of the real. Maleval's essential work on autism, *L'autiste et sa voix* (2009) points the way in developing this suggestion to the degree to which one might move from a discussion of the importance of rhythm to an elaboration of a specific autistic art of performance. In this chapter, this suggestion is followed with particular reference to David Byrne, who has, on a number of occasions, diagnosed himself with a form of Asperger's syndrome, the early work of Talking Heads, Byrne's reflections on his practice and music generally in his own book *How Music Works* (2012), and Naoki Higashida's *The Reason I Jump* (2013), the account of his own condition by a severely autistic Japanese boy who communicates through the means of a specially designed computer.

According to Maleval, autism is characterised by a disconnection between the master signifier and the *jouissance* that it fails to regulate. For Maleval, "this disconnection is a defence against the voice, which for Lacan is equivalent to enunciation", which, for the autistic subject, is "a real Other of jouissance" (Voruz, 2012, pp. 207–208). The disconnection between the signifier and *jouissance* corresponds to the disassociation between language and speech to the extent that autistic subjects are in language, but outside sense . . . Without access to sense the world is chaotic, and keeping things under control is a way to regulate jouissance. Everyone regulates the jouissance of the living through the signifier, i.e. the introduction of sense in the real through use of difference, except for autistic subjects. It follows that autistic subjects have to devise an alternative way of regulating jouissance. (Voruz, 2012, pp. 207–208)

Laurent, in an essay called "Spectres of autism" (2012b), observes that the "refusal of the signifier" means that language is reduced to a senseless noise resonating from the site of enunciation that has no specific designation as the signified subject of a statement. Without the distance introduced by the signifier of difference, the senseless noise can become an oppressive presence. This is evident, for Laurent, in the commonly noted extreme sensitivity shown by autistic subjects to ambient noise. Laurent cites "the case of a child who covers his ears when a plane passes overhead at thirty thousand feet" (p. 57), an image reminiscent of Edvard Munch's famous painting *The Scream*, whose figure also presses its hands against its ears in anguish at the "fundamental cry" that appears to scorch the sky in swirling flames of yellow and red. Given that there is no suggestion that autistics possess any physical difference in their auditory capacities, for Laurent this is an example of what has been observed in the Lacanian clinic: that "an autistic child is located in a space that is not constituted in terms of distance" (p. 57). The residue of noise left over by the refusal of the signifier is always close by. Indeed, as we shall see, rhythm formed on the basis of this noise can produce the sense of spacing (and time) necessary for the establishment of distance and, moreover, provide the basis for symbolisation. In another anecdote from the same essay, Laurent shows how noise, when subject to the regularities of repetition, can not only provide the vehicle for enunciation and a relation to the Other (as with the Goodall example), but may also supply the material support for articulate speech. In this anecdote, Laurent speaks of another autistic subject "who had two little sticks which formed the basis of his own system, two little sticks that he used to make a noise with all day long" (Laurent, 2012b, pp. 57–58). As part of his therapy, the child's analyst began vocalising the beats, the autistic subject's rhythmic noise, "ti-ti-ti-ti", in order to coax a similar verbalisation in his patient. "He was then able to pass from the exchange of the 'ti-ti-ti-ti' to the naming of other things" (Laurent, 2012b, p. 58).

The importance of musical rhythm and repetition can remain an essential support even to high-functioning subjects of autism such as those diagnosed with Asperger's syndrome. Amy Murphy, for example, writes on her blog about the "importance of music to autism [and] aspergers" in the following way.

> First and foremost, [music] is the largest and most sturdy of anchors. Mentally, I seem to frequently be allover [sic] the place and unable to focus and concentrate due to rampant and erratic running thoughts. I'm frequently lost . . . Music is a grounding force that helps me to bring my mind back in to focus by repeatedly playing the same song over and over again on, hopefully, a never ending loop. It's akin to being scattered from one end of the room to the other and the music brings all the pieces back into one cohesive unit. It allows me to focus and function. (Murphy, 2011)

For the autistic subject, then, the disconnection between the signifier and *jouissance* associated with the site of enunciation is supplemented by music from which voice has been successfully extracted to become purely a principle of organisation based on the regularity of repetition that satisfies the desire for stability and sameness. As we will see, the band in the heaven of autism plays your favourite song over and over again in a place outside space and time where nothing ever happens.

Fear of Music

Mulholland's *Fear of Music: The 261 Greatest Albums since Punk and Disco* (2006) is a collection of brief commentaries on his own personal pantheon of pop greatness from the late 1970s to its time of publication in which Talking Heads' *Fear of Music* (1979) is mentioned briefly as one of the featured albums. The title of Mulholland's book is curious and an unusual choice as an indicator of a "best-of" list. Mulholland justifies it by citing the "fear" that is apparently instilled in ordinary fans by most music criticism. Mulholland quotes television presenter Tim Lovejoy, who claims to have been "scared of music" because his own tastes did not cohere with those of the usual "all-time" favourites such as Van Morrison and The Beatles, for whom he had particular distaste. Mulholland uses Lovejoy's example to iterate the familiar journalistic complaint about the reduction of music to critical or "academic" categories and knowledge. "Critics turned jazz into academia", he laments, "if we're not careful we'll turn everything previously thrilling, irresponsible and gloriously, stupidly shaggable about pop into one enormous library of alphabetised lists of private ponderings" (Mulholland, 2006, pp. viii–ix). It is a strange way to introduce a book that consists entirely of Mulholland's own private ponderings on albums, albeit arranged chronologically rather than alphabetically. One assumes the critical disavowal is there to reassure the implied reader that the author shares our own "stupidly shaggable" idiotic *jouissance* with regard to popular music and that this connection both informs and authenticates his commentary.

Even more strange, then, to title the book *Fear of Music* (rather than "scared of music", say, which would have been the authentic quote from Lovejoy) when it cannot fail to refer to Talking Heads, a band whose music clearly offers a rather different relation to *jouissance* than that of the usual pop persona or rock band. Indeed, Mulholland accepts that the significance of Talking Heads' music does not primarily reside in its function as a soundtrack or *aide memoire* to one's amorous history or in its confirmation of one's attitude or worldview, but because "they fascinate and inspire and set off hours of contemplation of the meaning of meaning" (2006, p. 66). If the tautological "meaning of meaning" made any sense, it would imply a paradoxical position "outside sense" from which sense or meaning itself could be impossibly assessed. Insightfully, Mulholland argues that while the lyrical themes and topics of the band do not reflect the usual concerns in popular music—indeed it is usually difficult if not impossible to know what the songs are about—they are, nevertheless, recognisably articulated by a *way* of thinking, as Mulholland describes: "the way our minds flit from one subject to another, and alight on something, and obsess about it until we've excavated all its humours and horrors and realised we're driving ourselves recognisably insane" (pp. 66–68). Talking Heads' *Fear of Music* is about ways or modes of thought as much as it is often allusively about the contents or objects of thought.

Accordingly, the title of Talking Heads' third album does not concern music as an object of fear; rather, it refers to music as the medium of fear, or the vehicle that articulates and provides a means of negotiation of various objects of fear. This is a point emphasised by Lethem in his own book, also titled *Fear of Music* (2012): *Fear of Music* consists of "fear-of" music. Lethem writes that "It's been proposed that 'Fear of (signifier)' is the key to parsing the album: the 'real' subject being fear of air, fear of drugs, fear of heaven, fear of cities and animals and so forth" (pp. 17–18). Or, rather, the real subject is the music itself that tracks and organises the album's otherwise chaotic "quotient of free-floating dread" (p. 56).

Determining these themes is, of course, the main songwriter David Byrne, and from his initial appearance in 1977 as a clean-cut yet disturbing Anthony Perkins look-a-like (in his guise as Norman Bates, the lead character in Alfred Hitchcock's *Psycho*, 1960), Byrne's persona and performance brought a sharp definition to their first successful single, "Psycho Killer" (1977). Since then, Talking Heads' early albums have been indelibly associated with various types of "paranoia and psychological turmoil" (Mulholland, 2006, p. 68). The album *Fear of Music* is, indeed, rich in references to various phobias and forms of psychoses: schizophrenia (a mind's fear of itself) in "Mind"; the Cold War paranoia of self-styled urban guerrillas in "Life During Wartime"; obsessive concerns about the (in)adequacy of "Paper", the toxicity of "Air", the malevolence of "Animals"; multiple references to claustrophobia (see Lethem, 2012, pp. 20, 73, 80); agoraphobia (p. 42); insomnia (p. 68), and so on.

All of this is, of course, purely thematic and the stuff of art, but Byrne has, on a number of different occasions, acknowledged a particular distinction to his own thought patterns. In a short chapter titled "Is *Fear of Music* an Asperger's record?", Lethem notes that on his own website in 2006, Byrne acknowledged that "I was a peculiar young man. Borderline Asperger's, I guess", developing the point further in an interview with the *Guardian*, saying, "I'd only heard of Asperger's a few years ago, when a group out of Stanford proposed a spectrum that goes from autism to Asperger's to sort-of-good-at-math. I thought 'Wow, I see a lot of myself in that'" (Lethem, 2012, p. 96). It is an admission Byrne also repeats in his book *How Music Works* (2012, p. 33). He adds to this admission an anecdote concerning the name of the band he first joined with Chris Frantz, drummer of Talking Heads, in 1973. Frantz named this band The Artistics, but when the full extent of the social awkwardness of Byrne and another guitarist in the group became evident, Frantz joked that the band ought to be called The Autistics (Byrne, 2012, p. 36).

With the encouragement of these authorial hints, then, it is interesting to notice the elements of autistic structure evident in the songs and the self-reflexivity concerning certain symptoms and their broad political and cultural contextualisation. It is a context that seems to fill out this idea of the "borderline" in which, perhaps, subjective traces named as "Asperger's" or "autistic" play themselves out and have their effects in the context of a Punk or Post-Punk rock band and its oeuvre, that is, in a primarily musical enunciation that is collective and cultural.

Speaking beings and talking heads

As we have seen, according to Maleval, it is "the dissociation between voice and language that is the principle of autism" (in Laurent, 2012a, p. 22). A similar dissociation is announced by the name Talking Heads. It is well known that the name of the band comes from television broadcasting jargon. In an interview, the bassist Tina Weymouth recalled that "A friend had found the name in the TV Guide which explained the term used by TV studios to describe a head-and-shoulder shot of a person talking as 'all content, no action.' It fit" (Weymouth in Talking Heads, 1992). This distinction between "action and content" is analogous to the one at stake in the autistic relation to language in that while there is often a relation to *talk*, the content of speech, the action of speaking is too traumatic or burdensome. This is one of the key differences between the notion of a "speaking being", which lays the emphasis on the subject of the enunciation, and a "talking head", which is simply a sign indexing the taking place of an exchange of information, the precise nature or particular sense of that information being irrelevant. Both Middle English words, "speak" and "talk" appear to be synonymous, but in their primary senses they refer to two different aspects of the utterance. The *OED* takes the term "speak" to refer to the *act* of enunciation, the "action of speaking", its first medieval examples referring in different ways to the quality of speech and voice. "Talk", meanwhile, refers to the "exchange of ideas, thoughts and information" conveyed by speech, that is to say, discourse.

The name of the band also marks a clear disjunction between the activity of the group and what it normally designates, opening up a gap not only between speaking and talking, but also talking and singing. Even if the reference to "heads" might indicate that the band is more interested in the cerebral aspect of music than the body (the more conventional locus of stupidly shaggable pop music), the business of a rock band is generally to sing rather than talk. In its emphasis on the head, the phrase highlights the abstract exchange of cerebral contents in talk rather than action or the presentation of individual subjects or "personalities". As such, it is an image of speaking beings that have been rendered "other" to themselves in the mirror of television and the locus of televisual language and jargon. For Laurent, "autistic subjects are in fact very centred on this televisual Other" because it seems to guarantee the stability of talk, and he cites a subject who

> constituted his language out of catch phrases he had heard on the television, the scraps and ends of the discourse of the Other [but] as soon as it is extracted, it no longer refers to anything other than the statement itself, separated from its enunciation. (Laurent, 2012b, p. 59)

"Talking heads" is not simply a phrase drawn from the discourse of television, of course, but is a technical term referring to a particular television genre that implies knowledge about television even as the phrase is extracted from its original site of enunciation and deployed, apparently nonsensically, as the name of a rock band. Laurent writes that "when the autistic subject picks out this or that cantilena, he becomes, in a sense, an analyser of the common discourse that we repeat among ourselves" (Laurent, 2012b, p. 59).

An abstract term for a television genre that is extracted from the mirror of the televisual Other and then further abstracted as a *name* implying universal significance as the subject of a musical *oeuvre* could indicate both an analysis and critique of the reduction of human subjects to functions of television discourse or, as a point of identitification, "talking heads" could also resonate with Hans Asperger's own description of the subjects whose "syndrome" has been given his name: "to put it bluntly, these individuals are intelligent automata. Social adaptation has to proceed via the intellect" (cited in Maleval, 2012, p. 43). Many of the songs on the early Talking Heads' albums concern the difficulties of social adaptation, troubles with experiencing emotions (they exist but are difficult to manage), and, in particular, the problem of speech. On the first album, *Talking Heads 77*, the subject of "Tentative Decisions" announces that he wants to give the "problem" of speech to another; "Happy Days" similarly puts off the point of decision before he is able "to talk . . . like ev'ry . . .", though the sentence cuts off, implying he is not quite there yet. "No Compassion" again is obsessed with indefinite "problems", repeating the word insistently, particularly the problem of "decisions" that preclude his ability to feel compassion. And supremely, of course, the fractured, chaotic internal monologue of "Psycho Killer" itemises the subject's sensitivity to touch, his commitment to silence, even as he gives way uncontrollably to irruptions of garbled verbiage and snatches of French that disguise an apparent psychotic delusion. It is only here that, retrospectively, the wrong note is struck, since autism is not considered a form of psychosis (although this was a common view in the 1970s). While the characteristics of the subject of "Psycho Killer" (1977) are more autistic than psychotic, the latter more excitingly fits in with the "Anthony Perkins" persona. Beginning with his anguished confrontation with the "facts", the song's monologue builds to the point where it addresses an imaginary partner, complaining about his alter ego's inability to finish a conversation, of "talking a lot, but not saying anything", and of the speaker's own commitment to silence or, if pushed, his refusal to say anything more than once. With its clear distinction and dissociation between talking and saying, its commitment to silence with regard to enunciation which, as the song shows, is connected traumatically with *jouissance* (*"Realisant mon espoir / Je me lance, vers la gloire, OK"*), autistic structure could not be more evident. When the traumatic utterance occurs—here disguised and re-routed through French—it must not be repeated. As Maleval writes, "when the object of vocal *jouissance* is given up to the *jouissance* of the Other . . . There is no attempt to explain, no commentary, no retrospective return to what has been said" (Maleval, 2012, p. 39).

Heaven

Of course, many interesting questions arise here about how an undiagnosed autism can seemingly represent itself as the content of a song in the absence of any obvious self-knowledge. While Byrne has latterly diagnosed himself with a "mild" form of Asperger's syndrome, itself high on the so-called "spectrum" of "high-functioning" autism, he says he was unaware of the name or the syndrome itself at the time of his early career and records. Byrne was, nevertheless, characterising elements of the structure in songs and performance, presumably through emphasising certain traits or tendencies in himself or others so that they might form the basis of lyrical portrayals in "Psycho Killer" and other songs. It is, after all, what writers and songwriters frequently say when reflecting on their artistic practice. While Sacher Masoch would never have heard the term masochist, he nevertheless laid out in literary form a symptomatology for masochism, any more than Sade knew he was a sadist (I assume if he had an interest in such labels he would have thought of himself as a naturalist). As Deleuze suggests, writers and novelists can be great clinicians as well as artists, and perhaps the songs of David Byrne and Talking Heads indicate that there is an autism that knows itself even if it does not know that it knows itself, or that misrecognises itself, for example, for literary purposes, in the mirror of psychosis, thereby demonstrating a strong desire for recognition.

Along with "Psycho Killer", another extraordinary example of autistic structure can be found in the song "Heaven" from *Fear of Music*, which could almost be described as a hymn to autistic bliss in its celebration of sameness and repetition, where a celestial band has managed to personalise and reduce its set to each individual's favourite song which it then plays all night (and perhaps for eternity), presumably just for them. The chorus climbs ecstatically as it repeats its definition of heaven as a place where nothing ever happens. This characterisation of heaven chimes uncannily with its representation in a story called "I'm Right Here", which is part of a book-length memoire by Naoki Higashida, a thirteen-year-old boy with autism from Japan, written with the aid of a customised computer. The book is called *The Reason I Jump* (2013) and Higashida states that he wrote it in order to convince people that autism is a "personality-type" rather than a disability. This is, according to Maleval, a common trait in autism and in other testimonies of subjects who have written of their situation through the offices of an object-double, or writing machine. Maleval claims that all autistic subjects "write in order to be recognised as intelligent beings and to demand that their difference be better taken account of", citing, for example, Birgin Sellin, who wrote on his computer that "as an autistic person I serve as a spokesperson for other autistics" (Maleval, 2012, p. 35). As Maleval further notes, this is in stark contrast to psychotics, many of whom refute their diagnosis, are uninterested in representing other psychotics, and write mostly to pursue a type of conspiracy theory or other form of delusion.

Higashida's fictional narrative "I'm Right Here" appears at the end of his book and is written in order to help people understand "how painful it is when you can't express yourself to the people you love" (p. 154). It tells the story of a small boy, Shun, who discovers that he is dead, this state being the metaphor of his separation from his parents with whom he cannot communicate and who in the story mourn this separation as they mourn his death. Most of the story, however, takes place in heaven, the site to which Shun withdraws when he is not trying to make his presence felt to parents to whom he cannot speak and for whom he is "dead". Shun realises he is in heaven shortly after he works out that he must have been involved in a fatal accident. He is initially confused and anxious about what is going to happen to him, but God appears to reassure him that "Absolutely nothing's going to happen to you, because – well, look around you – you've gone to heaven" (p. 163). As in the song on Talking Heads' *Fear of Music*, heaven is a place where nothing happens but is also and as such a place of "perfect freedom" precisely because it is entirely empty. "There's nothing here" (p. 166) in heaven and yet at the same time it is described as "fresh and exciting" (p. 167). It "is a world beyond time, outside of space" that is intensely pleasurable, "blissful" (p. 167). Shun describes the "immortal stars", "numberless lights wrapped around [him], comforting him like a shimmering blanket" (p. 166). Eventually, however, he perceives that his parents are incapable of overcoming the loss of their child and his mother begins a physical decline towards the point of death herself. Asking God what he can do, Shun is told he can return to his parents in the form of another child but on condition he leave heaven and give up both his own identity and all memory of his previous existence, which he does with a heavy heart for the sake of his parents' happiness. The story then signifies both the suffering the autistic child feels about what he cannot be for his parents and their "loss" of a "normal" child, but also an elegiac sense of regret for the identity and *jouissance* that he would also have to lose should he be "cured" of his condition. This is the intense "worry" upon which he reflects in the very last paragraphs of the book: his concern about the problems caused by his autism, but also the worry about being "cured" and losing his identity, of being born again as someone different with another subject position entirely.

Autism as performance art of rhythm

As Naoki Higashida and others show, autism names a desire for recognition that has to take a different route than conversational speech. Significantly, Higashida attests that while it is still impossible for him to have a "real" conversation, a certain level of *performance* is necessary: "I have no problem reading books aloud and singing, but as soon as I try to speak with someone, my words just vanish" (p. 15). Again, it is repetition that is crucial in helping him negotiate the demands of words; repeating them over and over is "like playing with sound and rhythm" (p. 24). Higashida here sets out the conditions for an autistic art—something that I want to suggest is fully delivered by David Byrne and Talking Heads.

In his book *How Music Works* (2012), Byrne reflects very briefly on his subjective state as a teenager in his tentative beginnings as a performer. In so doing, he stresses the enabling aspect of performance relative to the incredible shyness of the world he inhabited as "a withdrawn introvert":

> I decided that making my art in public (even if that meant playing people's songs at that point) was a way of reaching out and communicating when ordinary chitchat was not comfortable to me. It seemed not only a way to "speak" in another language, but also entry into conversation. (Byrne, 2012, p. 32)

These snippets of autobiography are largely limited to one chapter called "My life in performance", which dwells for the most part on the technical aspects of performance, costume, choreography, and stage business. There are, however, one or two startling admissions, such as "performing must have seemed my only option" and "music saved my life" (2012, p. 32), as if life has only been possible through the efficacies of performance. Rather than autobiography, *How Music Works* mostly comprises a theory of music, a set of detailed reflections on the technical aspects involved in the production, performance, recording, distribution, and marketing of music that dwells topically on the fate of the business of the popular music industry in the wake of digital technology. Byrne's theory of music appears to owe a lot to a very anti-romantic, media studies' approach that forgoes ideas of individual genius and that often borders on the technical determinism of Marshall McLuhan and the Toronto school. For Byrne, what music is or can be is largely determined by the technologies that enable it and the spaces that shape and enhance or dampen specific ambient qualities and sonic possibilities, whether that be an outdoor tribal setting, a cathedral, a concert hall, a transistor radio, a club, a disco, stadium, car, or iPod. In so far as it tells his story, the book narrates the accretion of various competences and collaborations that again ultimately determine the form and quality of the music.

For Maleval, subjects with autistic structure function well in relation to the rest of the world where they can create

> a border involving three components: an imaginary double that can take on the responsibility of enunciation, an autistic object with which to regulate jouissance, and the creation of a synthetic Other designed through the accumulation of comprehensive knowledge of specified topics. (Maleval, 2012, p. 208

In the context of Byrne's own self-diagnosis concerning his autistic structure, his book suggests that his very successful life and career was largely an effect of being able to establish, as a young man, what he calls a stage persona that could take on and facilitate speech in the context of his band, Talking Heads, which constituted a collective site of enunciation; music, it seems, provided both an object for the regulation of *jouissance* (in "play and rhythm", as Higashida suggests) and a vehicle for the cultural articulation of various fears and anxieties. With its "air of list-making rigour", for example, *Fear of Music* could almost be, in the words of Lethman, "a kind of machine for coping" (2012, p. 98). Yet, at the same time, the play of music and rhythm enables a poetic problematisation of all lists and of the "monochord" factual language that characterises many high-functioning autistics but which, with Byrne, is rendered equivocal as it becomes part of his stage performance. In the song "Cross-eyed and Painless" (1980), for example, the rhythmical rant, rapidly spoken-sung sequence raps on the indispensability yet unruliness of facts that are (neither) simple nor straight, lazy, late, facts that are rebellious and come with their own point of view, and so on. The "synthetic Other" that results from the concatenation of specific topics to which one may dedicate oneself in establishing knowledge and competence are amply illustrated in Byrne's book *How Music Works* in detailed accounts of the architecture of the border, or rim, of musical *jouissance* that he has established in collaborations with other musicians, artists, producers, technicians, and entrepreneurs. By "Cross-eyed and Painless", that rim had thickened from the original three-piece band playing scratchy minimalist punk to a thickly textured, highly percussive, multi-instrumental sound dense with poly-rhythms. Talking Heads' songs were always rhythmic, "the groove was always there", says Byrne, "it served as a sonic and psychological safety net, a link to the body. It said that no matter how alienated the subject or singer might appear, the groove and its connection to the body would provide solace and grounding" (Byrne, 2012, p. 45). By *Remain in Light* (1980), however, the band had expanded and the "groove" multiplied to such a rich and elaborate state that it became transformative. Byrne writes,

> As I experienced it this was not just a musical transformation, but also a psychic one. The nature of the music helped, but partly it was the very size of the band that allowed me, even as a lead singer, to lose myself and experience a kind of ecstatic release. (2012, p. 49)

At the same time, as thick, rich and elaborate as the armature of musicians and sound became, the rhythm never once resembled the smooth or sinuous roll associated with African and African-American music. Similarly, in performance, Byrne studied a range of rhythmic dance styles in conjunction with choreographers, but only in order to "let my body discover, little by little, its own grammar of movement". Like the music, this often remained "jerky, spastic, and strangely formal" (p. 50). The characteristic indicators of his *jouissance*, then, still permeated the "rim" of sound and texture even as it accreted ever more layers.

This process is given stunning visual demonstration in *Stop Making Sense* (1984), Jonathan Demme's film of Talking Heads' concert tour promoting their fourth album, *Speaking in Tongues* (1983). The concert and film begins with Byrne alone on stage, playing an acoustic version of one of his earliest songs, "Psycho Killer", followed by "Heaven", to be subsequently joined by the rest of the band as, over the course of the concert, the stage fills with more and more instrumentalists as the texture of the music thickens and the rhythms multiply. Memorably, Byrne's costume inflated bizarrely as the concert drew to its climax with a performance of "Cross-eyed and Painless", his pale grey business suit expanding to an extraordinary proportion in a manner, he suggests, inspired by his research in Japanese Noh theatre.

In the process of constructing this elaborate rim, or border, comprised of a multi-dimensional performance through which Byrne's stage persona expressed itself in song, Talking Heads could be described as having produced a specifically autistic performance art that, at first sight, is little different from any other in its sophistication, wit, profundity, and fun—even if it lacks a little in "shaggable stupidity". By autistic art, I do not refer to an art that is naïve or deficient in any way, but, rather, an art that knows itself for what it is and that, on the basis of a specific subject position and certain constant traits, can produce, through definite measures, forms of aesthetic expression unavailable to other subject positions, that also offers analysis and insight into the cultural—and, by extension, the political—conditions of its site of enunciation.

From general psychosis to ordinary autism

In a short piece on the politics of autism, "Autism: epidemic or the ordinary state of the subject", Laurent discusses various responses to the alarming rise in cases of autism recorded by the Centre for Disease Control and Prevention in America, which has seen a 25% increase in cases since 2006 and 78% since 2000–2002. Various causes have been advanced to account for the rise in a condition that is still, for the most part, regarded as an "illness" that is at the same time both "genetic" and "epidemic" (2012, pp. 125–129, 127). Reasons offered range from an increase in better diagnoses in poorer communities, the encouragement offered by benefits and services, to the expansion of the "spectrum" to include other categories, and even a five-minute test offered by the Centre of Excellence of Autism in San Diego which, as Laurent remarks, now makes it possible to put any subject into the category. Meanwhile, various measures have been taken to reduce the increase, the major one being the decision of the *DSM* (the *Diagnostic and Statistical Manual of Mental Disorders*) to introduce stricter criteria, with the result that Asperger's syndrome is no longer located on the spectrum. It remains to be seen what difference this readjustment will make to the apparently inexorable rise.

For Soler, the new symptoms that are confronting contemporary analysts in their everyday practice, "which affect orality, action and mood, are almost all symptoms outside the social bond, bearers of autistic *jouissance*" (Soler, 2014, p. 183). This observation concurs with Laurent's comment concerning the very existence of the statistical debate about the so-called "epidemic" that in itself makes the case for "the quasi-ordinary status of autism". On the one hand, Laurent suggests, autism is simply an exacerbated effect of an originary human problem: "If we define the speaking being as a being of communication", he concludes, "we discover a radical flaw within it" (2012c, p. 129). On the other hand, when the form of communication is not just speech, but a complex regime of telecommunications, this flaw becomes deeper and multiply fissured as new forms of communication displace or reformat speech into digits, code, icons, talking heads on the multiple screens that constitute the dominant modality of the Other.

"I think that people with autism are born outside the regime of civilization", states Naoki Higashida (2013, p. 151), who has his own theory about the emergence of so many people with his condition. Higashida links this emergence to "a deep sense of crisis" in a civilisation that comprises flawed, discontented speaking beings whose basic "flaw" or division in language is being exacerbated and enabled (in every sense) every day by the increasing dominance of online existence. While the existence of networked computers enables communication in one sense (as it clearly does with Higashida himself), it also sustains solitude outside of traditional social bonds. In her book *Alone Together* (2010), Turkle writes about the increasing dependency on online forms of sociality and the growing use of social robots for purposes of work, entertainment, and even pastoral care and therapy. Turkle's concern relates precisely to the dimension of the autistic *jouissance* in this situation: we are essentially alone with our laptop, smart phone and robot; no one is really there. Similarly, for Lanier (2010), people are not only being defined by their gadgets, they are essentially rendered equivalent to them, becoming no more than conduits of information and data, "relays in a global brain", or hive mind. For Soler, the new symptoms bearing autistic *jouissance* are "the reverse side of the pressures of a triumphant capitalism" in which autistic alienation is hooked up and "inverted to the injunctions of discourse" that "do not subtract the subject from the common clamour" (Soler, 2014, p. 184). This "common clamour" consists, of course, as Turkle and Lanier attest, of a network of isolated nodes, each alone together in a social graph or network that reduces them to data streams.

As the next section will argue, new telecommunications essentially conform to, and intensify, an economic structure that was put in place in the last third of the twentieth century, establishing as a governing imperative the conditions for the generalisation of psychosis that has now mutated into a kind of ordinary autism. From the abstract, yet notionally paranoid, subject of game theory that underlies neoliberal economics to the phenomenon of the hikikomori via the psycho-pathologies distracted and inflamed by the *jouissance* represented by global celebrity, the following section tracks this movement from general psychosis to ordinary autism.

In a review of Maleval's *L'autiste et sa voix* (2009), Voruz under-scores the political importance of "a structural understanding" of the condition in contradistinction to remedial treatments based on norma-tive assumptions about subjectivity that engage in regimes of reward and punishment. While autistic subjects are "in language but outside sense", such systems are experienced as manifestations of the Other's own senseless malevolence (p. 209). From the perspective of civilisa-tion that has sought for so long to close off, master, and utilise it, "senseless malevolence" is an apt description of nature or of speaking beings' revelation of their own truth in "killings in the world and self-ish planet-wrecking" (Higashida, 2013, p. 151), the speech of speaking beings being nothing but a locus of delusion concerning their own de-natured nature and that of the real. This is never more so than in the discourse of science that seeks to explain, account, model, utilise, and exploit those aspects of the physical real it finds in formulae. In being located outside sense, the autistic subject is in a position analogous to the real, but the real of a different kind to science, a real that "seeks to knot" the being of communication "to the Eros of a possible, liveable bond" (Soler, 2014, p. 186). As Higashida writes of the dream-tale of his blissful death and its sacrifice, "I'm right here": "I wrote this story in the hope that it will help you to understand how painful it is when you can't express yourself to the people you love" and to "connect back to the hearts of the people with autism" (Higashida, 2013, p. 154).

Autism's real perspective is communicable but not, for the most part, through conventional forms of speech. Indeed, as we have seen, autistic communication can take place through music, a "language of the real" that conjoins, in its double nature, love and the cosmos. In what follows, we look at this potential of music, in the context of psychoanalysis as the "emergency discourse in civilization" (Soler, p. 186) to shape a social bond that both makes up for the relation that lacks and capitalist discourse that forecloses Eros in "the business of love" (see Soler, 2014, p. 185).

PART II

THE MADNESS OF
ECONOMIC REALISM

CHAPTER SIX

Primal scream: dissonance and repetition

I magine there is no heaven or hell, or earth. An undifferentiated peace prevails. Imagine no sound, no conflict to disturb a silence in which unimaginable power is suspended. All at once, and for no apparent reason, an almighty scream erupts from nowhere. It is the music of creation.

Whether someone or something was lacking, dying, or simply distracted, a strange and dissonant music constitutes and begins to fill all time and space. If a scream must always be interpreted as an appeal (Lacan, 1986, p. 569), this appeal is addressed to nothing but silence. There is no Other. The music of creation is the only sound and it is omnipresent, ubiquitous, has always been ubiquitous, and provides the condition for all imagination, alterity, and interpretation. This unearthly sound is only audible, however, when another piece of music, both more holy and more satanic, precedes it from a universe within itself. Both pieces of music resonate within each other as, indecisively, points of origin and emergence are at once dissonant and endlessly repeated. They inaugurate and delimit a particular threshold of existence, continuously. Although they could be said to have a specific date of emergence, within the particular threshold of existence they begin and constitute, they are quite literally—if in parallel—universal, constant, everywhere at the same time.

The first piece of music, immanent to the scream yet preceding it, is "that breezy little number that lets all your co-workers know you've finally gotten into the office", to quote a commentator on the Internet. It has a title. It is called The Microsoft Sound, and was produced for Windows 95 by Brian Eno. An avowed non-musician, Eno is also regarded as "one of the pivotal figures of twentieth-century music" (Prendergast, 2003, p. 115). Eno was one of a number of art school alumni who introduced the techniques and principles of Minimalism into rock music, and, in 1978, inaugurated and named a new genre of ambient music that was designed not simply as background, but as an environment, a universe in which to immerse oneself into new sonic worlds (Eno, 1995, p. 294). As the title of the first record, *Music for Airports* (1978) suggests, these new sonic environments were particularly suited to impersonal, anonymous spaces of communication, spaces located outside the traditional localities of home and abroad, region or nation. Moreover, in its mode of composition, this and the other early records anticipated the generative music and art that currently engages Eno, music that is designed by and for computers and their users.

In an interview in 1995, Eno spoke of his commission to produce The Microsoft Sound. Their missive, he recalled, said, "'We want a piece of music that is inspiring, universal, blah-blah, da-da-da, optimistic, futuristic, sentimental, emotional", this whole list of adjectives, and then at the bottom it said "and it must be 3¼ seconds long'" (Eno & Kelly, 1995). It was the challenge of creating a piece with such ambition and scope and yet with such a short duration that appealed to Eno. He created about eighty or so pieces and the people from Microsoft chose the one that is now familiar and provided the basis for subsequent versions and other imitations. It is kind of breezy, but other commentators have thought differently. Another blogger, noting already in 1996 that he had by now heard this tune thousands of times and that it had "become as familiar and mundane as the other audio of my daily life", suggested that there was still "something different about the Microsoft Sound—something eerie, disturbing, and disconcerting". Yet another commentator wrote, "I like Brian Eno, but I want to kill him for making the fucking Microsoft Sound". Ultimately, Pat Kane, in an article on Eno, wrote "this noise—like the waking murmur of an unimaginable machine intelligence; bloodless, precise, ending with a discord that hints of different menace—is what Bill Gates wants the future to sound like. To these ears, it sounds scary and inhuman" (Kane, 1995). In-human indeed; that is to say, it is a sound delineating an anorganism at variance with itself. The register of the "inspiring, universal, blah-blah" is dissonant, and its repetition lays out a locus of low level annoyance and irritation, delineating the discordance, within themselves, of the organic and inorganic elements of techno-bureaucratic assemblages.

The second ubiquitous, yet originary, piece of music is the sound of the so-called Big Bang: the sound of the origin of the universe and its first million years of existence. Ever since Robert Wilson and Arno Penzias of Bell Laboratories failed in their efforts to record silence in 1965, the world of science has known about the existence of cosmic noise, or background radiation. This noise, passing through nature as a faint microwave glow across the sky, also known as the Homedale Whisper, is now considered to be the echoing reverberations of the origin of the universe. Mark Whittle, a cosmologist from Virginia University, claims to have recorded it in 2004, and on his university website it is possible to hear what he purports to be "an accurate rendering of the first years of primordial sound, shifted up into the human range, and compressed into 10 seconds" (Whittle, 2007). Named by Fred Hoyle in the 1950s, the theory of the origin of the universe has been subsequently characterised as a huge aural explosion, but, as Whittle suggests, strictly speaking, the big bang itself was silent. Whittle describes the point at the beginning of time and space as "a moment of silence followed by a rapidly descending scream which builds to a deep roar and ends in a deafening hiss" (2007). To truly appreciate the sound, it needs to be played at the correct volume which, according to Whittle, is 110 decibels, which, as he also says, is "about as loud as a rock concert!" The rock concert culminates, after a hundred million years, in "a spectacular light show" in which "the highest pitch sounds dissolve into the first generation of exploding stars while the deepest bass notes slowly began to weave the tapestry of galaxies which now fills all of space". The universe begins, then, with a moment of profound silence followed by a "primal scream" (2007).

The scream remains audible. If it did not resonate well below the human range, it would be possible to hear it; the ambient sound of the universe, the noise that originated time and space: a deep, hissing scream. Indeed, although no one can hear, experience, or know anything about it without prosthetic means, these days a radio tele-scope and computer software, everyone *is* it. From "this cosmic sound came all of cosmic structure. Without it there would be no stars or galaxies. And without stars, there would be no elements and no plan-ets and no people" (Whittle, 2007). Computers are necessary to pro-cess and render audible the cosmic sound, which is one of the reasons why Eno's little refrain must take precedence. From the moment when Microsoft's economic power and ubiquity overwhelmingly defined the horizon of technological existence, The Microsoft Sound can be located as the origin of the origin, whether or not one listens to the big bang on a PC or a Mac. The Microsoft Sound, which resonates in all the subsequent variations, precedes and provides the work-a-day context and condition for the emergence of the origin of the universe and all time, space, and matter.

The juxtaposition of these two sounds, and their characterisation as music, illustrates a number of things, not least the establishment of a plane of consistency between music, science, and technology. The 1990s saw an increase in the application of scientific principles to music (not just maths and physics but also life sciences, evolutionary biology, and so on). That is to say to the making of music as well as the understanding of it, that took place less on conventional instru-ments than in computers, synthesisers, and sequencers. Further, this was connected to an understanding of music as an open rather than a closed system that "permeates and is permeated by the whole world" (Bogue, 2003, p. 14). There has been a correlation in aesthetic–scientific understanding or experience of the real. Music in the 1980s–1990s–2000s and beyond has been imagined not simply as a special mode of symbolisation, but a principle of integration through which the real might be known scientifically or experienced through simulation. But this further requires that it becomes decentred from the heart of human experience. Music is no longer centred on a human subject, composer, listener, fan, or subject-of-consciousness, but becomes ambient and ubiquitous, unheard as much as it is heard. Further, it is Eno's own ambition that such musical environments be generated autonomously without intervention from a musician or composer.

Eno's Microsoft Sound is one of many early experiments in an area in which the universe of sound clip provides, theoretically, the fullest realisation. The universe of sound is the most stunning example, the example of all possible examples, of the generativity of music, and indeed of the idea that all generation is musical, the effect of *natura musicans* that "pervades the physical and biological universe" (Bogue, 2003, p. 75). Born out of an interest in the ways in which machines and systems might be designed to produce musical and visual experiences, in 1995 Eno worked with Tim Cole's Koan software whose "authoring tool" enables a computer's sound card to be programmed to produce music autonomously (see Eno, 1995, p. 330–332). Such music can be generated indefinitely in series that are always different, and never repeated, even though the process itself is one of pure repetition. Composition is the effect of an endless repetition without memory, sounds, disposed and disposable, forgotten and replaced by new ones that are exactly the same. Conceptually, as he explained in a lecture at the ICA in London in 2001 that used the model of John Conway's Game of Life, Eno is interested in computer-generated music that emerges and develops according to the most basic principles of evolutionary biology.

This interest in generative music expresses, David Toop suggests, "the desire to make a music that exists in a state of being, theoretically without beginning or end" (Toop, 2004, p. 190). The music is, therefore, the manifestation of a desire for being; it is the sound or the clamour not *of* being, but *for* being. Philosophically speaking, this interest in generative music in the 1990s and beyond, which finds its ultimate metaphor in the universe of sound, provides the ambient soundtrack for a paradoxical ontology without being: the clamour of a desire for being or a want-to-be. Generative music, for which the universe of sound clip is, retrospectively, the primary model, takes up this contention, but with a certain nuance that suggests that such in-human univocity expresses a desire for being. Like the propositions made by Deleuze's canon of ontologists who proclaim the univocity of being, the generative music echoes in the clamour of a desire for univocity that renders it internally riven. It is the production of a process of auto-production that is the effect of the desire for an Other that is both the echo and the ordering principle of production. Ironically, the desire for univocity that consists in a multiplicity of echoing voices displaces and disguises the general economy of sound (or music as an open system).

That dissonance is a principle of repetition is evident, for Lacan, in the way in which *tuché* generates the automaton in Seminar 11 (Lacan,

1986, pp. 53–78). *Tuché* is described as "the encounter with the real", where that encounter is "essentially missed" (p. 55). Dissonance is the echo of that missed encounter, that big bang, the jarring noise of the singular (non)relation to one's own piece of reality. The function of the real in repetition, however, is rigorously distinguished, in Lacan, from the automaton that is "the insistence of the signs, by which we see ourselves governed by the pleasure principle" and the subject that is brought into social existence by the signifier. The missed encounter with the real is not the result of an action by a subject. But while the real is exterior to symbolisation, it is also "behind", or immanent to it: "the real is that which always lies behind the automaton" (Lacan, 1986, p. 54). We are essentially passive in relation to the encounter; it just happens. This is the function of the real in repetition. "What is repeated, in fact, is always something that occurs . . . *as if by chance*" (Lacan, 1986, p. 54). These two levels of repetition—the automaton of the signifier that determines the subject in relation to his or her social reality, and the *tuché* as the animating principle of the subject of the unconscious—are evident in Deleuze also:

> To repeat is to behave in a certain manner, but in relation to something unique or singular which has no equal or equivalent. And perhaps this repetition at the level of external conduct echoes, for its own part, a more secret vibration which animates it, a more profound internal repetition within the singular. (Deleuze, 1997, p. 1)

The dissonance that sounds in the singular chance encounter with one's own profound reality echoes in the repetitive everyday actions of social reality governed by the pleasure principle that seeks out a harmonious existence. Dissonance is the principle of excitation that is opposed to harmony only in so far as harmony diminishes the excitation. However, such diminution only leads to greater excitation in the disruption of another dissonance, the repetition of the disorientating encounter with the real that calls forth imagination and creativity in the different perspective on music that it opens up. What needs to be stressed, however, is that the automatism of a musical note or sequence in the locus of actual and virtual sound does not *represent* the function of repetition in the real. It is not a question of signifiers veiling a more profound reality even as they betray its presence in the dissonance between different aural events. While repetition may occur essentially for itself, it is not an objective property; it always occurs in this domain of experience and memory where it sustains the past's unconscious relation to the future.

Music is a singularly effective and affective vehicle in sustaining, through repetition, the unconscious relation between past and future. Repeated hearings of a particular piece of music, either expected or unexpected, can, in exquisite discomfort, suddenly disclose a forgotten past of pain or pleasure. This is perhaps particularly the case in the age of mechanical reproduction or recording that is so often maligned. Indeed, part of the rationale for Eno's generative music is his frustration with the "clockwork" repetitions of recorded music. Speculating on a future world in which every piece of music is different because it has been generated by a computer's difference engine, Eno thinks that "it is possible that our grandchildren will look at us in wonder and say, 'you mean you used to listen to exactly the same thing over and over again'" (Eno, 1995, p. 332).

The repetitive dissonance of Eno's generative music is an effect of a software programme that allows a finite number of tones/sounds to yield a practically unlimited diversity of combinations in which, however, each one is perfectly equivalent and exchangeable. This process promises a different relation between the subject and the real than that pertaining in the epoch of recorded music. This different relation is an effect of a scientific process generating a form of integrated reality in which music becomes continuous with milieu in a new order of (perhaps waning) affect. Baudrillard gives such music a privileged place in his account of integral reality, his name for the "perpetrating on the world of an unlimited operational project whereby everything becomes real", calling music composed on a computer "integral music":

> It is a music reduced to pure wavelength, the final reception of which, the tangible effect on the listener, is exactly programmed too, as in a closed circuit. It is, in a sense, a virtual music, flawless and without imagination, merging into its own model, and even the enjoyment of it is virtual enjoyment. Is this still music? (Baudrillard, 2005, pp. 27–28)

Music produced with computer software might sound "flawless" to Baudrillard, but his unmistakable discontent at its homogeneity (hinting at the survival of affect at the level of irritation) is not accidental and is an effect of the specific software that was designed, in the early 1980s, to represent musical notes. The designer was a music synthesiser designer called Dave Smith, who invented the MIDI system that is made of digital patterns representing keyboard notes. Designed to enhance the palette of sounds on a keyboard, it is not so effective in representing voice or wind and stringed instruments. Yet, as musician and Silicon Valley insider Jaron Lanier points out, in spite of its limitations, MIDI became the standard scheme to represent music in software which, because hardware was designed to work with it, quickly became entrenched and "locked-in" as standard, used ubiquitously by commercial and academic organisations around the world, becoming "a rigid, mandatory structure [that] you couldn't avoid" (Lanier, 2010, pp. 7–9).

The experiments in the digital molecularisation of music that went into the production of The Microsoft Sound in 1995 were almost certainly produced on MIDI software, as were the Koan software programmes that were being developed that produced the computer-generated music that inspired Eno to develop his generative music. It is, perhaps, no co-incidence that the music produced by the Koan software sounded uncannily like the ambient music Eno had already produced (which also sounds like MIDI, although produced through tape loops of recorded synthesised keyboard sounds). That Eno may be unconcerned about the relative monotony of this computer-generated music is for two reasons. First, because, following John Cage, Reich, and others, his interest is in "process not product". His interest is primarily in how technological innovation can transform the way that music is made; indeed, how music might make itself in such a way that the relative simplicity of the basis of this music is an experimental advantage. Second, as the final line of the sleeve notes for *Music for Airports* (1977) attests, Eno was keen to assure his listeners that the music itself should be "as ignorable as it is interesting" (1995). Indeed, it does not even need to be regarded as interesting. For Eno, "music is not actually that interesting in itself" (Young, 1996). Much more interesting for Eno are the technical systems that can generate sounds as if they were simple forms of cellular life. If Eno's ambient music does away with a conventional listener, just as it does away with a conventional idea of music, so it also does away with a conventional composer or artist. Some years before he experimented with computerised generative systems, Eno's ambient records were generated from self-designed machines using tape loops and numerical systems. Making and selling a machine that made numbers sing was the aspect that really interested Eno. "What I always wanted to do was actually sell the system to people, so that what they bought was the machine that made the music" (Young, 1996).

In 1995, as people all over the world logged on to their networked computers, Eno's The Microsoft Sound heralded a new world in which process rather than product was everything. The same process placed all productive activities on the same plane as art, work, and leisure, disintegrating traditional disciplinary boundaries and transforming the basis of value and meaning in society. The tinny machinic reveille of Eno's Microsoft Sound announces that the *avant-garde* ideas of Cage and Reich have become the operative principles of the new techno-capitalist order. It has been noted by numerous political commentators that systems of value have lost connection with traditional conceptions of art and labour. For the Italian Autonomist philosopher Paolo Virno, "the crisis of the society of labour consists in the fact that social wealth is produced from science, from the *general intellect*, rather than from the work delivered by individuals" (Virno, 2004, p. 95). Kevin Kelly, editor of *Wired* magazine during much of the 1990s, concurs. It is the "information economy", driven by science and technology, rather than the material and human resources of capital that create wealth (Kelly, 1998).

At broadly the same time that manual labour was displaced by machines as the major productive force in Fordist and post-Fordist factories, the work of art was displaced as the basis of value by a general process of innovation validated by a network of *avant-garde* intellectuals. And as soon as art becomes process rather than product, the space of art itself becomes evacuated as artistic processes migrate towards every other productive activity. In its wake, the *avant-garde* also loses its value and disappears along with its marginality. Throughout the 1980s and 1990s, Brian Eno occupied the ambiguous space where life management meets the aesthetics of existence, something clearly seen by Pat Kane in 1995. In his review of The Microsoft Sound, Kane suggests that "Eno's project is to provide the soundtrack, and perhaps even the logic, for twenty-first-century techno-capitalism" (Kane, 1995). He notes further that Eno's interest in systems and process, part of his early art school training in the 1960s and 1970s, is now perfectly consistent with an economic system which is more than happy to encourage us to be such "soft machines", manipulable and flexible to business impera-tives ... Are you beginning to see what Brian Eno is? He's actually pop culture's very own management guru: the Tom Peters of the digital sampler. (Kane, 1995)

In the 1990s, Eno was in the vanguard of those processes in which intellectual and artistic forms of production became increasingly auto-mated by computer software, algorithms, and robotics. The mighty music industry has all but been destroyed, and currently there are concerns, articulated by Lanier among others, that the intellectual labour of other professions, such as journalism, academia, and health care, are following in its wake and being replaced by automation (Lanier, 2013, pp. 77–97). Any object that can be reduced to the exchange of digital information will be, we are promised, effectively including people and their labour. The form and soundtrack for this process is, as Lanier suggests, MIDI software: "people are becoming like MIDI notes – overly defined and restricted in practice to what can be represented in a computer" (Lanier, 2010, p. 10).

The economic and political context that has defined and acceler-ated the conditions of this process is, of course, the situation created by the neoliberalism of the Reagan and Thatcher administrations in the 1980s. As we shall see, the essential role of government is to assem-ble a social machine, like one of Eno's generative systems, in which a formal structure can generate the music of economic growth all by itself. The art of neoliberal government, like the practice of Cage and Eno, looks primarily at processes, not end product, in which individ-ual subjects can be reduced to the level of digital MIDI "cells" that form the individuated units of generative systems in the game of (economic) life produced by neoliberal systems of governance.

CHAPTER SEVEN

Capitalism and psychosis I:
the Nash equilibrium

*A brief economic history of romance and
the* Verwerfung *of equilibrium*

In the film *A Beautiful Mind* (2001) directed by Ron Howard, John F. Nash Jr, played by Russell Crowe, is shown struggling to come up with the original idea that would form the basis of his PhD and future reputation. In 1950, Nash was awarded his PhD for a thesis he submitted titled "Non-cooperative games", which offered a formula that held that an optimum solution always exists in a situation where competitors not only seek their self-interests, but also calculate their best outcome on the basis of the others' similar interests. The formula, now known as the "Nash equilibrium", became, throughout the 1980s, "*the* analytical structure for studying all situations of conflict and cooperation from labor-management bargaining to international trade agreements" (Kuhn & Nasar, 2002, p. xvii). "By the late 1970s, game theory had become one of the foundations of modern economics. And at the center was the Nash equilibrium" (Samels, 2002). By the early 1990s, international recognition for the utility of Nash's equilibrium resulted in the Nobel Prize.

The practical example Nash used to formulate his equilibrium in his PhD thesis was poker, but in *A Beautiful Mind*, the film that was made of his life in the wake of his Nobel Prize, the example is more arresting and troubling, strangely cinematic and anti-cinematic at the same time. Having been advised by his roommate to leave the confines of his student lodgings at Princeton and seek inspiration "out there", Nash moves his desk and papers into what is presumably the bar in the basement of the Nassau Inn, popular with the Princeton mathematics department. This is not something that Nash ever did, of course, or could have done, but, nevertheless, in the film Nash moves his desk between the bar, pool table, and juke box as a means of seeking inspiration in real life. In the scene (scene 5 on the DVD), Nash is joined by male colleagues who draw his attention to the presence of a number of young women. In particular, a tall, blonde woman attracts his attention, someone with whom the audience has seen him have a previous encounter. The woman, who subsequently becomes the focus of all the young men, instantly suggests, in the way she is dressed and styled and fills the screen, the sex symbols of the 1950s: blonde bombshells such as Marilyn Monroe, Jayne Mansfield, and Mamie Van Doren. Nash and his colleagues begin to speculate on their chances of seduction, voices cutting across each other in competitive rivalry, "what shall we say, gentlemen, pistols at dawn?" But this anachronistic, almost chivalric suggestion of an aristocratic duel is immediately rejected by a more modern and enlightened suggestion. Characteristically, given these are young mathematicians and economists, the example of Adam Smith is invoked, "in a competition, individual ambition serves the common good", says one, "every man for himself, gentlemen", says another, "those who strike out are stuck with their friends". For Nash, sitting silently at the centre of the throng, it is a "Eureka!" moment. "Adam Smith needs revision", he murmurs, and with growing excitement begins to outline what will become his equilibrium theory:

> If we all go for the blonde, we'll block each other. Not a single one of us is going to get her. So then we go for her friends. But they'll all give us the cold shoulder because nobody likes to be second choice. But what if no one goes for the blonde? We don't get in each other's way, and we don't insult the other girls. That's the only way we win. That's the only way we all get laid. . . . Governing dynamics, gentlemen: Adam Smith was wrong. (Howard, 2001)

Leaving his colleagues to act on his suggestion, Nash does not bother to wait for empirical confirmation of his theory, but rushes off to express it mathematically. The cinema audience does not get to see whether or not all his colleagues give up on their desire for the blonde, but it is enough that the principle has been explained in a way conducive to popular cinema. The example is instructive, however, not just because it illustrates Nash's idea nicely, but also because it lays out very clearly in cinematic, but also in symbolic, form the condition of Nash's equilibrium. The condition that must be foreclosed in order for the equilibrium to be established is desire itself. Desire, and its signifier, has no place here other than to be by-passed. In the Hollywood cinema of the 1950s that is powerfully referenced in this scene in the form of the bar, the pool table and the Wurlitzer jukebox playing popular jazz music, the signifier of the Other's desire is supremely that of the blonde bombshell. Marilyn Monroe still regularly features at the summit of lists ranking the all-time most desirable woman in the cinema. The iconic blonde woman in this scene is not just a desirable woman, her blonde hair is a signifier of the sovereign good of America; her full figure embodies *das ding* around which its symbolic order circulates, the site of the erection of America's phallus, in Lacanian terms. In the film, she has no such significance for Nash. While he is minimally aware of her desirability relative to the other women, such desirability is simply an obstacle, something to be compromised in order to achieve the main goal that is to get laid, the satisfaction of the drives.

Nash's inability to understand the conventions of romance has, in the film, already been established in an earlier scene in a previous encounter with the same woman. The scene prepares the ground for the grand entrance of the blonde in scene 5, but it also serves to establish Nash's eccentricity, given that he was a man of striking good looks in his youth. Sitting at the edge of the bar, the woman gives Nash the eye and he is encouraged to approach her. At her side, Nash is unable or unwilling to speak, however. The woman suggests that he might like to buy her a drink, and, aware that this is his cue to begin his courtship, Nash remains silent for a few moments and then makes the following short statement:

> I don't exactly know what I am required to say in order for you to have intercourse with me. But can we assume that I have said all that?

I mean essentially we're talking about fluid exchange, right? So could we just go straight to the sex? (Howard, 2001)

Unsurprisingly, the woman calls him an asshole and slaps his face to general laughter in the room. But Nash was not playing to the gallery; it was not a performance. It was an acknowledgment of the impossibility of performance, a speech that disavows the possibility of speech before the Other, represented in sexualised form, by the desirable woman. "In psychosis", says Lacan, "the Other, where being is realized through the avowal of speech, is excluded" (Lacan, 1993, p. 162). Nash cannot locate himself through speech in the set of conventions that mediate sexual relations. He cannot engage in amorous courtship, banter, flattery, seduction, and so on. "There is no properly human desire at all in psychosis. Where the structure of desire is missing, desire too is missing" (Fink, 1999, p. 101). But something is speaking in Nash, even if it is not desire determined by language understood in Lacanian terms.

After the slap, the blonde woman walks off and Nash's English roommate, played by Paul Bettany, comments on his failure, expressing disapproval at the vulgarity of the "fluid exchange" reference. This character, the audience later realises, is only ever seen by Nash. He is a hallucination, an effect of Nash's schizophrenia. A Beautiful Mind is not, of course, just the story of a mathematics genius, it is the story of a genius cut short by a devastating descent into paranoid schizophrenia and his heroic management of his condition later in life. Indeed, retrospectively, and given the improbability of Nash setting up his office in a bar, the whole of scene 5 is no doubt meant to be delusional. The voices of his young male colleagues, expressing their sexual rivalry in terms of the history of economic competition, are perhaps just voices in his head, the equilibrium idea an effect of imaginary revenge at the original rebuff.

While neither scene in the Nassau Inn, actual or delusional, occurred in Nash's life according to Sylvia Nasar's biography that provided the basis for the film, it is, nevertheless, highly pertinent and instructive in the way that it not only makes the conception of Nash's Equilibrium an effect of his psychosis, but also in the way that it shows how the grounding of "modern economics" in the mathematics of game theory marks a profound break in economic history and, indeed, capitalism. No doubt one of the reasons that Adam Smith is in error for the fictional Nash in *A Beautiful Mind* is because, in *The Wealth of Nations*, Adam Smith finds the obscure origins of capitalism in courtly romance, in the understanding that there is no purely economic value and that exchange is always a modality of human rivalry—amorous, martial, and, ultimately, subject to symbolic laws and rules that are not purely economic (Smith, 1976, pp. 418–419). In this scene, however, objects are stripped of all symbolic value as if the drive had no *Vorstellung* other than numbers and was subject purely to a calculus of efficient satisfactions. But this, apparently, was indeed the assumption of Nash and many of his peers. According to his biographer, Sylvia Nasar, even before his psychotic break, Nash was

> Compulsively rational, he wished to turn life's decisions—whether to take an elevator or wait for the next one, where to bank his money, what job to accept, whether to marry—into calculations of advantage and disadvantage, algorithms or mathematical rules divorced from emotion, convention, and tradition. Even the small act of saying an automatic hello to Nash in a hallway could elicit a furious "Why are you saying hello to me?" (Nasar, 2001, p. 13)

Nash's compulsion to quantify everything was entirely consistent with many of his colleagues, particularly at the RAND Corporation, where mathematicians were reducing not just political and military matters, including nuclear war, to abstract formulae, but also the matters of everyday life. "RAND scientists tried to tell their wives that the decision whether to buy or not to buy a washing machine was an 'optimization problem'" (Nasar, 2001, p. 110), It is also, of course, entirely consistent with the American neoliberal attempt to extend the rationality of the market into every domain.

The issue here, in the correlation of some known facts and statements about and by Nash to Lacan's clinical structure of psychosis, as outlined in *Seminar 3*, is not one of attempting to iterate or revise a clinical diagnosis of Nash's condition; rather, there are a number of other reasons at stake. First, it seems to me important to show that the virtual subject of game theory and Nash's equilibrium have the same structure as psychosis; second, that this structure has been imposed, as a form of governance, across the economic and social field since the late 1970s, and third, that this development is an effect of the diminishing role played by speech and language relative to numbers and statistics in processes of techno-scientific individuation. Virtual individuals, possessed of imaginary drives, become the model for the subject, justifying systems of surveillance and management, based on minute calculations of advantage and disadvantage expressed in targets, incentives, and "optimization problems" that regulate everyone's actual lives working in the regime of techno-neoliberalism. Other aspects of Nash's case become pertinent here because of the role of other particulate systems—music and mathematics, particularly numerology—in mediating his relation to his social reality and other people. Perhaps, through looking at how music and numbers provide a resource for making sense and meaning (however delusional), correspondences can be drawn about the function of these and other particulate systems in the culture generally in the default of language.

From MIDI to me-me

It is well known that the defining characteristic of Chicago School neoliberalism that informed the Reagan and Thatcher administrations of the 1980s is the wholesale extension of "the rationality of the market, the schemas of analysis it offers and the decision-making criteria it suggests, to domains which are not exclusively or not primarily economic" (Foucault, 2008, p. 323). In his acute and prescient reading of neoliberal texts in 1978, Michel Foucault makes a clear distinction between the neoliberalism of the twentieth century and the liberalism of the eighteenth century—the physiocrats, Adam Smith, Jeremy Bentham, and British utilitarianism—to which the former so frequently refer. The essential difference concerns their understanding of the art or technology of government, on the one hand, and their extension of it to all forms of life, indeed life itself, on the other, thereby providing the framework for the intensification of modern biopolitics.

In his lectures, Foucault discusses both the German neoliberal texts of the 1930s and 1940s and the American neoliberal texts of the 1950s and 1960s that have shaped the political economy of western society since the 1980s. One of the essential differences between eighteenth- and nineteenth-century liberalism, laissez-faire capitalism, and neoliberalism is the understanding of the natural basis of exchange and the market. For traditional liberalism, the market is the key test and mode of veridiction that establishes both the truth of exchange and the fecundity of economic growth because it is regarded as a given of nature. As such, it must not be regulated by the state, which has merely to oversee and administer its spontaneous mechanisms. For the German neoliberals, however, these assumptions about the market constitute "naïve naturalism" (Foucault, 2008, p. 120). The market is not a natural phenomenon; on the contrary, its beneficial mechanisms—such as competition—need to be generated. Market mechanisms such as competition must be regarded not as something that is owed to the state of nature, but as part of a formal game with an internal logic. It is the role of government to produce the conditions in which these mechanisms can operate to optimum effect, including in government itself. The essential role of government is to assemble a social machine in which a formal structure can generate economic growth all by itself (compare Lacan's Discourse of Capitalism outlined in the Milan Discourse). There must be no other form of government intervention or planning than the institution of these formal rules of the market. Foucault's point is, therefore, that neoliberalism has a fully developed art of government and is highly "interventionist" in spite of its phobia of the state, an effect of the socialist and national socialist tyrannies of the twentieth century.

Anglo-American economists, traditionally less anxious about accusations of philosophical naïveté, did not, however, give up on justifying economic processes in nature, particularly evolutionary biology and genetics. Indeed, the metaphors of American neoliberals in the 1980s and 1990s are full of biological and genetic metaphors evident in the analysis of economic activity in terms of populations: "swarms", "hive minds", and so on. But there is absolutely no sense of a return to a seventeenth- or eighteenth-century understanding of a state of nature in this neoliberal "biological turn". On the contrary, with recourse to the formal rules of competition and game theory that inform both evolutionary biology and economic rationality, another form of freedom was envisaged, grounded in a new biotechnological conception of nature that can be generated from a general econopoietic process. Game theory, the new paradigm that unified the fields of biology and economics, became the theoretical basis and promise of the techno-neoliberal art of government and biopolitical management of the life it generates.

Developed in the mid 1940s in John von Neumann's circle in Princeton University, game theory was a branch of mathematics that found direct application towards the end of the Second World War, later becoming the basis of the cold war strategies of the RAND Corporation in the late 1940s and 1950s. Game theory seemed to provide a useful theoretical basis for nuclear weapons strategy because the stand-off between the USA and the USSR offered a very simple two-person scenario in which winner takes all. Two protagonists with the ability utterly to destroy the other exist in a state of implacable hostility with no possibility of mediation (for an account of the development and history of game theory see Poundstone, 1992). It is this absence of symbolic mediation, of a shared locus of value and law, that made the logic unfolded by game theory attractive to a whole range of other disciplines, such as economics, political science, sociology, and evolutionary biology, concerned to ground themselves in first principles. The proto-subject of game theory is an even more stripped-down version of Thomas Hobbes's inhabitants of the state of nature and Adam Smith's self-interested shop-keepers. Furthermore, the subject of game theory is entirely rational, totally consistent in its self-love, selfishness, and belligerence. At the same time, it has an almost infinite capacity to imagine its other and strategise against its motives and intentions entirely on the basis of its own.

Game theory also gave mathematical legitimacy to evolutionary biology, the gene individuated as the same kind of unit of calculating selfishness as the one at the heart of neoliberalism. This self-interested subject is never named as such, but is the pattern upon which each structure—the gene, the individual, the superpower—is built, a kind of me-me, not to be confused of the "meme" of Richard Dawkins. Me-me, since the "me" is an effect of an essential mirror relation, an interminable calculation of the other's motives on the basis of one's own: "I think he thinks that I think that he thinks that I think . . ." (Nasar, 2001, p. 97). Without the stability offered by a third term—a symbolic system of law, value, and social conduct—the me-me reflects and replicates itself endlessly, as if in a *mise-en-abyme*. For the economist Philip Mirowski, "The Nash equilibrium . . . is paranoid because it's the idea of a human being sitting alone in a room being able totally to reconstruct their opponent. Their opponent is totally implacable, totally hostile and bent on their destruction" (Curtis, 2007). While this is a popular, rather than clinical, picture of paranoia, there are elements of the me-me that, if it existed, would suggest a clinical structure of psychosis in Lacanian terms.

In psychosis, Lacan writes,

the Other with a big O, qua bearer of the signifier, is excluded. The Other is thereby all the more powerfully affirmed between it and the subject, at the level of the little other, of the imaginary . . . It's at the level of the between-I, that is, of the little other, of the subject's double, who is both his ego and not his ego, that words appear that are a kind of running commentary on existence. (1993, p. 194)

The Thatcher government of 1979 was revolutionary not because it sought to overthrow state institutions and elites, but in the way in which it sought to dissolve their symbolic authority and transform them, subjecting them to market forces and the immanent drives of the me-me. Mrs Thatcher's government was particularly interested in Buchanan's Public Choice Theory, which held that political idealism of any kind was a product of "zealotry" and the mask of tyranny. Zealots are just highly ambitious me-mes who strategically employ the ideology of public service and political virtue to gain power that, unchecked, will lead inevitably to tyranny. Zealots are dangerous if not properly managed. Unleashing the drives of a me-me, then, implies certain dangers and requires attentive and vigilant micromanagement. As Foucault writes, since liberalism is an art of government that deals fundamentally with self-interests, it cannot do this without "at the same time managing the dangers and mechanisms of security/freedom, the interplay of security/freedom" (Foucault, 2008, p. 66). Demystified, zealots and all the other me-mes can be held at a certain level and their drives channelled, regulated, and controlled through systems of incentives, targets, and performance indicators. Public servants were, therefore, encouraged to give up on the ideal of public service, the greater good being served best through me-mes following selfish interests that could be produced and channelled in planned incentives and enhanced by the rigours of the market. The goal of neoliberalism was to produce and multiply versions of this proto-subject as a means of extending competition into all areas of society, particularly public services and utilities. The example of the Reagan and Thatcher governments of the 1980s has been followed, over the subsequent thirty years, by governments around the world:

Advised by game theorists, governments around the world began to auction "public" goods from oil drilling rights to radio spectra, reorganize markets for electricity, and devise systems for matching doctors and hospitals. In business schools, game theory was becoming a staple of management training. (Kuhn & Nasar, 2002, p. xiii)

Establishing the conditions for working and consuming popula-tions to be transformed into a multitude of me-mes was one of the most profound acts of the Reagan and Thatcher governments. As far as possible, symbolic authorities, working-class collectives, cultural elites, and paternalist state institutions were assailed by a materialism that encouraged the pursuit of individual self-interests in the context of a "free market". These interests, however, have to be directed to officially sanctioned goals through the imposition of targets and performance indicators that are continually assessed in the "running commentary" of internal audit, the latter having no external rationale or reference other than the economic efficiency or "value for money" that is calculated on the basis of the same imaginary interests. This process reinforces and locks in competition as a formal principle. It is not through symbolic authority that the state seeks to normalise and control its citizens, but through the implementation of interests supposed to establish their own equilibrium in the way suggested by Nash, in which demand is rendered infinite and desire foreclosed.

In Lacan's terms, Nash's solution to economic conflict is purely imaginary, the construction of a scenario in which all the competitors are conceived as exactly the same, possessing the same goals, the same drives, imitating each other's actions. Nevertheless, this is the model of autonomy that has emerged out of the "discourse of freedom" that characterises modernity, a conception of autonomy even more "inex-pressible, fragmentary, differentiated, and profoundly delusional" as the one that Lacan, in 1953, argued possessed the same structure as psychosis (Lacan, 1993, p. 145). "It's classically said that in psychosis the unconscious is at the surface, conscious" (Lacan, 1993, p. 11). Since the me-me is both rational and totally pleasure-driven, there is no evidence of repression, no guilt, anxiety, or questioning that would betray the presence of symbolic prohibition controlling the drives. As there is no secret to the pleasures being sought, the Nash equilibrium assumes that the maximum of pleasure provides the threshold for every party in relation to which an optimum solution can be reached. In Freud and Lacan's terms, the absence of repression points to *Verwerfung*, or foreclosure, from the primordial signifier that activates the symbolic castration necessary for the regulation of the drives. There is, therefore, no relation to the symbolic order that is marked by paternal prohibition and authority, law, social customs, and the rules of civilised behaviour; indeed, for the advocates of neoliberalism— Hayek, Buchanan, Thatcher, Reagan—the me-me is the subject that can be generated and manipulated in a political rebellion against all forms of symbolic authority that in the field of economy provides an arbitrary, tyrannical, and inefficient regulation of the free market. Rather than symbolic, state or political control, Nash's equilibrium suggests that, in Lacan's terms, solutions to economic conflict can be based purely on an imaginary basis in which all the competitors are conceived as exactly the same, possessing the same aims and objectives, the same drives, imitating each other's actions.

The me-me is not just paranoid, however, but potentially schizophrenic, since, in the absence of law and prohibition, there is no security and subjective orientation can only be maintained by a kind of running commentary in which the me-me talks to itself, or, indeed, all the me-mes in the hall of mirrors comment on the me-me, on its existence, its acts and intentions, its utility and effectiveness in relation to an imagined hostile outside in which, in the play of mirrors, there is total confusion between self and other. In the absence of the consistency given to the symbolic order by the semblants and metaphors of paternal authority common to a particular culture and society, the psychotic may begin to generate its own delusional metaphor that gives meaning and consistency to the way he or she perceives the world. Lacan points out that the modern discourse of individual freedom and autonomy, which, of course, generates the idea of the me-me in the first place, has the same delusional structure as psychosis.

> With the impertinence that, as everyone knows, is characteristic of me I designated this the discourse of freedom, essential to modern man insofar as he is structured by a certain conception of his own autonomy. I pointed out its fundamentally biased and incomplete [*partial et partiel*], inexpressible, fragmentary, differentiated, and profoundly delusional nature. I set out from this general parallel to point out to you what, in relation to the ego, is apt, in the subject fallen prey to psychosis, to proliferate into a delusion. I'm not saying it's the same thing, I'm saying it's the same place. (Lacan, 1993, p. 145)

As Foucault argues, government provides the impetus for neoliberalism; it is the state that enjoins us all to act as if we were mad—

the better to manage us. "Freedom is never anything other . . . than an actual relation between governors and governed" (Foucault, 2008, p. 63). Liberal governance is not in the business of protecting abstract rights of freedom, "respecting this or that freedom, guaranteeing this or that freedom", it is, on the contrary, in the business of producing and generating freedoms such as the freedom of the market, freedom to buy and sell, the free exercise of property rights, and so on. The liberal art of governance involves producing and managing the conditions of economic freedom, producing and managing the creation of a free economic actor. It is in the business of generating and enabling an agent totally liberated to act in accordance with an economic rationality unrestrained by the "intervention of a third party, [or] of any authority whatsoever" (Foucault, 2008, p. 118).

"Freedom is the future of all humanity", announced George W. Bush, President of the USA at one of the high-water marks of the neoliberal discourse of economic freedom and market democracy. But, at the same time, the delusional nature of this freedom was marked by the increased anxieties concerning national security and the ever greater systems of surveillance and monitoring of subjects in the default of symbolic authorities impeached by this discourse of freedom and its worldwide extension. In their absence, the boundaries defining traditional forms of national identification and cultural distinction become inexpressible, fragmentary, minutely differentiated in a globalised world where friend and foe become increasingly indiscernible, immanent to the flows of information, commercial competition, and violence. The only form of rationality that might seek to manage and optimise such a situation is one that can convert everything into numbers, into digital information, data, and algorithms in the "mathematical modelling of humanity" that has become the major undertaking of the twenty-first century (Baker, 2009, p. 13). The me-me enables computing machines to turn subjects into numbers that can be calculated according to movements of data related to consumption and behaviour tracked through billions of traces left by receipts, emails, downloads, feeds from security cameras, and so on. The subject implied by this form of rationality is one who must seek the inexpressible in patterns and similarities, vectors, glimpsing meaning in the mass of shifting information in the absence of speech.[6]

Michel Foucault and the beauty of the absolute

Unlike Freud, for whom the pleasure of music was foreclosed by its imperviousness to rational enquiry, Michel Foucault's ignorance of music guaranteed its absolute beauty. He writes in a memoire, "The minimalist self" (in Foucault, 1988), about how he came to know intimately the generation of Pierre Boulez through the talented serialist composer Jean Barraqué. "A self-styled '*musician maudit*' . . . dedicated his life to a lonely and difficult quest for the absolute" until his untimely death in 1973 (Miller, 1993, p. 80). Although it "played a great role" in his personal life, music remained something of a mystery to Foucault, "a very importance experience" about which he knew little and could speak less.

> I had contact with the kind of art that was, for me, very enigmatic. I was not competent at all in this domain; I'm still not. But I felt beauty in something which was quite enigmatic for me . . . what is, for me, real beauty is a "*phrase musicale, un morceau de musique*", that I cannot understand, something I cannot say anything about. I have the opinion, maybe it's quite arrogant or presumptuous, that I could say something about any of the most wonderful paintings in the world. For this reason they are not absolutely beautiful. (Foucault, 1988, p. 13)

In his discussion of the French serialism of the 1950s in *The Rest is Noise* (2008), Alex Ross suggests that Foucault was almost the ideal listener or destination of the music's "objectified mechanical savagery" and "cerebral sexuality". Foucault, "the great theorist of power and sexuality", writes Ross, "seemed almost turned on by Boulez's music, and for a time he was the lover of Boulez's fellow serialist [Jean] Barraqué" (Ross, 2008, p. 396). Consistent with Foucault's interest in formalism generally, serialism adheres to strict yet simple mathematical principles related to tone and duration in order to make beauty the contingent effect of shifting tonal patterns. "The serialist principle", writes Ross, "with its surfeit of ever-changing musical data, has the effect of erasing at any given moment whatever impressions the listener may have formed about previous passages in the piece" (p. 396), leaving only, as Foucault suggests, the fleeting *"phrase musicale, un morceau de musique"*, that encapsulates absolute beauty because it absolutely escapes understanding. As such, it seems, the serialists represented for him "the first 'tear' in the dialectical universe" that Foucault inhabited in the French academy of the 1950s (Miller, 1993, p. 79).

Music also enabled Foucault to break out of the well-known impasse that his archaeological and genealogical studies had constituted in the mid-1970s. The "Death Valley" biographical anecdote documented by James Miller on the basis of Simeon Wade's detailed diary account is now famous as the event that transformed Foucault's project on sexuality, partly, it is claimed, through disclosing for Foucault a new understanding of his own sexuality (Miller, 1993, pp. 246–251). In the spring of 1975, Foucault was taken to the great outdoors in Nevada by Wade and his pianist lover, Michael. On Zabriskie Point, after having taken a tab of acid and with Stockhausen's *Kontakte* blasting out of a portable tape recorder so that it reverberated over the awesome rift of the Death Valley, Foucault contemplated the universe above the deep gorge separating humanity from the depths of geological time. Then, recalled Wade, "Foucault smiled" and "gestured towards the stars: 'The sky has exploded', he said, 'and the stars are raining down upon me. I know this is not true, but it is the Truth'" (Miller, 1993, p. 250). A beautiful vision of nonsense reveals the Truth in the explosion of the sky, the real unfixing of the laws of nature, a vision of the "outside" (outside-sense) disclosed by acid-enhanced Stockhausen (for the importance of the "thought from Outside", see Foucault, 1970, p. 50 and 1987, pp. 9–19). That is to say, a violence disclosed by an *a*musical experience that discloses the truth of the exteriority of the violence inherent to the purest, most beautiful form; it is an experience that registers, in its breaching of the (psychic) sensorium, the absolute contingently as either "absolutely beautiful", as Foucault suggests, or absolutely agonising. It is the *a*musical effect, no doubt, of an outside indifferent to us, an outside that means nothing to us, since we know nothing about it, but that nevertheless afflicts or delights us in the unbearable brilliance of its vibration.

CHAPTER EIGHT

Bach's Little Fugue

John Nash's paranoid schizophrenia became apparent at the age of thirty when he suffered a psychotic break. In his short auto-biography, written for *Le Prix Nobel* in 1994, Nash commented that the "mental disturbances originated in the early months of 1959 at a time when Alicia [his wife] happened to be pregnant" (Nash, in Kuhn & Nasar, 2002, p. 9). The prospect of fatherhood is a common trigger for the onset of psychotic delusions, since it exposes the subject to the gap, or void, where the paternal signifier should be, in the face of which things start to fall apart. Indeed, Lacan gives impending father-hood as an example in his seminar dedicated to psychosis, given in 1956, just three years before Nash's own collapse: "Which signifier is it that is in abeyance in his inaugural crisis? It's the signifier *procreation* in its most problematic form . . . the form *being a father*" (Lacan, 1993, p. 292).[7] Nash's crisis and the nature of its trigger was perhaps heralded by his appearance at a fancy dress New Year's Eve Party held on 31 December 1958. With his pregnant wife Alicia at his side, Nash turned up "naked except for a diaper and a sash with 1959 on it", waving a baby bottle full of milk (Nasar, 2001, p. 239). It is claimed that the idea for the costume was his wife's and babies are, of course, a conventional way of representing the New Year. For someone with

Nash's psychotic structure, however, it would have been a powerful way of replaying the site of maternal demand and dependency that had failed to become over-written by paternal law. Reports suggest that he spent most of the evening curled up in Alicia's lap, offering a spectacle to party-goers that some found "really gruesome" and "disturbing" (p. 240).

Nash's profound anxiety about fatherhood was no doubt exacerbated by the death of his own father a few months previously. As his biographer writes, Nash suffered a "one-two punch—losing [his] father and having to step into his father's shoes" (Nasar, 2001, p. 209). Furthermore, the premature death of his father from a heart attack was attributed in part by his mother to a devastating phone call they had received from Nash's mistress, Eleanor Stier, informing them that they already had a grandson from her but that Nash had refused to acknowledge him. "He did not offer to put his name on his son's birth certificate . . . he did not offer to marry Eleanor or support her" (Nasar, 2001, p. 176). Nash's neglect was such that Stier was ultimately forced to place her son into foster care. For Nash's father, John Nash Sr, a man with "a deep and ever-present hunger for respectability" because of the delinquency and abandonment of his own father (Nasar, 2001, p. 26), the actions of his son could not have been anything less than a profound shame and humiliation.

Nash's father, while "quiet" and "reserved" in comparison to his "adoring" mother, does not seem to have been in the least bit neglectful of his son (p. 27), although a reluctance to instantiate the paternal function may perhaps be found in the fact that, as a neighbour recalled, he "always spoke to his children as if they were adults", giving John Jr science books rather than toys for presents (p. 31). Indeed, in the last year of Nash's High School, the filial equality between them is signalled by their co-authoring an article for an engineering journal (p. 39). John Jr's repetition of his grandfather's irresponsibility, therefore, and his refusal quite literally to give his first child the name-of-the-father "Nash" is augmented by the repetition of giving both his first and second sons the forename "John". This name seems to render equivalent even as it subjectively obliterates generations of Nash males as they become filial rivals in relation to the dissolute great-grandfather, Alexander, "a strange and unstable individual, a ne'er-do-well, a drinker and philanderer" who abandoned his wife and three children, earning their "undying enmity" (p. 26).

The familial structure of schizophrenia seems to be extended over four generations, since Nash's son by Eleanor Stier, John David, also became schizophrenic. Now reconciled with the son that he initially abandoned, Nash nevertheless regards with suspicion John's claim to have visual as well as audio hallucinations since, in stark contrast to the film *A Beautiful Mind*, Nash never had any imaginary friends: "I never saw anything, but my son has said that he sees things, and I don't know what it's really like, because he doesn't say it very often. I'm rather suspicious of him that he might like to say that" (cited in Samels, 2002).

While there are many details that would support this clinical diagnosis, there is no space to rehearse all of them here. Rather, I wish to focus on two of Nash's main delusional vectors outlined in the biography that clearly seem to provide, in the default of language, the main means of establishing a relation with his psychic reality: music and mathematics, particularly numerology. The reason I do this is to highlight the role of these other particulate systems in psychotic structure and to suggest, speculatively, that there is evidence of a similar heightened role for these systems in contemporary society. While the "mathematical modeling of humanity" in the digital age has already been noted (see Baker, 2009, p. 13), the symbolic distinction between music and noise has broken down, with the result that music has become ubiquitous, an open system capable of constructing ambient environments altering mood and behaviour, affecting patterns of demand and consumption, and of being employed as a mode of identity and power, and even an instrument of physical and psychical torture.

Nash's audio hallucinations, his hearing of voices, did not occur until he had been involuntarily hospitalised a number of times in the early 1960s. In 1959, his delusions began a few weeks after the New Year's Party when he announced in the common room at MIT that "abstract powers from outer space, or perhaps it was foreign governments" were sending him coded messages in the *New York Times* (Nasar, 2001, p. 241). "Then he began noticing a curious pattern on the MIT campus: men wearing red ties. He was sure they were members of a secret communist organization" (Samels, 2002). Even more famously, on 9 February 1959, Nash interrupted a colleague's lecture to announce that he was on the cover of *Life Magazine*, although his photograph had been disguised as Pope John XXIII. He knew this in two ways, he said, "first because John wasn't the Pope's given name, but a name he had chosen. Second because 23 was his favorite prime number" (Nasar, 2001, p. 244). These delusions set the pattern for what was to become: a series of referential beliefs based on the perception of patterns and codes in newspapers and especially in particular numbers as his obsession with numerology took over from mathematics as his dominant language. Names and letters became equivalent to series of numbers, usually prime numbers, the significance of which only Nash's genius could perceive. When, in exasperation, a Harvard professor asked how a mathematician, a man devoted to logical proof, could believe that aliens were sending him messages, Nash replied that "the ideas I had about supernatural beings came to me the same way that my mathematical ideas did. So I took them seriously" (Nash, quoted in Nasar, 2001, p. 11).

There were other factors that could have triggered Nash's psychotic break or, indeed, contributed to it. By 1959, Nash had still, definitively, to make his name in the field of mathematics; his equilibrium theory went largely unrecognised until the 1970s. He had won no prizes, had not secured a coveted post at Harvard, or even achieved tenure at MIT. For Lacan, making one's own name through artistic or scientific endeavour can be a way of supplementing, for someone with psychotic structure, the absence of the paternal function and, therefore, provide a means of warding off a psychotic break. He had also just recently reached the age of thirty, the mythical year by which mathematicians mark the beginning of the waning of their powers. Nash's thirtieth birthday was an event that apparently produced a kind of cognitive dissonance in him (Nasar, 2001, p. 229). Desperate to secure his reputation as a genius, Nash had embarked on an attempt to solve the Riemann hypothesis concerning prime numbers, the "holy grail of pure mathematics" (p. 229).

Generations of mathematicians have, apparently, been broken on the wheel of Riemann's hypothesis and it is regarded as quite a dangerous mountain to climb. This is especially the case for someone like Nash, whose psychotic structure determined an almost complete indifference to authorities and subjects-supposed-to-know. Nash famously never went to lectures or read books, but sought the solution to problems in his own way, "rediscovering their truths for himself". While this enabled Nash to show startling originality in some areas, this is a particularly foolhardy approach to take to Riemann's hypothesis, which "is not the sort of problem that can be attacked by elementary methods" (Nasar, 2001, p. 232). There is an extensive literature documenting ideas and revelations that have got nowhere. Nash got nowhere, but his mind and the revelation of numerical patterns intensified.

In the mid to late 1950s, Nash's homosexuality was also beginning to blossom in a series of relationships that he regarded as the most important of his life. While these encounters were exciting, they were dangerous in the context of his work at the RAND Corporation at the height of the McCarthy era. Indeed, Nash had recently been dismissed from RAND because of a charge of indecent exposure, the effect of an entrapment exercise by the LAPD on Muscle Beach. Nevertheless, in a "poignant and introspective letter" written to his sister Martha in 1965 about his life in 1959, "he was seized by a terrible sense of regret" at the struggle between his "merciless superego" and the "special friendships" in his life. He admits that "away from contact with a few special sorts of individuals I am lost, lost completely in the wilderness . . ." (Nasar, 2001, p. 317).

Freudian doctors at McLean clinic put the psychotic break down to Alicia's pregnancy, and explained his psychotic structure as an effect of "fetus envy" and "latent homosexuality" (p. 259). In a general way, this diagnosis does not seem to be far off the mark, though the treatment, in common with most others, was geared towards reducing the symptoms through therapy or, more commonly, through various drugs. The Lacanian approach to the treatment of psychosis is completely different because it does not attempt to treat or cure the delusional symptoms, but, on the contrary, regards them as the path towards successful management of the condition. Paraphrasing Freud, Lacan remarks that "psychotics love their delusion like they love themselves" (Lacan, 2001, p. 157), and it is a mistake to dismantle them, sometimes leading to suicide.[8] His biography notes that Nash's "regretful tone" concerning the forced interludes of rationality

> brings to mind the words of Lawrence, a young man with schizophrenia, who invented a theory of "psychomathematics" and told Rutgers psychologist Louis Sass: "People kept thinking I was regaining my brilliance, but what I was really doing was retreating to simpler levels of thought" (Nasar, 2001, p. 295; see also Sass, 1992).

Accordingly, it is the imaginary dimension of self-love, love, and friendship that can support the psychotic in the absence of symbolic mediation and orientation. "The goal", as Bruce Fink writes, "is to return the imaginary to the stable state it was before the psychotic break" (Fink, 1999, p. 101). After the psychotic break, which involves not just a major break with the Other that is the consensual locus of symbolic reality, but the disorientating emergence of hallucinations and other delusions, it is the latter that can provide the basis for reorientating the subject.

> Delusional activity, when it is allowed to run its course rather than being silenced by a therapist's intervention, eventually leads – and this process may take years – to the construction of what Lacan calls a "delusional metaphor" . . . a new starting point on the basis of which the psychotic establishes the meaning of the world and everything in it. (Fink, 1999, p. 109)

Lacan writes, with reference to Judge Schreber, who believed he was becoming a woman as a means for God to repopulate the world, "isn't it better, after all, to be a spirited woman than a cretinous man?" (Lacan, 1993, p. 256). This clearly anticipates and pre-empts Deleuze and Guattari, for whom a schizophrenic out for a walk is a healthier specimen than a neurotic on a couch. Nash himself agreed that "normal" subjectification to the conventional understanding of rationality and symbolised reality is limiting and constraining. In his autobiography, Nash commented that "rationality of thought imposes a limit on a person's concept of his relation to the cosmos" (Kuhn & Naser, 2002, p. 10), comparing it unfavourably with the world of his delusions, and, in an interview, he repeated this idea: "to some extent, sanity is a form of conformity. People are always selling the idea that people who have mental illness are suffering. But it's really not so simple. I think mental illness or madness can be an escape also" (Nash, quoted in Samels, 2002).

One of the most affecting aspects of Nash's story, which made it successful both as a biography and a feature film, is the way in which he eventually became able to manage his delusions, overcome the most alienating aspects of his condition, return to some kind of professional life, and even remarry his estranged wife. Throughout all the psychotic's delusional activity, reconstructing the world on an imaginary plane, there remains, for Lacan, "a certain . . . sense of reality" that has been retained through "the learning by rote, of the refrain, of empty sense" to which the delusion can become reconciled and to which the psychotic can return, albeit problematically (Lacan, 1993, p. 256). Lacan writes,

> The register in which the onset of psychosis is played out is located between these two poles – the word of revelation, which opens up a new dimension and gives a feeling of ineffable understanding, which corresponds to nothing previously experienced, and on the other hand the refrain, the same old song. (Lacan, 1993, p. 255)

Lacan presumably uses the metaphor of the refrain to refer to the experience of shared reality because, for the psychotic, this experience is empty, and, like music, is essentially meaningless and learned by rote, by imitation. "Thanks to imitation, a psychotic can learn to speak the way other people speak, but the essential structure of language is not integrated in the same way" (Fink, 1999, p. 91). Elsewhere in Seminar 3, *The Psychoses*, Lacan refers to the two poles of the word and its opposite, which is

> the form that meaning takes when it no longer refers to anything at all. This is the formula that is repeated, reiterated, drummed in with a stereotypical insistence. It's what we might call, in contrast to the word, the refrain. (1993, p. 33)

It is interesting that here the refrain is also a formula. Having repeatedly used this formulation, it is clear that this is more than a routine metaphor for Lacan and that he is suggesting that the experience of music and mathematical formula is directly analogous to the psychotic experience of language precisely because, devoid of a paternal metaphor, there is no anchoring point for the subject, no "permanent monologue", just "some kind of music for several voices" (p. 250). Music becomes the model both for the repetition that provides some kind of hold on reality and the dissonant voices that constitute the major hallucinatory part of delusional activity.

Accordingly, there do indeed appear to be two poles for Nash, but, rather than aspects of a deficient relation to language analogous to music and mathematics, they *literally* concern them and, therefore, concern quite different structures to language. The "word of revelation" was not, for Nash, a word so much as a prime number, the number twenty-three, delusions becoming based in ever more elabo-rate numerological systems based around this number.[9] Meanwhile, the refrain was not just "the same old song", the habitual activity of everyday life mimicked from others, it was indeed a refrain: a piece of music. Throughout his whole life, Nash sustained a degree of consis-tency via music since this refrain functioned "symbolically" as the vehicle of personal significance and a means of relating, of signifying himself, to others. Even at the height of his illness, musical structure lent a degree of consistency to his delusions so that he was able to sustain a measure of self-knowledge through his "B Theory". In this theory, music and mathematics conjoined to produce, in approved Lacanian fashion, a formula that expresses the inexpressible, that gives a place to the subject through introducing into knowledge "what eludes understanding, the point of anchorage epitomized by the matheme" (Dolar, 2006, p. 139).[10]

In both his biography and his autobiographical fragment, Nash's earliest memory, as a child of about two or three, is "listening to his maternal grandmother play the piano" (Nasar, 2001, p. 25; Nash, 1994, p. 6). Indeed, his infancy seems to have been dominated by this kind of maternal influence, Nash spending "a good deal in the company not only of his adoring mother, but also of his grandmother, aunts, and young cousins" (Naser, 2001, p. 30). Interestingly, his most signifi-cant relationship with a woman, his wife Alicia Larde, mother of his second son, was also mediated by music. Larde developed a crush on Nash while his student at MIT and sought him out in the music library on his return visits from RAND, eventually getting a job as a music librarian. When Nash was finally ejected from RAND in disgrace following arrest for indecent exposure

> Nash escaped to the music library almost every afternoon. The library, on the first floor of Charles Hayden Memorial, had an impressive collection of classical recordings and sound-proofed, private cubicles where one could sit and play records, surrounded by deep-blue walls that made one feel as if one were floating in water. Nash would go into one of these and listen to either Bach or Mozart for hours on end. (Nasar, 2001, p. 26)

While the music library provided the sanctuary of a maternal, even womb-like space in its amniotic, deep-blue wateriness, so that he was even able to find comfort in the warm embrace of a woman, music, for

Nash, was not limited to this "pre-symbolic" maternal realm. Bach, in particular Bach's Little Fugue, was almost Nash's signature, his calling-card; it is the thing that most people remember about him, according to the biography and most other accounts of his life, providing the point either of sympathy or, more often, annoyance in his relations with others. At Princeton as an undergraduate, "Nash soon acquired a reputation for being both brilliant and odd. In the quadrangle, he rode a bicycle in figure-eights, over and over, and paced the hallways obsessively whistling Bach's Little Fugue" (Samels, 2002).

> The ten or so first year students were a cocky bunch, but Nash was even cockier. He loved sparring in the common room. He avoided classes. He was rarely seen cracking a book. Pacing endlessly, whistling Bach, he worked inside his own head. (Kuhn & Nasar, 2002, p. xiv; see also Nasar, 2001, pp. 12, 113–114, 163, 315, 323–333)

Associated indelibly with his thought, his arrogance, and his annoying presence, Nash's whistling produced a number of complaints. Nasar reports that the mathematics secretaries at Princeton complained about his whistling to his tutors and superiors. (Nasar 2001, p. 69) The whistling was annoying, no doubt, because of its monotony, but perhaps also because it established a relation of disconnectedness with people. It heralded his presence but also his absence, his indifference to those around him, being lost in thought. But there is evidence that Nash was also very aware of this effect, that the refrain had a representative function. It seems to have been in some ways analogous to speech, a statement not to anyone in particular, but to the Other, concerning his existence: "I am thinking", or "genius at work". Therefore, it established a relation to the Other even though, in the context of the members of the mathematics faculty, the relation was perceived as one of rivalry and provocation.

According to Bruce Fink, in his book on the fundamentals of psychoanalytic technique, because psychotics have foreclosed any relation to a governing paternal metaphor, they are incapable of forming new metaphors or of representing themselves metaphorically, that is, symbolically. "The properly symbolic dimension of language, involving a potential gap between signifier and signified, is missing in psychosis" (Fink, 2007, p. 240). This dimension of language crucially involves the separation between words and things, allowing the subject to talk about something as "present when absent and absent when present" (Fink, 2007, p. 241). This is what occurs with Freud's nephew's "fort" and "da" game, where the words, in substituting the appearance and disappearance of the cotton reel, and the comings and goings of the mother, become the basic elements of a shared symbolic system, the Other, in which desire is bound up with the desire of the other, an alter ego (see Lacan, 2006, p. 262). For the psychotic, however, this dimension of absence/presence is apparently impossible because "meaning and sound, signified and signifier, are inseparable" (Fink, 2007, p. 240). Yet Nash, "knowing that his whistling irritated one particular music-loving mathematician, who frequently asked him to stop . . . once left behind a recording of his whistling on the man's Dictaphone" (Nasar, 2001, p. 114). Here, it is not just that Bach's Little Fugue comes to signify Nash or his thought, but that it can do so in his absence and in the absence of his interlocutor, and, moreover, through the vehicle of a dictaphone. It is a joke (something of which psychotics are also supposed to be incapable) in which Nash's own whistling substitutes for the other's voice through the mechanism of the machine whose functioning betrays the presence and symbolic mediation of the Other.[11]

On a later occasion, when Nash was teaching at Princeton and managed to solve a particularly intractable and coveted problem posed to him by colleague and rival Warren Ambrose, "Is it possible to embed any Riemannian manifold in a Euclidian space?", Ambrose was generous and "took to telling his musical friends that Nash's whistling was the purest, most beautiful tone he had ever heard" (Nasar, 2001, p. 163). Nash's whistling, therefore, as both irritating noise and beautiful tone, is the point of *a*musia by which Nash is established in an extimate relation with the Other, something that, as a psychotic, he would be unable to achieve in language. Even after his psychotic break, Nash continued to whistle the fugue, and it continued to sustain this ambivalent symbolic function. In the biography, Nasar records his eldest son remarking, seemingly in mild annoyance, about the constant whistling, and during 1967–1970, while living with his mother at Roanoke, various townspeople still recall him wandering around town whistling (2001, pp. 323–324).

Bach's Little Fugue in G Minor is more than just a simple refrain, as recognisable as it is to lovers of classical music. It has a characteristically precise and mathematical structure in which initially two and then four "voices" or tunes are counterpointed. No doubt the mathematical precision appealed to Nash; Bach, along with Mozart, was his favourite composer. Bach's Little Fugue has a precipitous momentum, starting relatively simply and sedately and then increasing its tempo, voices imitating and cutting across and undercutting each other. It could be easily imagined that these voices offer a model, even a metaphor, for schizophrenic subjectivity, described by Lacan as "some kind of music for several voices" (1993, p. 250). Except, of course, that the four voices are held in exquisite aesthetic tension by Bach's "math-musical" structure.

In 1968, deep in the heart of his lost years of mental illness, Nash came up with his own metaphor for his subjectivity, "a metaphor that he couched in his first language, the language of mathematics" (Nasar, 2001, p. 168). On a postcard, Nash wrote of himself: B squared + RTF = 0. This "very personal" equation represents, according to his biographer, "a three-dimensional hyperspace, which has a singularity at the origin, in four-dimensional space. Nash is the singularity, the special point, and the other variables are people who affected him— in this instance, men with whom he had relationships' (Naser, 2001, p. 168, see also p. 204). They were the highpoint of a narcissism that was noted by one of Alicia Larde's confidantes, who recalled that he was far from being infatuated with his wife, "he was infatuated with himself" (Nasar, 2001, p. 201). This self-infatuation became the basis for increasingly intense but brief relationships with young men like himself that culminated in his arrest, and, no doubt in reaction, marriage, fatherhood, and breakdown in 1959.

The narcissistic, libidinal intensity of this psychic structure is revealed in a letter he wrote to his sister. As Sylvia Nasar writes,

> After John Nash lost everything—family, car the ability to think about mathematics—he confided in a letter to his sister Martha that only three individuals in his life had ever brought him any real happiness: three "special sorts of individuals" with whom he had formed "special friendships". Had Martha seen the Beatles' film *A Hard Day's Night*? "They seem very colorful and amusing", he wrote. "Of course, they are much younger like the sort of person I've mentioned . . . I feel often as if I were similar to the girls that love the Beatles so wildly since they seem so attractive and amusing to me". (Nasar, 2001, p. 169, see also p. 317)

The four young men that he loved at MIT, the "RTF" that culminates in the "B" (for Jack Bricker, his greatest love of all the young
men) are squared by The Beatles, four voices singing in counterpoint
and in harmony, like Bach's Little Fugue. At the other side of the
equation is Nash at the 0 point of a singularity, screaming like the
thousands of Beatles' fans featured in *A Hard Day's Night*, at Kennedy
airport, at Shea Stadium, Nash's Beatlemania opening up a fourth
dimension. This structure can easily be mapped on to Lacan's Schema
L that features in Seminar 3, *The Psychoses*.

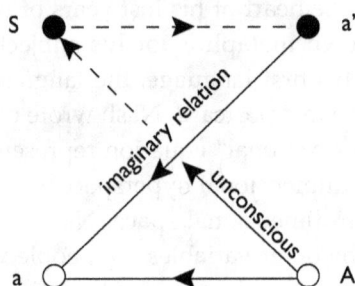

S = the Subject
a' = the other
a = the ego
A = the Other

Figure 8.1.   Lacan's Schema L (Lacan, 1993, p. 14).

This schema (Figure 8.1) "represents the interruption of full speech
between the subject and the Other and its detour through the two
egos, *o* [*a*] and *o'* [*a'*], and their imaginary relations" (Lacan, 1993,
p. 14). The diagram represents the "triplicity" of the subject, that is
supported by the Other, the locus of the unconscious. The subject's ego
appears as an effect of the mirror relation with the other, the alter ego,
but its "full" speech is determined by the Other in the unconscious. In
the verbal hallucinations characteristic of psychosis "the subject literally speaks with his ego, and it's as if a third party, his lining, were
speaking and commenting on his activity" (Lacan, 1993, p. 14). But, as
Nash himself avers, "You're really talking to yourself is what the
voices are" (Samels, 2002).

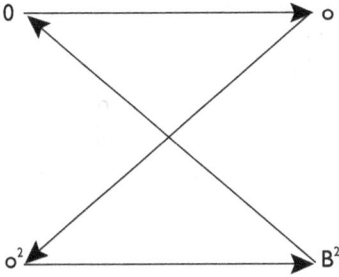

0 = Nash as singularity / void
o-o^2 = Nash's objects RTF, the sum of which is B for Bricker
B^2 = the musical locus of the social bond from Bach to The Beatles

Figure. 8.2.   Nash's B Theory.

Here (Figure 8.2) we can see the shape of the figure eight that Nash traced "over and over" on his bicycle in the Princeton quadrangle while "obsessively whistling Bach's Little Fugue" (Samels, 2002). It expresses Nash's own equation B squared + RTF = 0 in the form of Lacan's diagram. The 0 of the subject devoid of a signifier nevertheless manages to locate the egoic image of its self-love in its objects, the young men designated by RTF that find their ideal image in the "B" for Bricker. This is squared by The Beatles and Bach's Little Fugue, the latter providing the "speech" of the subject in Nash's whistling. However, here the Other is a *locus* not of signification, but of music, the canon of music from Bach to The Beatles that runs from the fugue to the screams of Beatlemania that issue from the infinity of the singular point "0" that opens up the fourth dimension (for other references to Nash's *B Theory* see Nasar, 2001, pp. 290, 326).

This narcissistic structure and its homoerotic, libidinal ambivalence is evident in the game theories he developed years earlier in Princeton, most particularly in his foray into the theory of non-cooperative games in which he devised a strategy called "Fuck Your Buddy" (Nasar, 2001, p. 102). His life reached the point of its nadir around 1968 and this ambivalence was fully blown and invested the totality of his paranoiac delusions. By the late 1960s, he had lost his wife and most of his friends, had nowhere to live, and no option but to return to his mother, who lived in the small town of Roanoke. As his mother recalled in 1994, "Roanoke was not a good place to be. There were no intellectuals there. He'd be too much alone. He would wander around whistling" (p. 323) His delusions of persecution grew to cosmic scale, informed by theories that were "astronomical, game theoretical, geopolitical, and religious" (p. 326). The dominant theory, however, remained B theory: "I've discovered a B theory of Saturn", he wrote in one of his many

> Joycean monologues [that were] written in a private language of his own invention . . . the B theory is simply that Jack Bricker is Satan . . . the root of all evil, as far as my personal life is concerned (life history), are Jews, in particular Jack Bricker who is Hitler, a trinity of evil of Mora, Iblis and Napoleon [these are all] Jack Bricker in relation to me. (Nasar, 2001, p. 326)

All the while he was working through his theories, and B theory, the theory of theories, he would for days pace "round and round the apartment, his long fingers curled around one of [his mother's] delicate Japanese teacups . . . sipping Formosa oolong, whistling Bach" (pp. 323–324).

Making numbers speak

After Nash's mother died in 1969, Nash was fortunate enough to be allowed back to Princeton, where he became the "Phantom of Fine Hall", a semi-mythical figure, the mathematical genius who had "flipped". He spent his time ghosting around the faculty leaving cryptic messages and mathematical formula that no one understood on the walls, blackboards, and windows. It seems that as his delusions became less affected by Cold War "paranoia" and amorous relations with young men and more closely bound up with mathematical problems and purely theoretical speculations, his aberrant behaviour diminished and he managed to avoid "the direct attention of psychiatrists" (p. 335). Nasar gives a mind-boggling account of his attempts to find meaning in mathematical formulae, even to the point of devising highly complex calculations that, if they came out "right", would "produce actual words" (Nasar, 2001, p. 336). In the context of Princeton, and with a semi-symbolic "name" as the mythical mad genius, Nash's mathematics provided the sinthome that stitched together his theoretical identity in a symbolic pattern and stabilised the "singularity" of the zero or void that he considered himself.

This desire to make numbers speak, which, of course, depends upon the fact that they do not, is, like the desire for musical speech, the essence of delusion and common to culture generally. The desire to make numbers speak leads to God and the prospect of divine revelation.[12] For Nasar, Nash's numerological delusions were not the ravings of a madman but a "conscious, painstaking, and often desperate attempt to make sense out of chaos" (2001, p. 334). For Nash himself, numerology precisely provides a bridge over the short gap between the essentially meaningless abstract formalism of mathematics and a world full of meaning and portent:

> You don't have to be a mathematician to have a feel for numbers. . . . the relation to numbers is not necessarily scientific, and even when I was mentally disturbed, I had a lot of interest in numbers . . . there's a transition from really having more of an enthusiasm for the numbers, like maybe magical or representing a divine revelation, and just a more scientific appreciation of numbers, and these are not necessarily entirely far apart. (Nash, 2006)

Being able to read the speech of God in his language of prime numbers means that one must begin to take on a "Messianic godlike feature" oneself (Nasar, 2001, p. 335). The narcissism of someone acknowledged by one of his peers as "the greatest numerologist the world has ever seen" (Nasar, 2001, p. 335) took on divine proportions. Making a comparison with the ecstatic theory of love of the Middle Ages, Lacan argues that

> in order to understand the psychoses we have to make the love relation with the Other qua radically Other, and the mirror situation . . . overlap . . . for the psychotic a love relation that abolishes him as subject is possible insofar as it allows a radical heterogeneity of the Other. But this love is a dead love. (Lacan, 1993, p. 253)

It is dead because it is doomed to remain silent and sterile. "The psychotic's Eros is located where speech is absent", but it is nevertheless "there that he finds his supreme love" (Lacan, 1993, p. 254)

No doubt, as the social bond established in speech declines relative to the coded flickering of digital screens, God and Eros increasingly find their location there; that is not the problem, both having always been "hospitable to a certain spectral virtuality" (Derrida, 2002, p. 62). The problem is what happens when the neo-liberal faith in numbers to speak the truth, in the default of God and Eros, and answer to the infinite demand for the optimum in efficient satisfactions collapses and loses all credit and credence?

For Nash, music speaks for and to him and through this he retains contact with the Other, albeit an Other describing an *a*musical locus from the fugues of Bach to the screaming of Beatlemania.

CHAPTER NINE

Decomposing the voice

D avid Schwarz begins his book *Listening Subjects: Music, Psychoanalysis, Culture* (1997) by arguing that music has significance for psychoanalysis because of its function as a sonic envelope. In particular, music is pre-eminent in providing the pleasures of oceanic fantasies of absorption or immersion (along with swimming, floating, religious experiences) that involve the imaginary crossing or dissolution of the boundary between the subject and the external world. This idea is, of course, based in Freud, where, at the beginning of *Civilisation and Its Discontents* (1930a), he alights on this fantasy that some consider the basis of religious feeling, and begins to speculate on its origin. For Freud, the oceanic feeling is a relic of the baby's sense of continuity with the mother. "An infant at the breast does not as yet distinguish his ego from the external world as the source of the sensations flowing in upon him" (Freud, 1930a, p. 64). The ego develops its sense of unity and autonomy from the external world through a process of relative privation of maternal care that becomes signified by the cries and screams that mark its departure and summon its return. Further disengagement with the external world is precipitated by "the frequent, manifold and unavoidable sensations of pain and unpleasure the removal and avoidance of which is enjoined by the pleasure principle, in the exercise of its unrestricted domination" (Freud, 1930a, p. 70). Pleasure itself thus becomes a principle of separation and avoidance of pain, the pleasure-ego enclosed by the pain that waits at the door of what Lacan would call the *jouissance* of the Other. Freud, therefore, traces back the oceanic feeling to the earlier phase of the ego prior to its sense of separation. If the oceanic feeling becomes the support for religion, then Freud can only suppose that this is because, even as it seeks "the restoration of limitless narcissism" in which the self is one with the world, it is the correlate of the "infantile helplessness" that desires paternal presence. And Freud "cannot think of any need in childhood as strong as the need for a father's protection" (p. 72).

In *Listening Subjects*, Schwarz uses the related concepts of the sonic envelope and the acoustic mirror to analyse pieces of music, notably Steve Reich's piece "It's Gonna Rain" and The Beatles' "I Want You (She's So Heavy)". Steve Reich's piece is an early example of process music and has been cited on a number of occasions by Brian Eno as inspiring his desire to develop the idea of ambient and generative music.

Reich's "It's Gonna Rain" and "Come Out" are early voice works for tape that "explore the strange accretion of phenomena that occurs when two identical tape loops play in sync but then run progressively out of phase due to slight variations in motor speed in the tape machines" (Toop, 2004, p. 184–185). "It's Gonna Rain" is constructed out of two tapes of the same brief speech by a street preacher from the southern states of America that are played in a loop simultaneously. The piece of music, which consists entirely of the speech of the preacher, unfolds as the tapes go out of phase, and the phrases are cut so that the tapes loop faster, going further in and out of phase, the repetitions producing a powerful musical effect. For Schwarz, as with other examples of Reich's oeuvre, this piece of music represents "sonorous space as regressive fantasy in which threshold crossing undermines the (apparent) stability of conventionality" (Schwarz, 1997, p. 16) This presumably means that Reich's music unconsciously tells the story of his infantile subjective development, "It's Gonna Rain" representing the move from Imaginary to Symbolic registers. The duplication of the preacher's voice represents the acoustic mirror, but it is the repetition that makes the moment of threshold crossing possible, in two ways.

The piece of music is divided into two parts. In the first part, the threshold crossing occurs in the way in which the edited tape "repeats the word *gonna* over and over again, cutting the word down to the syllable *go*" that, for Schwarz, suddenly takes on an imperative voice, "calling to the listener" (Schwarz, 1997, p. 17). The listener, hitherto caught in the rapid reverberations of the acoustic mirror, is able to break out of the Imaginary echo chamber through perceiving the truncated "*go*" as some kind of paternal command from the Other. In the second part, different elements of the preacher's speech are condensed further and the threshold crossing occurs because the repetition of the words "open the door", "sure enough", and "Hallelujah" causes the words to lose their meaning so that they reach the point of pure sound. In this way, "Reich represents the noise within the sonorous envelope", the "disordered sounds that support the Symbolic Order" (Schwarz, 1997, p. 18).

While Schwarz's reading of the piece illustrates well the conventional psychoanalytic understanding of music, he ignores what Reich himself has to say about the significance of the piece. Neither, apart from a purely psychoanalytic meaning, does he relate his analysis to any political or musical relevance the piece might have. That is, he ignores what is important—seminal—about the piece formally and conceptually. Yet, it seems to me that it is precisely in these areas that the piece resonates most strongly with psychoanalysis, particularly in some of Lacan's speculative work that was being articulated in seminars in the early 1960s.

Perhaps the most significant aspect of Reich's two pieces in this regard is the way in which music appropriates and decomposes speech. Both "Come Out" and "It's Gonna Rain" comprise speech solely. But speech is cut up and decomposed in a process that is mechanical and aleatory into musical elements that are repeated over and over again. In this process, speech becomes separated from voice as the latter is turned hypnotically into music. If there is anything left of speech, it haunts the tape machines like a ghost. This is, I think, what Schwarz is getting at when, in his analysis of "It's Gonna Rain", he focuses on the truncated syllable "go", suggesting that it produces what he calls a "listening gaze" that assembles "a sonorous fantasy space in which the listener feels directly addressed by the music" (Schwarz, 1997, p. 17). Instead of constructing the catachrestic figure of a "listening gaze", however, that yet again negates voice and sound in favour of vision, it is strange that Schwarz does not turn to Louis Althusser's aural transposition of the Lacanian gaze. It is precisely through "hailing", through calling out "hey you!" that ideology interpellates individuals as subjects, according to Althusser. This is the paradoxical effect of the decomposition of speech in music that the piece produces. Paradoxically and miraculously, Reich makes music "speak" through the musical destruction and decomposition of speech. If, as Schwarz seems to suggest, Reich's piece does indeed hail its listeners through the uncanny effect of producing the imperative "go!", it can only be through summoning, perhaps in the unconscious of the listener, the apocalyptic dimension of the piece. For Reich,

> "It's Gonna Rain" is about the end of the world. In those days, the voice was recorded in '64, you had the Cuban Missile Crisis and so it was very much a part of many people's thinking at that time. We were at the point where we could all turn into so much radioactive ash at any given time. So while this guy is preaching about Noah, it's not something abstract that has nothing to do with what's going on in your life. (Reich, 2000)

For Reich, this piece defines his own technique in relation to other experimental music of the time, such as *avant-garde* electronic music or *musique concrète* that used real sounds such as trains or car crashes. However, the latter were always lowered an octave, speeded up, run through a ring modulator, or played backwards in order to produce a more musical noise. For Reich, it was important that the tape recording of the preacher's voice was heard *as* a voice and not turned into something else. At the same time, the voice is subject to the twin forces of machinism and chance. In this way, the voice produces its "emotional resonance" not through speech in the conventional way, but precisely as an effect of the process of dissonance and repetition through which speech is transformed into music. It is vital that the voice is not transformed by the direct intervention of the composer or technician; its transformation occurs as an effect of the musical process itself. The voice becomes musical, therefore, not as an effect of song, but because it departs from the domain of speech and language as an effect of the tape loops. In fact, it becomes *a*musical, entering a domain where it is properly neither speech nor music. This process, in which a voice is broken down into segments, doubled and repeated, then redoubled and repeated yet again, on and on in a relation of endless dissonance with itself, disorientates the listener. But this stereophonic disorientation begins to resonate in the skull and body of the listener as it becomes faster and faster and more rhythmic, as if voice, utterly decomposed, were on a sonorous line of flight away from itself.

The second half of "It's Gonna Rain", recalls Reich, "is very bleak. You are literally hearing the world come apart . . . going from two then to four then to eight voices and never coming back together again, which is more in keeping with the text" (Reich, 2000). However, it is not so much that, as Schwarz suggests, "repetition tears meaning away from language by the end of the piece to reveal the disordered sounds that support the Symbolic Order". The sounds no longer support the symbolic order at all. In keeping with the apocalyptic theme of the piece, the disintegration of speech into a multiplicity of schizophrenic utterances splitting apart gives way to pure mechanism that, nevertheless, in its *a*musicality, seems to appeal to another Other, the impossible according to Lacan: an impossible silence, perhaps, that provides the caesura for the birth of another entirely musical Other. The music, if it is music, gives way to a drive to go beyond the "fort/da" and evoke "a desire to begin again – to cast away the world, nature and all its works so that it can return again but this time differently, created anew from zero" (Lacan, 1992, pp. 212–213). But this is no longer in an address to the symbolic order as such. The symbolic order is not cast away in a beckoning summons; at this point, the apocalyptic theme of the piece no longer matters. Rather, the "creationist sublimation" concerns a different, purely musical form of creation that is itself here created for the first time out of nothing, out of the gap between two reels of tape going off kilter. Reich describes the process of creation in an interview with Jason Gross, thus:

> I put on headphones (which were stereo with each ear with a separate plug going into the two machines). By chance, two machines were lined up in unison. So what I heard was this unison sound sort of swimming in my head, spatially moving back and forth. It finally moved over to the left, which meant that the machine on the left was slightly faster passing in speed than the machine on the right. So the apparent phenomenon in your head is the sound moving to the left, moves down your left shoulder and then across the floor! (laughs) . . . I thought to myself "this is unbelievable". Instead of a particular relationship, here is a whole way of making music . . . (Reich, 2000)

Through the mediated and conventional techniques of tape-recording, splicing, and phase motion, voice is taken into a different register and disintegrates into swirls of oscillating vibrations that begin to create new circuits in the psyche and, no doubt, in the brain. The audio unconscious hooks up the body to the external world immanent to a purely machinic and aleatory process of creation. As Reich says, "focusing in on the musical process makes possible that shift of attention away from *he* and *she* and *you* and *me* outwards towards *it*" (Reich, 2002, p. 35). Thus, the relation that structures the drives of the audio unconscious concerns the outside, the non-human and the anorganic, rather than the sexual relation. Or, to put it better, the erotic register is desexualised, shifted away from a concern with "he and she and you and me" on to a plane of *a*musical joy in which *it* connects with *it*.

This is precisely what excites Eno about these early Reich pieces, and why he regards them as so important. David Toop notes Eno's frequent reference to "It's Gonna Rain" and "Come Out", emphasising that it was not the interventions of the composer or the producer that provides the revolutionary importance of these pieces, but his withdrawal.

> I thought the economy of them was so stunning . . . There's so little there. The complexity of the piece appears from nowhere. You think, my God, it's so elegant to make something like that . . . to realise that it was made from just a few molecules of sound – that really impressed me. (Eno, cited Toop, 2004, p. 185)

Decomposed speech, broken down into a few molecules of sound, becomes the bare stuff of a new musical order.

Pushing the sonic envelope

In a short piece titled "Ambient music", written as sleeve notes to the album *Music for Airports* (1977) and reproduced as one of the appendices to his 1995 diary published as *A Year with Swollen Appendices* (1995), Brian Eno reflects on the emergence of the musical genre that he named. Eno noticed that in the early 1970s, with the novelty of records and radio wearing off, he and his friends had begun listening to music in a different way. "My friends and I were making and exchanging long cassettes of music chosen for its stillness, homogeneity, lack of surprises and, most of all, lack of variety" (1995, p. 293). Eno and friends wanted music that would surround them and be continuous with, or constitute, "the ambience of our lives". They began to make music in which they could become completely immersed: "Immersion was really the point: we were making music to swim in, to float in, to get lost inside" (Eno, 1995, p. 294).

That music and environment could become continuous became clear, Eno recalls, in a defining experience in 1975 when he had been confined to his bed following a serious accident. He was visited by a female friend, who gave him a record of seventeenth-century harp music. She put the music on as she left. Alone and incapacitated, Eno

> realized that the hi-fi was much too quiet and one of the speakers had given up anyway. It was raining hard outside, and I could hardly hear the music above the rain – just the loudest notes, like little crystals, sonic icebergs rising out of the storm. I couldn't get up and change it, so I just lay there waiting for my next visitor to come and sort it out, and gradually I was seduced by this listening experience. I realized that this was what I wanted music to be – a place, a feeling. (Eno, 1995, pp. 294–295)

What is interesting about this evocative description is the way in which an initially disagreeable situation transforms itself into a seductive and pleasurable one. Clearly in discomfort, unable to move after his accident, Eno is confined to his bed. He is in a passive situation that he is unlikely to have experienced since he was a small child. Dependent upon the comings and goings of nurses, friends, and visitors, the female friend in the anecdote compensates for her departure by putting on the harp music at his request. In the anecdote, the harp music substitutes for the woman's absence, functioning like the mechanical musical mobiles that were introduced in the mid-1970s, designed to amuse and lull a baby to sleep in the absence of the mother. Initially, the experience is unpleasant. The music is barely perceptible and obscured by the rain outside. The music merges with the rain, but even then the sonic environment remains chilly, even icy and tempestuous. Eno has no choice but to give in to his situation. "I couldn't get up and change it, so I just lay there." Gradually, the storm abates and the ocean settles to produce a more seductive and pleasurable all-enveloping experience, one that changes his relation to music and his understanding of what it can do or be.

There is no obvious reference to religion or fathers in Eno's anecdote; rather, there is the icy harp and rain-music of the world. Neither the harmony of the spheres nor a scream passing through nature, it is perhaps the noise-music of a father who does not know he is dead, the music of his harp-playing angels fading away, indistinct from the rain. Confined to his bed, following his own near-death experience, dependent on the presence and absence of friends and relations, Eno, in his anecdote, has clearly been returned to a state similar to Freud's grandson whose famous game with the cotton reel seemed to suggest that the drive conformed to a principle that went beyond pleasure in an "instinct for mastery" that overcomes pain and recovers pleasure via an identification with sounds (Freud, 1920g). From an original position of maternal dependence and passivity, the child exerts itself actively and begins to distinguish and identify himself in relation to a signifier, an utterance, "fort!", with which he can address an imaginary or real partner whom he makes disappear. The exertion of imaginary mastery, therefore, is a repetition that replaces passivity with activity and compensates for the disappearance of the mother.

There is obviously a temptation to hear in Eno's anecdote how the harp music, in substituting for the presence of his female friend, takes over the function of maternal presence in the form of a substitute voice, a lullaby perhaps. But there is nothing warm and comforting about it. It is chilly, icy. Following his accident, Eno has been reminded of his own mortality and this rain and harp music has more of the austerity of the symbolic order that is, of course, cemented by the name and law of the dead father. The music of the harp and rain is no more an echo of the mother's voice than the fort! and da! that is uttered by Freud's grandson as his cries fill the empty space vacated by the mother. For Lacan, these utterances are testimony to the violence of the symbol that "first manifests itself as the killing of the thing, and this death results in the endless perpetuation of the subject's desire" (Lacan, 2006, p. 262).

For Eno, music is not, in itself, very interesting. Rather, he is more "interested in . . . what happens when music hits its culture, what it does to people, what new types of thought it allows" (Eno & Kelly, 1995). It is not, then, the formal qualities of music's specific organisation of sound that is important, or the timbre, the quality of its "voice". Rather, it is the way music "hits its culture" and transforms it, creating a gap for new kinds of thought. In his own anecdote, Eno is describing the power of sound to change the world, to change the feeling and perception of the world of symbolised reality in a way that is both outside language and analogous to it. Music is no longer something that is composed, performed, and listened to; it is all around us, a place, a feeling that induces calm and "creates a space to think . . . it must be ignorable as it is interesting" (Eno, 1995, p. 296). The music is much less important, therefore, than the space it creates, the effect that requires naming.

This transformative force of music, a force that transforms even our understanding of music itself, is not without its sensuous compensations, and as the sounds become more seductive, the thought that they solicit quickly turns to symbolisation proper and the power of naming. As he struggles with the here-and-there of the notes of the harp coming in and out of hearing beneath the heavy rain, Eno masters the situation in his imagination by synthesising everything into the field of his own "pleasure-ego". Eno's mastery takes the symbolic form of a whole new function and genre of music. The musical seduction is essentially a self-seduction in which he becomes at one with his environment even as he masters it, wallowing in an oceanic joy of limitless narcissism that is secured by his act of naming: Eno has invented and named the world: it is ambient music.

American Psycho and Phil Collins

*A*merican *Psycho* (1989), Bret Easton Ellis's satire on the rise of neoliberalism in 1980s America, draws a direct causal link between the ambient vacuity of corporate rock and violence— or at least the fantasy of violence. It is not just that, as part of the satire on the vapidity of his class and generation, long passages and three whole chapters are given over to Patrick Bateman's critical appraisal of Phil Collins, Whitney Houston, and Huey Lewis and the News as the highest achievements of liberal culture. Rather, it is that each of Bateman's bursts of rage or violent fantasies are preceded and apparently prompted by the ambient noise of rock and pop. Belinda Carlisle has him reaching for his serrated knife ready to gut and slice open a colleague (p. 50), MARRS' "Pump Up the Volume" prompts him to fantasise about stabbing a waitress (p. 57), The Lovin' Spoonful suggests slitting the throat of another woman (p. 74), George Michael accompanies and drowns out his announcement that he's going to cut the arms off another (p. 75), and so on. When eventually, in the narrative, he commits his first murder, this is immediately juxtaposed to his four-page peroration on Genesis (pp. 128–131). If he is not wired into his Sony Walkman listening to Bon Jovi, at a club being blasted repeatedly by INXS, U2, or Madonna, he is at home playing repeatedly the

Broadway cast recording of Les Misérables on his latest state-of-the-art hi-fi (p. 165), music that, when whistled by a colleague, causes him to try to strangle him in the men's room (pp. 152–153). The novel seems to suggest that Bateman's violence, whether actual or fantasy, is the inevitable outcome of the ubiquity of a certain type of standardised popular music, the garish expression of its evil banality.

Maybe. But there seems to me something abyssal or contagious about this banality, and the banality of naming it, that sees it reproduce itself over the perceived void of contemporary culture. The psychological structure of American Psycho is not psychosis; the book is hysterical in its appeal to literary authority that has lost all purchase and meaning. Yet, the satire is crassly simulated in the same smug irony and faux shock that characterised the marketing strategies of 1980s advertising and MTV. It is not just that American Psycho was the literary equivalent of Phil Collins, it is that Phil Collins was the general equivalent of all culture, including literature. Hollowed out as the pure form of cultural exchange, this meant that poor Phil Collins lost all specificity except as an excremental remainder, a stain on the cultural memory of the 1980s.

However, there was a happy ending. In 2007, Phil Collins triumphantly returned as the apotheosis of modernity in his overcoming of the history of western metaphysics in the form of an animatronic gorilla in a television commercial for chocolate. In this advertisement, a favourite on YouTube, he is playing karaoke drums to his own track, "Coming in the Air Tonight". The song, once scurrilously assumed to be about masturbation, is here the occasion for the full, dignified presentation of humanimality, as the camera pans in close-up over the gorilla's intense concentration and contemplation, poised to erupt into an explosive rhythm. In the gorilla's embodiment of the continuity between music and violence, Collins is disclosed as the extimate heart of consumer culture's amusical ecstasy. "Joy in a glass and a half."

CHAPTER TEN

The Ride of the Valkyries

I t is one of the most famous and chilling scenes in cinema. A fleet of Hueys, assault helicopters of the 19th Airborne Cavalry, appear over the horizon at sunrise. As they approach the apparently peaceful Vietnamese village, an eerie sound can be heard above their engines and beating rotors: a kind of screaming or wailing, or perhaps even singing. For the commander of the fleet, Lt Colonel Bill Kilgore, this noise is his signature and accompanies every airborne assault because he believes "it scares the hell out of the slopes". For this reason, the Hueys are not just equipped with rockets and guns, but an elaborate sound system linked to a reel-to-reel tape machine that can blare out the beginning of Act III of *Die Walküre*, by Richard Wagner, "The Ride of the Valkyries". Part of the original screenplay by John Milius, the scene is one of the highlights of Francis Ford Coppola's *Apocalypse Now* (1979), but it is a curious scene that bears no relation to any actual event in the Vietnam war. Certainly, the US military used loudspeakers, but, as would be expected, they broadcast propaganda in Vietnamese, and if they played music, they played Vietnamese music. While soldiers and armies have, no doubt, since time immemorial, shouted, screamed, hollered, bugled, piped, and drummed on their march into war, the sinister sound of rotors signalling the helicopters' approach would in itself have terrified a Vietnamese village far more than some weird foreign music almost certainly drowned out by the noise of the engines. The scene is purely cinematic and what it conveys has significance only for a cinema audience.

Dolar begins his book *A Voice and Nothing More* (2006) with another military call to arms in a joke at the expense of the Italian army. Ignoring their commander's call to attack, the opera-loving infantrymen merely sigh, "*Che bella voce!*" "What a beautiful voice" (Dolar, 2006, p. 3). Dolar's point is to illustrate how the aesthetics of voice can be heard in a way distinct from any message it might convey. But in his conjunction of the army and the opera, Dolar adds another term, psychoanalysis, in order to elucidate a third dimension of the voice. This is the voice as "blind spot in the call and as a disturbance of aesthetic appreciation" (p. 4). Rather than the Italian commander's battle cry, Dolar finds this third dimension in the effect produced by a speaking machine constructed by Wolfgang von Kempelen. The machine's voice inspired awe not because of the clarity or beauty of its speech, but its incongruity. The voice, emanating from a crude machine, evoked a sense of the uncanny as if it had become somehow separated from its bodily support in a human being, and left to haunt the machine.

Returning to Coppola's conjunction of war and opera, is it possible to locate in this scene these three dimensions of the voice? The American example is more complex than the Italian, but at first sight it seems to involve a simple reversal. Rather than a military command being appreciated for its aesthetic qualities, an aria is deployed as a battle cry. Moreover, particularly in the exterior aerial shots, the voices of the sopranos seem to emanate from the helicopters themselves, as is no doubt Coppola–Kilgore's intention. The Hueys become the Valkyries, bearing death from above; it is the intention to inspire shock and awe through this uncanny effect as much as through the bombs and rockets. Yet, there is more to each of these levels than this. At the level of meaning, the musical extract connotes much more than its ostensible message were it to be taken as speech and received in the context of the opera as a whole within the confines of an opera house. In order for the music to have its effect, it is not necessary for the soldiers, the Vietnamese, or the cinema audience to know that they are listening to the daughters of Wotan and Erda carry dead warriors from the battlefield to Valhalla, as appropriate as that scenario might be. For the soldiers and the cinema audience, it is more likely that the music is familiar from other films, its military heritage generally, and Wagner's association with the Nazis. It is well known that Wagner was Hitler's favourite composer and apparently "his music was played over the loudspeakers in the Nazi extermination camps" (French, 1999, p. 201). Among a number of previous films, "The Ride of the Valkyries" features prominently in the original score of D. W. Griffith's *The Birth of a Nation* (1915) at the climactic scene of the third act when a number of white Americans, threatened by a group of liberated slaves, are rescued by the Klu Klux Klan. The message of Milius and Coppola, therefore, conveyed by the inclusion of this extract from Wagner in this scene, can, no doubt, be read as a comment on Kilgore and the US commanders that he may be taken to represent. Following Groucho Marx in *Duck Soup*, the "authorial" message, therefore, might be: "while Kilgore may strut like a Nazi, act like a Nazi and like Nazi music, don't let that fool you, he really is a Nazi". But that ignores a number of Kilgore's specific qualities that, judging by subsequent events, are characteristically American. The use of music in the midst of war, the delusion of indestructibility evident in his complete indifference to enemy gunfire, and the staging of the battle purely in order to facilitate surfing, testify to the "madness" caused by such a confusion of boundaries in which war as an instrument of foreign policy becomes simply an ecstatic mode of non-productive expenditure. That war is utter joy for Kilgore is evident in the melancholy of his sigh that "someday this war will end".

The aesthetic dimension of the helicopter attack is more complex still because, again, it operates cinematically in excess of its purely operatic context in an assemblage of audio-visual elements. As the voices of the sopranos drift in and out of earshot above the engines and, later, the explosions and carnage of the attack, singing becomes indistinguishable from screaming. The screams of the helicopters, the villagers, and the soldiers both set off and merge with the daughters of Wotan and Erda as the death they bring is borne off to Valhalla. Amidst the clamour, the voices illuminate the silence of the death drive through providing the point of uncanny, familiar strangeness around which the drive pulsates. The sound of the divas bears more than an operatic beauty, since their unearthly singing is poised on the edge of screaming. It is that dissonance, for the American soldiers and the cinema audience, that eerie foreign noise singing–screaming in a foreign language that provides the traumatic affect that ensures the scene makes such a strong impression. Taking their cues from the reaction shots of Willard's crew, it is the cinema audience that registers the terror, assumed for the "slopes", in the alterity of Wagner's Valkyries. It is the uncanny shock of hearing this foreign dissonance within the repetition of the same old scene of movie-military triumph, surfing on a foaming plume of napalm, that renders the scene memorable and even traumatic; as so often, the trauma of such a dissonance provides the basis of a series of repetitions.

Apocalypse Now is a film that is routinely voted one of the most powerful war films of the twentieth century. In these days of globalisation, moreover, the USA's enemies are much more likely to be familiar with Hollywood film and their conventions than the Vietnamese in the 1960s. Indeed, as Jonathan Pieslak recounts in *Sound Targets* (2009), his book on the recreational and operational use of music in the Iraq war (2003–2004), it was the knowledge that "Saddam Hussein liked old American movies" that inspired US soldiers to blast Wagner's "Ride" on the outside of their trucks as they attacked Baghdad (p. 85); that and the desire to persuade the Iraqis that they were "freaking insane" (C. J Grisham, US soldier in Iraq, quoted in Pieslak, 2009, p. 85). While one assumes that Hussein was a Coppola rather than Griffiths fan (one imagines *The Godfather* films would also have been favourites), the use of this music was more than simply ironic. It was part of a systematic approach to the deployment of music, especially popular music, as an instrument of war and torture.

The effective use of music as a psychological tactic was decisively confirmed for the US military by the success of Operation Just Cause in Panama in 1989, where it was used as both a barrier to President Manuel Noriega's communications with the outside world and a powerful incentive for his removal by the local residents of and around the Vatican consulate. It also had the added benefit of driving Noriega himself nuts. Aware that Noriega was a fan of opera (no point in Wagner, then), but hated rock music, the military blasted the Pope's House with AC/DC, Mötley Crüe, Metallica, Led Zeppelin, and others, with satisfying results. "Operation Just Cause became a seminal event in the practice of utilizing music as a distinct psychological practice" (Pieslak, 2009, p. 82). Subsequently, the hard rock/metal genres have, along with rap, been the music of choice for the military, paradoxically perhaps for both recreational as well as operational purposes. Tanks, Strykers, and Humvees, equipped with audio and communication technology that soldiers customise into throbbing sound systems, pound out mainstream rap and metal while on patrol. In interviews with troops, Pieslak shows how music has various functions in the theatre of war: in recruitment videos, in combat training, motivational preparation, as a battlefield weapon, post-operational recreation, and extreme interrogation tactic. The most famous use of rock as a battlefield weapon came in the battle for Fallujah, which, because of the extensive use of music, became known by the troops, after Lollapalooza, as LalaFallujah (AC/DC and Guns 'n' Roses featuring prominently). Along with concerts and festivals, Pieslak notes the crucial importance of MTV from the 1980s as a model for army recruitment advertisements, although, as with the television station, the advertisements featured mainstream rock and metal rather than rap, presumably for similar reasons. With these examples and others, American popular culture is disclosed not just as the vanguard of American Empire, but as its shock troops in battle; the Iraqi conflict was very much MTV at war.

Just as music fought with the GIs and the aircrew, it worked also for the CIA and its employees. In her essay on the use of music as a torture and battlefield weapon, and in the area of interrogation, Suzanne Cusick notes that there was a "torture playlist" of tunes that guards and interrogators liked to use when they sought to disorientate detainees or deprive them of sleep. Again, paradoxes arise with the choice of music concerning whether it is actually pleasurable to the interrogators (along with favoured heavy metal acts like Metallica, Eminem, and Bruce Springsteen featured) or intensely annoying (like Neil Diamond, apparently, or the theme tunes to *Sesame Street* and *Barney*). Pieslak is scrupulous and perhaps a little too credulous in insisting that the use of such music did not constitute cruel and unusual treatment, or torture, accepting at face value the interrogator's claim that every aural assault inflicted on the detainee was equally suffered by the interrogator. Wagner-user in battle, music aficionado C. J. Grisham also deployed some of his MP3 collection during interrogations, and, in a rather gruesomely comic way (though no doubt unintentionally) describes the process as a sort of stand-off, a competition in musical endurance and sleep deprivation: "we can't treat them any worse than we treat ourselves . . . you can't, the purpose—it's sleep deprivation [that's] me staying up just as long as they stayed up" (Pieslak, 2009, pp. 88–89). In this marathon dual by musical ordeal and red-eyed wakefulness, Grisham starts off with Britney Spears and Metallica, adding later some Mudvayne, ultimately cranking up the pressure with Slipknot. The use of pop, however, was prohibited because it ran the risk of turning the tables should the detainees' toes start tapping. On his patrols, Grisham had previously seen Iraqis wearing N'Sync T-Shirts and doing the Moonwalk:

> And I'm like "what's that kid saying?" Then he started doing the little moves, the foot moves and stuff like that, and I'm like "Holy Cow!" ... I never used any of that because, you put on a Michael Jackson tape, which to me would make me talk, but you put it on for those guys and like, "Oh Michael Jackson", and it doesn't do anything [to] them. But you put on the hardcore, heavy metal American music from the Deep South or wherever. They don't want to hear that stuff, they think it's Satanic. (Pieslak, 2009, p. 89)

In George Gittoes' documentary *Soundtrack to War* (2006), multiple soldiers make the claim that "War itself is heavy metal" (cited in Pieslak, p. 53), perhaps not simply as analogy but also as substitution. For the US bomber pilots who, Christopher Coker notes, "flew missions with heavy-metal music pumping through their headsets while graphic-simulated displays helped guide their bombs to their targets" (Coker, 2004, p. 117), music functions simultaneously as simulation and barrier to the reality of war. As Baudrillard argued in a different way for the first Gulf War against Iraq, music compensated for the fact that for many US combatants, the war did not wholly take place. Pieslak reports, "one woman I spoke to said that since her brother came back from Iraq he listens to death metal constantly even though he was not a dedicated fan before he left" (p. 53). Heavy metal, the musical illusion of Iraqi massacre, is also the compensatory repetition of the trauma that for many American combatants was essentially missed.

In war, metal seals off Americans from the real world of their own un-making in another world of pleasurable sonic madness and pumping aural carnage – a world of their own. Commenting in 1986 on Louis Wolfson, the schizophrenic translator who, years before the appearance of the Walkman, used to wander around wearing a stethoscope plugged in his ears attached to a tape recorder, Gilles Deleuze claims him as the device's true inventor: "a makeshift schizophrenic object lies at the origin of an apparatus that is now spread over the entire universe, and that will in turn schizophrenize entire peoples and generations" (Deleuze, 1998, p. 13). Or, as a soldier in *Sound Targets* says,

> music was a huge thing for me while in the war, music played a great deal in deployment. I listened to it as much as I could. I really don't know what I would have done without my iPod over there. The military ought to issue an mp3 player to every soldier. (Pieslak, 2009, p. 3)

The Internet and networked technology that enabled the revolution in military affairs that informed the Iraq wars and that also enables MP3 players and music downloads establishes the front line and the home front on the same plane of consistency.

In her essay on music and torture, Cusick consults various discussions and exchanges in the online blogosphere in order to assess the cultural resonance of such usage on the home front. While opinions on its morality, legality, and effectiveness differ, few doubted that music could be used as torture and numerous examples of favourite hates—rap music, disco, Bill and Hillary singing "I Got You Babe"—are exchanged. There is one artist, however, universally deemed beyond the pale, Yoko Ono. One blogger wrote "you might as well stick panties on the head of everyone in the village. At least THAT would be more human than using Yoko Ono as a weapon of torture". Another posted a parody of Article 13 from the Geneva Convention to prohibit the use of her music, while yet another wrote:

> No dude . . . we gotta have some limits . . . I mean . . . just damn. I mean . . . pork fat, shredded Koran, menstrual fluids . . . I see the usefulness there. But I gotta draw the line at Yoko. I mean, we're not barbarians. (Cusick, 2006)

In the characteristic singing of Yoko Ono, the sound of operatic screaming returns in the voice of a woman from Japan, another historical Asian foe of the USA, to disclose, uncannily, the barbarous limits, the *acheronta movebo*, or infernal regions, of American culture.

PART III
SCREAMADELICA

CHAPTER ELEVEN

Flower of hate: the lack in The Beatles

In an interview in 2007 with Beth Ditto, Yoko Ono relates a little fable in order to convey to the singer of The Gossip the formative nature of her early years in Britain with John Lennon.

> Did you ever hear the story about three pots of plants? Three pots of plants, each watered with certain thoughts: one watered with nothing, just water, the other watered with love and the other with hate. Which one do you think grew better?

Ditto replies, somewhat predictably, love, and Yoko confirms that the plant that died was the one treated with water and indifference. But the plant fed with hate did just as well as the one given love.

> Hate and love was equal ... You see many people hated me ...
> Well I used that hatred as a power, as an energy, and it's a great power, my God. As long as you don't get distressed about it ...
> The whole world was giving me bitter medicine for 40 years, and it was probably better than if they gave me sugar. (Ono, 2007, p. 39)

She's so heavy

Following his analysis of Steve Reich in *Listening Subjects* (1997), David Schwarz turns to the song "I Want You (She's So Heavy)" from The Beatles' album *Abbey Road* (1969) in order to deepen his discussion of the voice as a maternal echo, reverberating the acoustic mirror or sonic envelope of the mother's voice. For Schwarz, the enunciation of sexual desire in the song activates the retrospective fantasy of sonorous union with the voice of the mother, sexual difference and the desire for union being figured in the echoing tension between voice and music. In the initial part of the song, John Lennon's "scat" style of singing is perceived as the echo of the sound of the guitar and other instruments that all repeat the same riff. Meanwhile, the

> knocking motives that follow the lines "I want you" and "I want you so bad" in the verse . . . turn this difference within echoing voices into an extended representation of frustrated desire for a female object – an attempt to break through a barrier. (Schwarz, 1997, p. 28)

Schwarz's analysis draws on a notion in psychoanalysis that Silverman suggests has become something of "a theoretical commonplace . . . the maternal voice as a blanket of sound, extending on all sides of the newborn infant" (Silverman, 1988, p. 72). For Silverman, this notion is marked by ambivalence both in its effect as fantasy and also in the way that it has divided psychoanalytic commentators who understand it as either a nurturing, warm, and enveloping space or a suffocating zone of dependency and entrapment (pp. 72–73). As it progresses, "I Want You (She's So Heavy)" couples the (frustrated) desire for unison with the voices in the chorus that sing "*heavy* repeatedly like voices echoing into the distance". The verse–chorus structure, therefore, seems to perform the oscillation between two ambivalent fantasies "that trap the male subject" into both a desiring dependency and the "oppressive presence" of the maternal object in whose voice the subject's own demands are always already echoed, reverberating and fading away in the acoustic mirror.

In his account of "I Want You (She's So Heavy)", Schwarz's emphasis is more on the oppressive nature of the maternal voice, but, rather than a woman's scream, it is Lennon's own screaming voice that becomes the focus of analysis. "At the end of the fourth repetition of the verse, Lennon emits a searing scream from 4:27 to 4:30 . . . it sounds poised between the traditional, affirmative rock-and-roll *Yeah!* and a nonlinguistic scream of horror" (Schwarz, 1997, p. 30). However, he considers it to be more akin to the latter than the former, citing as evidence Lennon's own comments concerning the meaning of screams in his work: "When it gets down to it . . . when you're drowning you don't say 'I would be incredibly pleased if someone would have the foresight to notice me drowning and come and help me', you just *scream*" (p. 31). For Schwarz, Lennon's scream suggests "the primal enunciation of communication" which is not just the instinctual cry for sustenance, but also the cry that is enunciated as a demand in imitation of the speech and cries of others. This is the "primal" demand not just for the satisfaction of need, but also of love and anxiety at the oscillating absence/presence of the mother.

In his analysis, it is odd that Schwarz makes no mention of the song's presumed referent, Yoko Ono. This is particularly the case given that it is very well documented that Lennon's songs at this time and subsequently were avowedly personal. Although it is credited to Lennon and McCartney and all four Beatles played on the track and regarded it as a favourite, "I Want You (She's So Heavy)" is over-whelmingly a Lennon as opposed to a McCartney song. It is also well known that he referred to Ono, both in song and more familiarly, as "Mother", or "Mother Superior". Indeed, the highly personal nature of Lennon's songs more or less from the point of his engagement with Ono is something that Beatles commentators specifically credit (or rather blame) her for. "Of all the most dangerous ideas Ono unloaded on her spouse around this time, the most damaging was her belief that all art is about the artist and no one else" (MacDonald, 2005, p. 346). Here, Lennon's elaboration of a personal voice in contradistinction to his collective identity as a Beatle is regarded as entirely negative and false, a dangerous foreign import, the echo and imitation of another's voice. MacDonald's analysis of "I Want You (She's So Heavy)" in *Revolution in the Head* (2005), his highly acclaimed song-by-song commentary on The Beatles entire *oeuvre*, pulls no punches when it comes to the meaning and significance of the song:

> Lennon's passion for Ono had shaken him to the core. His long dreamed-of erotic mother had finally arrived and the reality was almost too much for him. Sexually addicted to her, he was helplessly

dependent, a predicament grindingly explicit in his chord sequence
... Nightmarishly tormented, this is a musical tryst with a succubus.
(MacDonald, 2005, pp. 343–44)

Schwarz's timidity with regard to biographical analyses is, in some
ways, admirable, but his reading bumps up against one of the most
powerful myths concerning John-and-Yoko that, if addressed, might
raise it to a different level and, thereby, connect his account of the
structure and dynamic of this specific song to that of a cultural symptom generally. Instead, through leaving the reader to fill in the maternal gap, Schwarz silently reproduces the structure of absence/
presence in which Ono's influence on her husband is regarded as
suffocating. The maternal envelope in which Ono enfolds Lennon is
generally regarded by fans of The Beatles as entirely malign and is
usually characterised in a very familiar, if contradictory, way. On the
one hand, she is a talentless gold-digging parasite, and, on the other,
a dominating and controlling figure imposing abstract and over-intel-
lectualised ideas on to a natural genius.

Over forty years after the break-up of The Beatles and thirty years
after Lennon's murder, during which time Ono has been afforded
sympathy for her bereavement and blessed with a softening of atti-
tudes among Beatles' commentators, her essential place in their myth
has remained undisturbed. Examples are legion, but if references
are necessary, then perhaps it is enough to cite the recent Beatles biography by Bob Spitz. Spitz both quotes and comments extensively
on Ono's harmful influence, iterating the idea that "Yoko was drawn .
.. to the girth of his chequebook" (Spitz, 2007, p. 748), and that
she wanted to exploit and manipulate Lennon into furthering her
career—"No one was going to derail her grand designs, especially
now that she had a weapon like John Lennon in her arsenal" (p. 820).
At the same time, these "grand designs" are dismissed as "loopy",
"screwy", "avant-garde crap" (Spitz, 740–741), "annoyingly adoles-
cent" (p. 743), and "mumbo jumbo" (p. 778). Given this, some account
has to be given for how the sharpest and most streetwise of The
Beatles could have been taken in by such self-evident self-serving
nonsense, so Ono must have in some way bewitched him or sapped
his will. Thus, Spitz laments how the other Beatles had no choice
but to become co-dependants in "John's addiction" (2007, p. 777),
noting Lennon's "zombielike regard" for her (p. 784) even as she

herself is described as "a zombie [who] had claimed his tormented soul" (p. 813).

This dependency introduced a fatal rift into the life of the group, Ono's "destructive airs" (Spitz, 2007, p. 805) and "negative vibes" (George Harrison, quoted by Spitz, p. 813) signalling its break-up. From the first full biography (Davies, 1981, p. 376) to the latest (Spitz, 2007, p. 783) to the most respected and scholarly (Lewisohn, 2004, p. 276), Ono is the cause of The Beatles' demise. Spitz, interestingly, uses Ono's voice as a metaphor for the disharmony she introduces. "Hardly a day went by when one of the Beatles—*or more*—wasn't at one of the other's throats. The pitch of antagonism in the studio ran about as high as a Yoko Ono vocal" (p. 783). The bitterness and pain that, bizarrely, is apparently still felt by Beatle fans at this break-up is strongly evident in the affectivity of Spitz's own subjective response and characterisation of Ono's voice. He remarks on its "high-pitched, almost painful wailing . . . the kind of jarring vocals that reminded listeners of 'the Babel inside an insane asylum'" (Spitz, 2007, p. 765). Her voice "grated like fingernails on a chalkboard" (p. 784), "screech-ing like a wounded animal" (p. 809). Ono's voice is cause, metaphor, and, here in this visceral and excessive characterisation, *a*musical symptom linking the cleavage of Spitz's imaginary relation with The Beatles to the echo of some old scene of maternal deprivation retained in the unconscious, perhaps. But to suggest this and relate Spitz's phantasmatic characterisation of Ono's voice back to some primal site of enunciation and maternal ambivalence, I would be repeating Schwarz's own analysis of Lennon's voice in "I Want You (She's So Heavy)". Like Lennon's voice, according to Schwarz, Spitz's stridency is captured by, and echoes within, the voice of Yoko Ono. This repeti-tion is, as I will show, one of many that reverberate throughout accounts of the encounter between Yoko Ono and The Beatles. How-ever, rather than gather them all together in one group or cultural fan-tasy and relate them back to the same primal scene, I want to discuss them as the effect of the convergence of two heterogeneous series, a Yoko Ono-series and Beatles-series, of discordant repetitions in which screaming provides the line of auditory cleavage, that is to say, of (dis) connection and (non)communication, music and noise, hearing and deafness, love and hate. In these series, even the notion of the "primal scream" can be seen as yet another repetition. In this story, it is not in relation to some primal scream or inaugural cry of enunciation that one scream or utterance relates to another; there is no first term that is repeated: rather, dissonance resounds as an effect of the repeated scream. The primacy resides in the dissonance *of* repetition. This requires looking at the various series of screams and sonic milieu that they constitute, irrupt and deterritorialise.

Beatlemania

It was, indeed, the sound of screaming female voices that established The Beatles as a unique cultural phenomenon and provided the conditions for their rapid disintegration. None of these voices had anything to do with Yoko Ono, however, but were the referent of what was called Beatlemania. As they reached national recognition with a series of number one records in the British music charts in the early 1960s, concerts by The Beatles took on a paradoxical nature. They became less about music, its performance and enjoyment, and more about the frenzied noise generated by the audience. This noise was produced by an audience that consisted for the most part of young women screaming their heads off. American popular music had generated this kind of excitement before in response to acts like Frank Sinatra and Elvis Presley, but never to this intensity. To a degree, the screaming was a continuation of the excitement of The Beatles themselves, who were initially and above all *fans* of American popular music. Their early sets consisted mostly of imitations of their favourite records by American artists. The Beatles' versions of the Isley Brothers' "Twist and Shout", or Barrett Strong's "Money (That's What I Want)" being notable examples that exceed the originals in energy and enthusiasm, if not in finesse.

Sublimely ignorant or indifferent to the racial segregation that marked the production, dissemination, and reception of popular music in America at the time, The Beatles' covers of rock and roll, rhythm and blues, and soul records nevertheless conveyed the sexual excitement of an enthralled European encounter with American exoticism. John Lennon does not so much sing "Money (That's What I Want)" or "Twist and Shout" as *scream* them, conveying the latter, according to MacDonald (2005, p. 76), in the manner of a sexual challenge that "adapts the song to a white female audience for whom such primal abandon was frenziedly thrilling in 1963". The "primal abandon" owes less to the original record by the Isley Brothers as to The Beatles' own performance of an encounter with an imaginary American otherness that is conveyed to the audience in a contagious screaming that is returned a thousand fold.

Such screaming became a worldwide epidemic, spreading even to America itself as The Beatles generated their own frisson of cultural difference by returning the message of African-American popular music to the USA in an inverted (white) form. Even in America, The Beatles quickly became less about music than about noise, money, and a terrifying white ecstasy of (non)communication. It reached its crescendo at the concert held in Shea Stadium in August 1965, home of the New York baseball team, the Mets. The fact that the concert was being held in a sports stadium, playing to 56,000 people, by far the largest audience to which any musical act had performed in history, already indicated that this event had transcended the merely musical. The possibilities of electronic amplificationmade it conceivable, of course, but before they had uttered a syllable or played a note, The Beatles realised that music would be neither possible nor necessary.

Upon walking on stage, The Beatles were greeted by a "tsunami" of ear-splitting sound. Over fifty thousand American kids screamed in unison in the crumbling concrete bowl of the stadium. The *New York Times* reported that

> their immature lungs produced a sound so staggering, so massive, so shrill and sustained that it quickly crossed the line from enthusiasm to hysteria and was soon in the area of the classic Greek meaning of the word pandemonium—the region of all demons. (Spitz, 2007, p. 577)

Another description compared the sound to "a dozen jets taking off" (p. 577), as fellow British musicians Mick Jagger and Keith Richards looked on in awe. Shea stadium represented both the pinnacle and the pit of The Beatles' experience as live performers, their presence being totally effaced by the screams of the audience that needed only the semblance of an appearance to erupt.

According to his school friend, Pete Shotton, Lennon "very quickly realized that . . . he was getting cut off from the world—and that it was [only] going to get worse. He realized very early on that this was the penalty" (Spitz, 2007, p. 456). Indeed, in the April preceding the Shea stadium concert, The Beatles recorded the song "Help!" that Lennon later claimed was indeed a genuine cry for help in the midst of the mayhem caused by the mania surrounding the group. MacDonald writes that "lyrically 'Help!'" distils Lennon's misery, marking a watershed in his life.

> Here the shell that he had grown around his feelings since his mother's death finally cracks as he admits a need for others. Musically … the song opens on an unhappy B minor, climbing stepwise via a sixth to a pleading scream as A major arrives to stabilise the harmony. (MacDonald, 2005, p. 153

This harmony is only momentary, however, as "'Help!' perpetually slides back to the anxiety and tension of B minor" (p. 153).

By the time of Shea stadium, all the Beatles had become tired of acting like the mannequins that they had become for their audience. Completely surrounded, enclosed by an ocean of screams, The Beatles were reduced to pure soundless image. The screaming of Shea stadium provided the ultimate experience of disconnection and discordance with the world that held The Beatles in its suffocating embrace. And it was into the bubble formed by this dystopian envelope of sound that Yoko Ono applied her verbal incision, bursting open a hell of execration and hatred.

Dissatisfied with the boredom and pointlessness of touring, The Beatles retired from public performance and, as is well known, concentrated on recording, undertaking a series of innovative, influential, and highly regarded studio albums. The studio in Abbey Road used by The Beatles has become regarded by fans as something of a sacred space, the birthplace of a number of timeless pop classics. It is represented, for The Beatles, as "an ideal environment and refuge away from the madness outside" (Lewisohn, 2004, p. 277). That is to say, an all-male, yet strangely womb-like, space negatively defined against the pandemonium of the world outside represented by the screams of young women. Spitz affirms that at this time, "The Beatles were an unconditionally exclusive fraternity—one for all and all for one. Cynthia Lennon, envious of their rapport, called it 'a marriage of four minds … [that] were always in harmony'" (p. 736). No one, not even Brian Epstein, their manager, or Dick James, their music publisher, was permitted to breach the sacred studio space in which The Beatles worked with their producer and engineers. And yet, in 1968, as The

Beatles began work on what would become their eponymous "white" album, this sanctuary was breached by Yoko Ono (Spitz, 2007, p. 777).

Ono's inaugural appearance in The Beatles' recording studio on 30 May 1968 resulted in screaming, but not from her. Amid increasing tension, the session dedicated to recording the first version of "Revolution #1" resulted in something resembling an *avant-garde* happening consistent with Ono's work with Fluxus. Mark Lewisohn, who has exhaustively chronicled The Beatles' recording sessions, relates the event thus:

> By the end of this session, the last six minutes of this 10 minute 17 second recording was the sound of pure chaos – the sound of a 'Revolution' if you will – with discordant instrumental jamming, feedback, John repeatedly screaming "alright" and then, simply repeatedly screaming, with lots of on-microphone moaning by John and Yoko, with Yoko talking and saying such off-the-wall phrases as "you become naked", and with the overlaying of miscellaneous, home made sound effects tapes . . . [eventually this] last 6 minutes would be hived off to form the basis of Revolution #9. (Lewisohn, 1988, p. 135)

This session came just eleven days after Ono and Lennon had consummated their affair following a similar all-night improvisation and recording of an assemblage of music and noise that would be released as *Unfinished Music No 1: Two Virgins* (1968) with the famous naked cover. "Comprised of [*sic*] an uninterrupted wash of *avant-garde* sound effects, beyond the ken of pretty much everyone", it was, Lewisohn notes, "banned, mercilessly criticized and attacked" (p. 283). Incomprehensible to fans of The Beatles (or western ones at least; the reception in Japan was different, as we shall see), the title of this work relates directly to a central theme of Ono's art and clearly exemplifies John Lennon's loving embrace of her work and, given its likely reception, provocative and courageous participation in her approach. The extension of such an approach to a Beatles session was indeed even more provocative, but unquestionably liberating for Lennon. For MacDonald,

> the shift towards simplicity registered in REVOLUTION 1 . . . [and the] shedding of pretence became progressively more obsessive until, two years later, it reached an agonised climax in the naked "primal" expiation of his first solo album. (MacDonald, 2005, p. 286)

Primal scream therapy

One of the ironies of Ono and Lennon's participation in Arthur Janov's primal scream therapy was that they were, at the time, the recipients of a collective howl of rage and pain drawn, it could be suggested, from the same kind of structure of feeling, the imagined separation from a source of pleasure and plenitude associated with maternal presence that informs Arthur Janov's quasi-Freudian therapy. Janov's somewhat Rousseauean idea is that the renunciation of instinctual satisfaction that Freud regarded as the child's "great cultural achievement" is the wellspring of all pain and evil. The point of differentiation and separation from the source of instinctual satisfaction, the mother, is regarded as the most primal formative experience in which such satisfaction is supplanted by pain. When that pain is repressed and instincts are sublimated in symbolic substitutes, neurosis is inevitable. Subsequently,

> in the neurotic, the real feeling self is locked away with the original Pain; that is why he must feel that Pain in order to liberate himself; feeling that Pain shatters the unreal self in the same way that denying the Pain created it. (Janov, 1970, p. 35)

Janov's therapy involves somehow connecting with the unconscious "intolerable pain" that provides the lining and support of consciousness, and which is an effect of disconnection and symbolisation, and unleashing it in a primal scream. Such screaming, one might say, phantasmatically acts out the *jouissance* of castration, in Lacanian terms. Rather than refusing *jouissance* and seeking it on the "inverse scale of the Law of desire" determined by the symbolic order and the signifying chain (Lacan, 2006, p. 700), Janov wants his subjects to reject speech and access the *jouissance* of suffering directly by smashing through the symbolic order in an orgy of screaming.

For John Lennon, such a process provided a means of conceptualising, writing, and performing some of the songs for his first solo album *John Lennon/Plastic Ono Band* (1970) that thematised his fraught relationship with his parents, particularly his mother, and the latter's premature death when he was a teenager. But that does not mean that these songs and Lennon's screaming on them are somehow more primal or primary in relation to Lennon's earlier vocal performances.

His screaming on the tracks "Mother" and "Well, Well, Well" is consistent with previous performances with The Beatles on "Twist and Shout", "Help!", "Revolution #1", "I Want You (She's So Heavy)", and so on. They are rock and roll screams, part of a series not limited simply to Lennon or The Beatles, but equally to Little Richard or Jerry Lee Lewis. Each scream in the series, each repetition, takes music or harmony into a zone of rock and roll excess, disharmony or discordance in its own way in relation to another character, another object of desire. Each scream relates to the virtual object denoted by the "*a*" that marks the place of the *a*musical subject's discordance with itself and its desire, its clamour for being. "In short, there is no ultimate term – our loves do not refer back to the mother; it is simply that the mother occupies a certain place in relation to the virtual object in the series" (Deleuze, 1997, p. 105), as Deleuze writes in *Logic of Sense* (1989), during his Lacanian phase.

Yoko Ono's vocal performance on her companion album, *Yoko Ono/Plastic Ono Band* (1970), is completely different from Lennon's, even though forms of screaming are extensively employed. They do not have very much to do with Janov's ideas or therapeutic techniques, either, and neither do they have much, if anything, to do with rock and roll, even though they are introduced into a rock and roll setting. This is partly because Ono apparently found "less in Janov's work than John" and partly because, like Lennon but in relation to quite a different tradition, that of the *avant-garde*, "she had long been exploring the scream vocality far beyond Janov's remits" (Clayson et al., 2004, p. 150). In so far as the psychoanalytic framework invoked by Janov resonated with Ono's experience in 1970, however, and in so far as she was being consistent with her belief that "all art is inescapably self-referential" (MacDonald, 2005, p. 332), Ono's musical screams possibly take their bearings from a position that was unique with regard to the *jouissance* of the Other in Britain at the end of the 1960s.

It is difficult to overstate the importance of The Beatles to the baby-boom generation and to the new sense of British identity being forged in the 1960s after the austerity of the immediate post-war period and the end of empire. To adapt a Lacanian term in a familiar way, they were—and, indeed, still are—an exemplary instance of *das ding* in the national narrative of Britain at the end of the twentieth century (see Lacan, 1992, pp. 100–114). Giving a sense of vivacity, plenitude, youth, and glamour to an old nation, they are an instance of that precious

Thing, popularised by Slavoj Žižek , that becomes invested with *jouis-sance* as it grounds national identity in the real of desire. For years The Beatles enjoyed the benefits of the intense narcissistic attachment of the British people, including the notorious British Press, who indulged them completely. Spitz notes that "the Stones were routinely hounded by the press and police, as were other rock bands with a bad-boy image" (Spitz, 2007, p. 799), but this was never the case with The Beatles. The journalist Ray Connolly recalls that

> they were considered untouchable, by the police also. No one wanted to spoil the party . . . no bad word was ever written about them in the daily papers . . . it was an unspoken contract. The press was rooting for them—and protecting them. (Connolly, cited in Spitz, 2007, p. 799)

All this changed with the appearance of Yoko Ono. While Lennon was always provocative—this was part of his charm—and the press and the fans "could deal with John's outbursts, his rebellious nature, his opinions about the [Vietnam] war. But with Yoko, apparently, he had crossed the line" (Spitz, 2007, p. 799).

Yet, in this way, Ono's appearance did not destroy the quasi-sacred, untouchable nature of The Beatles; she actually confirmed it. She cemented it through her desire for Lennon and the imaginary threat she represented, the threat that this foreign woman would "steal" Lennon away from the nation, break up The Beatles, and spoil the party. By the end of 1968, Lennon and Ono were arrested for possession of marijuana amid wide publicity and hostile crowds (the arrest is now widely assumed to have been a police set up, the chief investigating officer having subsequently been convicted for corruption relating to other matters). This was evidence for the Beatle that "everyone—the press, the police, even the fans—'were out to get' him" (Spitz, 2007, p. 799). In the news footage that survives of the arrest, in which the couple are surrounded by over twenty members of the Metropolitan Police and a crowd of onlookers, a shrill female voice screeches above the throng, "She's 'orrible! Cynthia's better than her!" (The Beatles Anthology 6, 1995). In interviews, Lennon later said he was taken aback at the abuse his wife took and the number of people who called her "ugly", yet again highlighting not only the aesthetic dimension of racism but also the ugliness it discloses in the racist. Yoko's perceived ugliness concerned her difference from the western standard of female beauty, of course, but more than anything it was the *voice* of "John Rennon's famous gloupie" that cut to the quick of the aesthetic basis of British and American racism. For Philippe Lacoue-Labarthe, all racism "is primarily, fundamentally, an aestheticism. (In his essence, 'the Jew' is a caricature: ugliness itself.)" (Lacoue-Labarthe, 1990, p. 69). With Yoko, it went further than simply aesthetics; it was not just an "oriental" appearance, but, above all, Ono's voice, grating "like fingernails on a chalkboard" or "screeching like a wounded animal" (Spitz, 2007, pp. 784, 809), that provided the extimate point of excruciating dissonance defining British *a*musia. This *a*musia is the symptom through which British discordance with the world is experienced in relation to Yoko Ono, beyond all rational measure or aesthetic criteria, in unbearable noise, tunelessness, and the pain of its misogyny, racism, and abjection. And Yoko Ono had not even begun screaming in earnest yet.

It was in 1969, a few months after their drug bust at the end of 1968 but before undergoing the primal scream therapy with Janov, that Ono decided she "was ready to begin screaming again" (cited in Munroe and Hendricks, 2000, p. 234). Ono had last screamed with intent back in the late 1950s and early 1960s in the midst of the New York *avant-garde* scene in the circles of John Cage, La Monte Young, and Fluxus in instructional and performance works like "Voice Piece for Soprano". Reflecting in 1992 on her performance of the latter in 1961, Ono commented that "the avant-garde guys didn't *use* the voice. They were just so cool, right? There was also this very asexual kind of atmosphere in the music. And I wanted to throw blood" (Kemp, 1992, p. 78). By 1969, Ono was ready to start throwing some more blood. The context this time would be different, however. This time, rather than in the midst of *avant-garde* gallery cool, she conceived of an idea of a rock band that would be a kind of anti-Beatles. It would be an idea for a band that was not bound by the kind of exclusivity that had caused so much friction and bad feeling surrounding her presence at Abbey Road. Indeed, it would be a concept "for a band that would never exist . . . that didn't have a set number of members . . . that could accommodate anyone who wanted to play with it" (Edwards, 1971, p. 35). The name of the group was the Plastic Ono Band.

In her album that takes the title of her conceptual band (comprising, in this instance, Lennon on guitar, Ringo Starr on drums, and Klaus Voormann on bass) Yoko adapts her previous vocal style and vocal improvisations into a new form. Writing of her improvisations in a non rock and roll setting on *Unfinished Music No. 1: Two Virgins*, Jungr suggests that her

"screaming" is a much more complex sound than the word suggests. In fact, she draws on many elements of the sound palette within that rubric. Sometimes animal-like, child-like at points; passionate, grieving, desperate, open, closed, higher, lower. Weird yes, but never, ever dull. (Clayson, 2004, pp. 143–144)

It has even been suggested that Ono's voice bears the force of the unconscious, but not as the scream of a long suppressed primal pain. Writing about the soundtrack to Ono's film *Fly* (1970), which focuses on houseflies feeding on the sugar-coated body of a recumbent naked woman and was produced the same year as *Plastic Ono Band* (1970), Alexandra Munroe writes that "Yoko's voice suggests the unconscious, otherworldly life of the woman's knocked-out state, a life that is oblivious to yet omnipresent in the activities that occupy the flies" (Munroe & Hendricks, 2000, p. 29). Citing Jonathan Cott of *Rolling Stone*, Munroe writes that Ono's "legendary vocals ... the screams, wails, laughter, groans, caterwauls" evoke "the feeling of being inside one's own body cavities" (p. 29). The body, traversed by a voice-music that is both interior and exterior, speaks, or, rather, screams, laughs, and howls in a clamour for being.

On *Plastic Ono Band*, this sound palette is stretched and extended as it is pitched against amplified instruments, a driving drum and bass beat, echoing and fusing with "Lennon's ferocious guitar work" (Munroe & Hendricks, 2000, p. 235). Ono takes the basic format of rock and roll into a completely new direction through changing the function and relationship of the voice to lyrical expression, liberating it from the form and structure of the song. In their use of the example of vocal music to deconstruct the speech-language distinction which "is used to relegate all kinds of variables at work within expression and enunciation to a position outside language", Deleuze and Guattari unwittingly provide an apt description of Ono's practice in the albums *Plastic Ono Band* and *Fly* (1971):

The voice in music has always been a privileged axis of experimentation, playing simultaneously on language and sound. Music has linked the voice to instruments in various ways; but as long as the voice is song, its main role is to "hold" sound, it functions as a constant circumscribed on a note and *accompanied* by an instrument. Only when the voice is tied to timbre does it reveal a tessitura that renders it heterogeneous to itself and gives it a power of continuous variation: it is then no longer accompanied, but truly "machined", it belongs to a musical machine that prolongs or superposes on a single plane parts that are spoken, sung, achieved by special effects, instrumental, or perhaps electronically generated. (Deleuze & Guattari, 1988, p. 96)

The first two tracks on *Plastic Ono Band*, "Why" and "Why Not?", were developed in jam sessions during which "recording engineers routinely walked out" (Munroe & Hendricks, 2000, p. 235), no doubt fellow sufferers of the British fear of music. Yet, for Andy Davis, the first track, "'Why' seethes with a confrontational menace not heard again in Britain until 1976 punk", Ono's voice matching Lennon's "scratchy, razor-wire guitar" which is "harder and more experimental than anything he ever managed for his own recordings" (Clayson, 2004, p. 150). "Why" and "Why Not?" pitch the question of desire into infinity, a *mise-en-abyme*, voice and guitar distorting, extending, and deterritorialising the so-called acoustic mirror beyond any point of identification, stability, sense or meaning on a line of continuous variation infused with a suffering and joy that is addressed to no one. The voice and guitar do not imitate each other; they do not construct a sonic envelope, but, rather, engage in a process of constant sonic unfolding, an evacuation of meaning in an ascetic eroticisation of the scream.

The solitary good review, by Bill McAllister of *Record Mirror*, that was included on the sleeve notes of later pressings of the album emphasises the point of moving beyond aesthetic boundaries, the territories delimited by form, reflection, and even the margin of excess that delimits them. "Yoko takes music beyond its extremes, into the realm of non-music you might say . . . Yoko breaks through more barriers with one scream than most musicians do in a lifetime" (McAllister, December 19, 1971). In subsequent tracks, the basic voice–guitar–drum–bass assemblage is thickened up with tape fragments, sound effects, and improvisation tapes that develop textured audio events that nevertheless exist on the same plane of intensity. For Edward Gomez, these tracks are like "evocative sound poems [that] blended train, bird, and dog-howl sounds into Ono's chanting voices, which were multi-tracked in overlapping waves" (Munroe & Hendricks, 2000, p. 235). Beyond extremes, Ono generates sound that is a modality of excess, neither conventional music nor noise, but a form of screaming that renders music completely strange, takes it into another dimension (see also Clayson, 2004, p. 142). Deleuze and Guattari continue, again as if with Ono in mind,

> It should not be thought that music has forgotten how to sing in a now mechanical and atomized world; rather, an immense coefficient of variation is affecting and carrying away all of the phatic, aphatic, linguistic, poetic, instrumental, or musical parts of a single sound assemblage—"a simple scream suffusing all degrees" (Thomas Mann). (Deleuze & Guattari, 1988, pp. 96–97)

This scream, as sound assemblage, both suffuses and is suffused by the audio unconscious. From one of its main points of enunciation, located as a symptom of British amusia, Ono's voice becomes an assemblage in which the racist *jouissance* that it bears is transformed into an audio sign of joy. From "Why" to "Why Not" and beyond, a continuous process of desire is established that draws out the *jouissance* of the Other along a path of ex-sistance. It establishes a plane of amusical intensity determined by, and exceeding, the audio unconscious for which it is, nevertheless, a sign: a joy-sign that signifies nothing but is filled with the singular life that animates it. For Ono and Lennon, this joy-sign reinscribes the real into the purely imaginary and symbolic space to which they had been consigned by the system of celebrity that had rendered them soundless images reduced to silence by the cacophony of an enamoured hatred, the ambivalent symptom of British amusia and racism that heard only its own noise in reverse form. Seething with confrontational menace, the opening track declares the album's intent of reintroducing the real, in the form of war and the question of war, into the autonomised world of aestheticised exchange to which they had become confined as celebrity commodities.

CHAPTER TWELVE

The murder of John Lennon

Imagine

It is not known whether Mark Chapman killed John Lennon in order to hear Yoko Ono scream or because he objected to the song "Imagine". Chapman certainly hated "Imagine", and years before he undertook to kill the ex-Beatle "engaged in a vendetta against" the song "warning that Lennon's message – to imagine a world with no heaven or religion – was blasphemy . . . friends remember that he would sing his own foreboding lyrics to the Lennon tune: 'Imagine John Lennon is dead'" (Jones, 1992, p. 144).

But Yoko Ono did not scream on the night of Lennon's murder, or in the film made of the killing that, if it were a classic Hollywood picture, according to Michel Chion, should have demanded it (Piddington, 2006) There was no scream from Ono, no voice, just gaze. Three silent stares: one as she got out of the car and saw that Chapman still remained outside the Dakota building even though Lennon had given him his autograph hours before, another as she turned to face the source of the gunshots, and a final piercing stare through the window of the NYPD squad car where Chapman was being held, a gaze from which "he could not avert his eyes" (Jones, 1992, p. 59).

Ono was struck dumb by the gunshots that made audible Chapman's desire to echo the screams of her husband in his music. By his own account, Chapman was enveloped in the Lennon–Ono screams that defined his own silence, screams that were returned to Lennon in the form of five hollow-point bullets in the back. In Jones' biography, based on interviews with Chapman in Attica prison, Chapman recalls that

> I needed to scream but I had no mouth. John Lennon, when he was going through a tremendous time of confusion and depression in the sixties, from what I've read, in his own words, about the song "Help!" that he wrote: the song was a genuine cry for help. . . . That was a kind of preprimal scream therapy for him. But with me, I couldn't mouth the word *help*. I couldn't even scream. Listen to some of Lennon's records. Listen to the background of some of the Beatles songs. That screaming in the background, that's John Lennon. Listen to him scream. (Jones, 1992, p. 213)

Made famous by his music-screams in The Beatles and with Yoko Ono, Lennon's voice enveloped Chapman, he seems to suggest, it rendered him silent, sunk in quasi-autistic *jouissance* until it became echoed by the voice of a superegoic, demonic child screaming "Do it! Do it! Do it! Do it! Do it!" in a voice that exploded in the Manhattan night in the form of five gunshots (Jones, 1992, p. 55). "And that was what came out that night in December when John Lennon stepped out of his limousine. What came out of the barrel of that gun was that giant scream after all those years" (Chapman, in Jones, 1992, p. 55).

It is possible that Mark Chapman committed the first *amusical* assassination. Although many musicians have been murdered before (in the field of American popular music Robert Johnson, Sam Cooke, and Marvin Gaye spring to mind), "Lennon was the first in America to be murdered purely because he was a famous musician, the rationale for the killing being 'predicated on somebody's art'" (Jones, 1992, p. 74). But it is not just hatred of Lennon's art that defines his killing. Lennon's music provided Chapman, someone with psychotic structure, with an ambivalent relation to a world of symbolised reality outside himself. Chapman's profound narcissistic dissonance with his own psychic reality repeated, through its *amusical* (non)relation to Lennon, the amorous discordance of the formative forces outside himself. Beyond the particularities of his family romance, Chapman's *a*musia articulates psychotic disharmony with the culture generally, the state of affairs that he inhabits.

The form and reception of Lennon's song "Imagine" is a significant point of interconnection. The incongruity of a millionaire piously imagining a world of no possessions is the central contradiction that establishes, for Chapman, Lennon as "king of the phonies" (Jones, 1992, p. 220), allying him with Elvis Costello, Robert Elms, and countless others hostile to the song; Elms cited Lennon's possession of a single "temperature-controlled room in his Manhattan mansion just to store his fur coats" in order to highlight its apparent hypocrisy (Elms, 2005). Indeed, it was precisely photographs of Lennon posing in the luxurious surroundings of his apartment in the Dakota building featured in Antony Fawcett's memoir *One Day at a Time* (1977) that Chapman claims particularly enraged him. Chapman came across this book in a library at a point of personal crisis at the same time as he rediscovered J. D. Salinger's *Catcher in the Rye*. *One Day at a Time* is a very slight and fairly insignificant book exploiting its author's brief period as Lennon's personal assistant at the end of the 1960s supplemented by publicity photographs and biographical notes on Lennon's life in the 1970s. Next to Salinger's text, however, Fawcett's memoir took on an inordinate significance for Chapman. The images of Lennon "on the roof of the sumptuous Dakota building: the decadent bastard, the phony bastard, who had lied to children, who had used his music to mislead a generation of people" enraged Chapman (Jones, 1992, p. 219). "I devoured page after page of that John Lennon book. And at that moment something in me just broke" (p. 219). His rage initially extended to the world that he says he would have destroyed if he had had nuclear weapons. Soon it distilled into a desire simply to destroy Lennon, its imaginary king, as he played the *Imagine* album and its precursor, the "primal scream" album *Plastic Ono Band* repeatedly. The music was the thing "after the *Catcher* and the Lennon book. I would listen to this music and I would get angry at him" (p. 221).

"Imagine" provides a point of articulation between the two texts not just because its lyrical sentiments highlight Chapman's belief in Lennon's hypocritical "phoneyness", but also because the simple two-note basis of its musical structure, reminiscent of nursery tunes like "Twinkle-twinkle Little Star", evokes childhood. Childhood is, of course, the sacred object of *Catcher in the Rye*'s hero Holden Caulfield that is, in the novel, impossibly both lost and threatened by the phoney adult world. "Imagine" manages to evoke the lost maternal intimacy of the nursery even as its singer threatens it with his phoney adult lies. Significantly, Lennon and The Beatles were present in Chapman's own childhood in Roanoke, Virginia (Jones, 1992, p.114). Disturbed by his parents' rows and fighting, the young Chapman lost himself in his own imaginary world, a utopia populated by "little people" who adored him (p. 119). Chapman's means of pleasing his little people was to conduct concerts by The Beatles. "He would sit, sometimes for hours, playing *Meet the Beatles*, his only rock album, while rocking back and forth in front of the tiny stage (of the Little People)" (p. 120). It seems to have been Lennon's indelible association with Chapman's lost childhood that became inverted in the image of its "betrayal" in the post-Beatle Lennon lounging on the roof of the Dakota building, as if taunting Chapman with his nothingness. It was this juxtaposition between the Lennon of his childhood and the Lennon living in the Dakota that Chapman says triggered his desire to murder the singer and make a name for himself, as if removing his body would enable him to steal Lennon's identity and his world renown. "I thought of the repercussions that would occur around the world . . . I felt that perhaps my identity would be found in the killing of John Lennon" (p. 223).

Ironically, "Imagine" is a song by a "somebody" imagining a world of nobodies. It is a paean to nothingness, a nihilistic hymn. It offers no positive vision, but begins with a series of negations: no heaven, no hell, no countries, no religion or values worth dying for, not even any possessions. The song provides the template for a conceptual country called Nutopia that is practically a Nul-topia in its absence of qualities. Appropriately, its "national" anthem, featured on Lennon's album *Mind Games* (1973), is a few seconds of silence, and its flag a plain white.

All of these featureless features are, of course, consistent with Yoko Ono's art and practice, influenced as it is by John Cage. The song's imperative to "imagine" is drawn directly from Ono's book *Grapefruit*, first published in 1966, with its commands to "Imagine the clouds dripping / Dig a hole in your garden to put them in", or "Imagine your head filled with pencil leads / Imagine one of them broken" that Lennon himself found both irritating and inspiring, depending on his mood. Ono's instructions are intended to "instructure" rather than structure, but in so doing they can become what Deleuze and Guattari

call *mots d'ordre*, or order words, that command obedience by implying certain implicit presuppositions. In "Imagine", for example, obedience is commanded through the implicit presupposition of the evils of
nations, religions, and possessions. Supremely, obedience is commanded through the presumed virtue of the dreamer and the dream: "You
may say I'm a dreamer", begins the famous last verse that ends with
the equally famous expectation: "I hope one day you will join us".
Who could refuse? But the dream, in its evocation of a fictional or
purely conceptual reality and in its invocation of an indeterminate
future, condemns the life of the present both in its actuality and in its
potential. For Deleuze, the dream is another form of judgement,
another eschatology, in which life is condemned and rejected for a
deathly world of shadows. "The dream erects walls, it feeds on death
and creates shadows, shadows of all things and of the world, shadows
of ourselves" (Deleuze, 1998, pp. 129–130). For all its advocacy of a
secular existence and "living for today", "Imagine" substitutes a land
of conceptual shadows for a world of actually existing people.
Musically, its childlike simplicity is flattened out by Lennon's characteristic drone-like tonal "horizontality" as if the song were an organ-
ism inhabited, from the very beginning, by a drive seeking out its own
death not just in its own way but in the negation of all things, all life,
even an afterlife.

The utopia, or Nutopia, that listeners are instructed to imagine, so
curious in its vacuity, is often compared to communism (including,
apparently, by its author), but there is no mention of any workers.
Ironically, since Lennon's assassination, the song has become sancti-
fied as an unimpeachable utterance of secular piety. Former USA
President Jimmy Carter is said to have heard it used in over 125 countries as an alternative (or, no doubt, supplementary) national anthem.
As journalist Jon Dennis writes, "Imagine" is "so ubiquitous that it is
hard to hear with anything approaching objectivity, or indeed without
racing for the dial" (Dennis, 2005). This global ubiquity suggests that,
far from being a radical or extreme political statement, "Imagine" is
perfectly in tune with the current state of affairs, its message of
universality at one with the forces of globalisation. Dennis notes that
in some countries "it is played on the radio at times of national crisis,
such as the death of a member of the royal family, as it is perceived
as non-threatening to public order". And, indeed, he notes that, most
remarkably, Errol Brown of Hot Chocolate led the whole of the UK

Conservative party conference in a collective rendition of the song in the mid-1980s at the height of Mrs Thatcher's neoliberal revolution. Dennis suggests that "the popularity of Imagine is so great that people tend to pin whatever meaning they want on it", but perhaps there is more to it than that. Perhaps the lyrical sentiments of "Imagine" are consistent with Friedrich von Hayek's ironic call for a neoliberal utopia, or Paolo Virno's paradoxical worker-free "communism of capital" driven by its immaterial "free" labour (Virno, 2004). Indeed, the imperative form of "Imagine" is another version of Yoko Ono's seminal advertising art, such as her *Isreal* campaign for a non-existent art gallery and the world-wide billboard campaign War Is Over! (If You Want It). "Imagine" is an advertising jingle, not for any particular product, but for globalisation itself. Imagine a purely global capitalism, a globally free market with no intervention from nation-states, no religious restrictions, asceticism, or terrorism. Imagine a capitalism of no possessions, just activities defined by the desire for pleasure linking income with output. The American neoliberal theory of human capital does precisely this through extending economic rationality into every domain and aspect of human life, thereby dissolving the situation where individuals are defined by their possessions or by the price of their labour. The theory of human capital analyses human behaviour and the internal economic rationality of that behaviour. It is directed towards "the strategic programming of individuals' activity" and correlating an income with an ability, skill or "income stream" (Foucault, 2008, p. 224). The neoliberal *homo economicus* is not, therefore, "the man of exchange" who is defined by his possessions. He or she is "an entrepreneur of himself", producing himself, his satisfactions, and his values through the act of branding and self-promotion. Imagine. Just Do It. Do it.

Do it. Do it. Do it. Do it. Do it. Mark Chapman's assassination of John Lennon was, by his own admission, an act of pure self-promotion indifferent to the prospect of material reward. It would, of course, be facile to suggest that Chapman's act was conditioned by a utopian tendency in neoliberal desire, even if the "identity" he sought can only find definition on the horizon of an aesthetic–economic system of self-promotion and "celebrity" that has created its own order. The aetiology of Chapman's act lies in the structure of his own psychopathology, but this structure is itself conditioned by the economic and cultural forces that shaped it.

The (self-) diagnosis that emerges from Jones' book, *Let Me Take You Down* (1992), based on two hundred hours of interviews with Chapman, is characteristically self-obsessed and self-serving. But his reflections have clearly been informed by his conversations with therapists at Bellevue Hospital in New York as they sought to establish his legal responsibility for his crime. The account of the views of Chapman's therapists, given by Jones, is interesting and presents a fairly clear picture which seems quite close to what one would imagine, from the limited information, a Lacanian diagnosis might be like.

Various psychiatrists visited him at Bellevue Hospital in New York, and were contracted to the cause of the prosecution and defence. Dr Daniel Schwartz, while concluding after his interviews that Chapman was schizophrenic, "knew the nature and consequences of his conduct" (Jones, 1992, p. 98). Indeed, his intention was to achieve fame because, according to Schwartz, the killer also "suffered from a narcissistic personality disorder that caused him to crave attention and fame" (p. 98). However, Schwartz complicates this view by adding a nuance that locates Chapman in a pantheon of "self-punishment" paranoiacs that dates back to Lacan's doctoral thesis of 1932, *De la psychose paranoïaque dans ses rapports avec la personnalité*. In this thesis, Lacan argued that the attempted murder of Huguette Duflos, a celebrated actress, by a thirty-eight-year-old woman, Marguerite Pantaine, nicknamed by Lacan "Aimée", was the effect of a personality disorder. For Lacan, personality is defined in a significant way, positively and negatively, by "ideal" images. Noting that "the ranks of paranoia are swelled by those unjustly denigrated as inferior or limited", ideal images reflect social aspirations as well as accentuate, by contrast, their inaccessibility. As such, they can become bound up in a cycle of self-recrimination and self-loathing driven by the superego. Suffering from increasing delusions of persecution from various famous actresses and a novelist, along with fantasies concerning the Prince of Wales, to whom she sent poems and love letters, Aimée eventually attempted to murder Duflos, whom she imagined to be her rival in her royal romance. For Lacan, "Aimée's entire delusion" could "be understood as an increasingly centrifugal displacement of a hate whose direct object she wished to misapprehend" (Lacan, 1932, p. 282), The famous actresses, the objects of her persecutory fantasies, represented her ideal images that supported her "Ego-Ideal". In the sanatorium after she was apprehended, Lacan noted that her

delusions dissipated and vanished. Through her crime and its consequent punishment, she had brought about her own "cure". In striking
Huguette Duflos, Lacan wrote, Aimée

> strikes at a purely symbolic value, and the act brings her no relief.
> Nonetheless, by the blow that rendered her guilty in the eyes of the
> law, Aimée has also struck at herself, and this brings her the satisfac-
> tion of fulfilled desire, and the delusion, having become superfluous,
> disappears. It seems to me that the nature of the cure reveals the
> nature of the disease. (Lacan, cited in Roudinesco, 1997, p. 48)

In striking Duflos, Aimée essentially struck out at herself as a result of
her "self-punishment paranoia".

Daniel Schwartz perceives a similar structure in the case of Mark
Chapman. He notes that Chapman's personality disorder was based
around a confusion of identities in relation to images of John Lennon.
Schwartz observed that, like Lennon, Chapman had married a Japanese woman a few years older than himself and that he had put
Lennon's name on a nametag and in a logbook at his job site several
weeks before he left Hawaii for New York intending to kill Lennon.
Like Lennon, he had become a "househusband", although without the
millionaire comforts of life in the Dakota. Nevertheless, Chapman's
apparent total identification with Lennon "caused Schwartz to theo-
rize that the murder was a surrogate suicide" (Jones, 1992, p. 98). To
this diagnosis could be added Chapman's own self-dramatisation of
his act in which his personality is split between a "child" bent on
murder and an "adult" reluctant to carry it out. The "screaming" child
drives the adult on to do it, only to vanish after the act, the "shallow
hulk of the phony adult . . . left there to pay the price" (Chapman,
quoted in Jones, 1992, p. 55). By this rationale, it was not fame that
Chapman was looking for so much as punishment; he was looking
for law.

Why Chapman should have felt that law was lacking and needed to
be summoned from its slumber by the assassination of a global super-
star is disclosed by the therapist for the defence, Dr Richard Bloom.
Bloom also concluded after extensive interviews that Chapman was
schizophrenic, and that he suffered from delusions of grandiosity, but
that the delusions sprang from a profound sense of inadequacy
produced as an effect of his own particular family background (Jones,

1992 pp. 100–101). Broadly consistent with Lacanian assumptions concerning the aetiology of psychosis, Bloom attributes Chapman's psychotic structure to his (non)relationship with his father. Jones writes that

> Chapman talked in detail to Bloom and other psychologists and psychiatrists of the times his mother had cried out to him for help when she was abused by her husband. He told Bloom he would wake up many mornings to find his battered mother in his bed. (p. 102)

Shortly after the murder in 1981, Chapman told his psychiatrists that his mother had "told me she hated my father. She said the only reason she married him was so she could have me" (pp. 118, 157). The father's agency is impeached by the mother and his marital role given to her son, leaving the child deep in the embrace of maternal demand. Bloom argued that

> Chapman was permanently scarred by the role his parents unwittingly placed on him as his mother's protector and surrogate spouse. The responsibility of a job he was powerless to fulfil caused him later to abandon hope of gaining control of his own life. (p. 100)

For Bloom, this further accounted for his creation of the fantasy world of the Little People in which The Beatles would star so prominently and his fascination with the Wizard of Oz. Ultimately, this trajectory would lead to his obsession with *The Catcher in the Rye* and Holden Caulfield, with whom he identified, according to Bloom, "as somebody that would rescue the children, which is something that nobody would do for him" (p. 101). Chapman's delusions of grandiosity were generated in the same way, as an effect of the full exposure to maternal demand without paternal mediation. His mother's response to the questions of his existence and his destiny were fully indulgent. "He was born to greatness, she told him; he could be anything he wanted to be" (p. 109). He was born to greatness because his conception was immaculate. "She told me that God planted a seed inside a woman's stomach and then it grew to become a baby. I thought that was a really nice way of explaining the facts of life to a child" (p. 110).

After growing up with The Beatles and following their example into experiments with psychedelic drugs, Chapman began, in the early 1970s, to explore his connection with God, undergoing a "spiritual conversion" and becoming an evangelical Christian. At about the same time, "he began to express an intense loathing for the musical heroes of his childhood: John Lennon and the Beatles" (Jones, 1992, p. 143). The focus of his loathing was predictable, as a friend, Mark McManus, recalled: "Imagine" and "that comment by Lennon, about the Beatles being more popular than Jesus, that really pissed him off" (p. 144). Then and later, in 1980, while he was redis-covering his hatred for Lennon prior to killing him, Chapman found that Lennon's track "God" from the *Plastic Ono Band* disturbed and infuriated him. Chapman states how angry at Lennon he became

> for saying he didn't believe in God, that he just believed in him and Yoko, and that he didn't believe in the Beatles. Even though this record had been done at least ten years previously . . . I just wanted to scream out loud, "Who does he think he is". (p. 221)

In these examples, Lennon does not just deny God, he substitutes him-self or locates himself in the place of his absence: The Beatles rather than Jesus, Nutopia rather than heaven, stating that he believes in himself rather than God, thereby drawing an equivalence between the two. As the son of God himself, according to his mother, Chapman can see Lennon not just as his imaginary double and oedipal rival, but also as a threat to his paternity and existence.[13]

Apparently settled in Hawaii with his wife, Chapman was un-enthused about his mother's decision to join them there on the island. He was even less pleased when she embarked on a series of embar-rassing affairs with much younger men. Following the logic of his psychotherapist Richard Bloom would suggest that the intrusive and disturbing presence of his mother at this time in his life triggered the psychotic break that precipitated the murder of Lennon. It is at this time when Chapman suffers the repetition of the religion-inspired hatred of Lennon nearly ten years before, reframed by *Catcher in the Rye*, "God", and "Imagine", and his subjectivity fractures into differ-ent "voices".

His wife, Gloria, recalls Chapman listening to headphones and bellowing along, in a weird voice, to The Beatles' "I Want You (She's so Heavy)". Then, another voice starts bellowing "Must die! . . . The phony bastard must die". Gloria Chapman told Jones, Chapman's biographer, that

The voice seemed to be coming from two people at once—one of them trying to scream and the other trying to call back the awful words. It shifted into a dull, staccato chant:

"The phony must die, says the Catcher in the Rye.

The phony must die, says the Catcher in the Rye.

Don't believe in John Lennon.

Imagine John Lennon is dead, oh yeah, yeah, yeah.

Imagine that it's over".

The music stopped and the voice was silent for several minutes, before it began muttering quietly to itself.

"The fool" . . . "The goddamn phony fool. He doesn't even realize that soon he's going to be dead."

"Just imagine that." (Jones, 1992, pp. 233–234)

John Lennon is only ever an image for Chapman. After receiving Lennon's autograph on the day of his death, Chapman is taken by how "nice" and "kind", "courteous and polite" Lennon is to him. "'But he wasn't real', said the child inside. 'You *know* he wasn't real'"(Jones, 1992, p. 45). Lennon is pure depthless image, associated by Chapman with the erasure of the law. The only thing that is real for Chapman is the scream: the dissonant scream that repeats from the background of The Beatles songs of his childhood to the gun that summoned up symbolic law by ripping out those five fatal shots.

This is to say that not only did he succeed in attracting the attention of the NYPD, he at last managed to make some kind of a name for himself. But the law that gives value to his name is not the *non/nom du père* that grounds its authority in prohibition. His name accrues value as it is screamed in banner headlines and in media outlets throughout the world in a manner that, of course, does nothing but affirm his act. This is the sound, the music of a purely aesthetic–economic law that can only scream, like The Beatles and their manic fans, "oh yeah, yeah, yeah". Born on this wave, Chapman takes over the destiny of the image from Lennon and becomes a film.

In the cybertopia that has realised much of Nutopia's requirements—no national or religious limits, no possessions, just streams of digital information—everyone is transformed into an image/profile in a world of generalised minor celebrity. There are no more stars like John Lennon or Elvis Presley, or indeed, further back, John Wayne or Greta Garbo. While there are few Lennons left to kill, the pattern for the universal subject of cybertopia is, nevertheless, more the half-life of Chapman than Lennon: anyone in any room anywhere, an ambiguous support for text and image, engaged in self-promotion. Lennon or Beatles-scale stardom was itself an effect of limited access to global telecommunications, one of the first live satellite broadcasts around the world being their live-to-air recording of "All You Need Is Love" in 1967. Already dead without knowing it, animated and destroyed by an infinite scream passing through the mediascape, Lennon's stardom flashed for an instance, filling skies across the world. It is now fading away, the scream of a dying star dissolved into the clicking keyboards of a billion fractal web identities.

Echo

To accompany and promote a major retrospective of Yoko Ono's art and life at the Walker Art Center in Minneapolis in 2001, a new musical work was produced based on an old score from 1961 that is collected in her famous book *Grapefruit* (2000). The work, "Laugh Piece", was performed for 100 days, between 10 March and 17 June, concurrent with the duration of the exhibition entitled "Yes Yoko Ono". The piece did not take place in a gallery, however, but in the virtual spaces of the Internet and the telephone network. For 100 days the website of the PBS arts show EGG invited visitors to call a telephone number, listen to a recorded message by Yoko Ono, and leave a response. The message was "Voice Piece for Soprano". In this piece, again from 1961, Ono invites the reader (or, here, the listener) to "Scream". Against the wind, wall, and sky. The responses were recorded on to an old 1980s answering machine and redirected away from the message tape into a computer and made immediately available online. As such, the piece not only recalled the original "Laugh Piece" (with the instruction "Keep laughing a week", 1961 winter), but also practically enabled an approximation of another of Ono's instructional musical works, "Echo Telephone Piece" (Ono, 2000), which demands that the reader find a telephone that only echoes back the speaker's voice. The speaker then is further invited to call every day and talk about whatever she or she likes. Respondees to "Laugh Piece" 2001 could "roll over a dot" on the site and play back their contributions as many times as they wished, just as they could listen to others in real time and respond in turn. A bulletin board was created so that performers could email the Walker Arts Center and comment on their contributions. These included a man and his eighty-three-year-old female friend, an artist and teacher, who "gave a wonderful loud high pitch scream, that was long in length"; three young artist friends and a parakeet who "just started to freak when we were jamming, beating his head on the side of the cage"; "all the screams of crazy drunk people roaming towards the big market" down High Bridge Street in Newcastle, England; a man from Minneapolis who dialled in "the bizzare [sic] screams of a self-modified Yamaha drum machine via a cell phone whilst walking down Nicollet Ave" (Sonic Flux, 2007).

The piece is authentically Ono, even if it was created by Justin Bakse and Justin Braem, and produced by Trudy Lane. Drawing on her work in the 1960s, "Laugh Piece" combines many of its characteristic elements and further demonstrates how they anticipated their general combination in the virtual space of the Internet in the 1990s to create a sphere in which art and commerce are indistinguishable. It is not clear whether "Laugh Piece" was a work of art or a promotional gimmick, a new media event designed to publicise the Walker Arts Center, the television show EGG, and the exhibition itself and its merchandise that included a handsome coffee table book with reproductions and essays, and a CD.[14] This is consistent, however, with the advertising art, culminating in the "War Is Over" billboard campaign, that Ono pioneered along with others in the 1960s and 1970s. With the online "Laugh Piece", advertising art is combined with the form of her instructional and deliberately unfinished works that demand completion by their audience. As Alexandra Munroe writes, Ono produces a "social art that relies on participants — not just to be appreciated in the abstract, but to be actually made real, completed" (Munroe & Hendricks, 2000, p. 12). In its new location on the Internet, this piece links Ono's earlier participation pieces with one of the important new laws of the digital economy introduced in the 1990s that exploits the free labour of users who, through their accessing of sites, actually build and maintain them, keeping them visible and profitable through consuming bandwidth.

"Laugh Piece" establishes a plane in which art and commerce are perfectly consistent with one another in their dissolution of the boundary between production and consumption, labour and creativity through assembling a "desire machine", in the terms of Deleuze and Guattari. Indeed, one of Guattari's prime examples of a desiring machine is a telephone exchange that would enable, through dialling a number connected to an automatic answering device,

> the overlay of an ensemble of teeming voices, calling and answering each other, criss-crossing, fading out, passing over and under each other, inside the automatic voice, very short messages, utterances obeying rapid and monotonous codes. There is the Tiger; it is rumored that there is even an Oedipus in the network. (Guattari, 1995, p. 123)

In "Laugh Piece", it is not simply a tiger or an Oedipus directing the flow of voices in the network; rather, it is the machined voice of an artist, a businesswoman, a famous millionaire and widow whose erotic agency functions as deterritorialised part object "in the sphere of chance and multiplicity [that] connects up with a flow that irradiates a whole social field of communication through the unlimited expansion of a delirium or a drift" (Jean Nadal, also on the telephone exchange as desiring machine, cited in Guattari, 1995, p. 124). Yoko Ono's instructions in "Voice Piece for Soprano", the recorded message, provides the point of agency for an operatic cacophany of men and women screaming, a demented parakeet and a distorted drum machine (at the very least); it is an assemblage of human, animal, and machine elements whose screams echo and reverberate in amusical disharmony throughout the worldwide web. Yoko Ono's "Voice Piece for Soprano" and the extraordinary machinic assemblage that it produces in the midst of the system of global telecommunications clearly deterritorialises and expands the subject of *a*musia across a very wide, trans-national, and even trans-human, social field.

It deterritorialises the screaming soprano at the extimate heart of the *a*musical subject even as it dissolves the distinction between opera and screaming, music and non-music, and turns the sound into the expression of multiple creative desires at the econopoietic conjunction of art and commerce. Multiple screams echo in the clamour for being in the network as voice undergoes an incorporeal transformation into data, archive, and information flow. The virtually free space of art and

economy is, of course, absolutely the same as the plane of total recording, commodification, digitalisation, and infinite surveillance. The
general incorporeal transformation of the subject into a data profile
across the range of social, commercial, bureaucratic, and financial
networks supports the fantasy of the total aestheticisation, codifica-
tion, and control of identity and desire. The screaming that, in "Laugh
Piece", echoes throughout all these networks reverberates with the
memory of Yoko Ono's art and life, the subject, of course, of the retrospective exhibition that ran throughout the duration of the piece.

More than perhaps anyone in the latter part of the twentieth
century Yoko Ono experienced the process of transformation in which
her body became art, commodity, news, information, and brand. From
the second half of the 1960s, Ono became the focus and symptom of a
constellation of discontents produced by the conjunction of art,
money, celebrity, and its global expansion across telecommunications
networks, suffering the effects of flows of multiple desire, mass
hatred, generalised psychosis, and the paranoia for which her husband paid with his life. Well might she scream, and hail an Internet
chorus of ghostly screaming throughout the frequencies of the various
wired and wireless networks. But multiple screams, collective and
singular, were enunciated throughout the life and work of Yoko Ono
and John Lennon, separately and together, their own and that of
others, musical and amusical, visceral and aesthetic, anguished and
erotic, therapeutic and terrifying. From Beatlemania to Arthur Janov,
these screams proceeded from a demand for love and a delusion that
was amplified on a global scale, to become a screamadelica, both
actual and virtual, that constitutes the ground and symptom of global
telecommunications then and now.

CHAPTER THIRTEEN

Unlistenable

a*music*

By definition, it ought to be impossible to produce literally un-listenable music, unless it were produced at frequencies that were audible only to dogs or aliens, in which case it would be listenable at least to them. At a certain point fairly early in his career, Masami Akita, the "Godfather" of Japanese noise-music otherwise known as Merzbow, consciously set out to produce a music that was accessible, designed to be heard, and yet was unlistenable in the sense of unmasterable, uncompletable, too formidable to encompass. (Akita, in Woodward, 1999, p. 40). It would be affirmed as music, but of such a degree of dissonance and discordance as to be unlistenable even to the *avant-garde* cognoscenti familiar with Varese, Cage, *musique concrète*, Stockhausen, free jazz, or, indeed, fans of the extremes of rock, Hendrix at his wildest, the Who at their most auto-destructive, heavy metal, industrial metal, grindcore, death metal . . . By reputation and critical reception, Merzbow exceeds them all.

Not even the most satanic headbanger or receptive connoisseur of extreme music can meet the challenge posed by Merzbow and its unmasterable oeuvre. When played at the correct volume, listeners are "pulverized" (Hegarty, 2005) by its "death scream of electronics" (Morley, 2003, p. 150). Katharine Norman claims, in *Sounding Art* (2004), that Merzbow's "noise obliterates the senses: it overwrites them gradually until there is only whiteness and empty parenthesis (a feeling that something was there but has gone)" (Norman, 2004, p. 168). Such subjective disintegration is not caused simply by volume or disabling frequencies enabled by high-tech electronics, but by a low-tech art of the unconscious:

> My first motivation for creating sound was the anti-use of electric equipment: a broken tape recorder, broken guitar, amp etc. I thought I could get a secret voice from the equipment itself when I lost control. That sound is the unconsciousness, the libido of the equipment. Then I tried to control them with a more powerful process. (Akita, in Woodward, 1999, p. 10)

Akita's conception of the audio unconscious is that it is the trail of sonic detritus left by music and its instruments. The audio unconscious lies in the virtual locus of sounds that may be produced in the disuse, anti-use, and abuse of musical instruments and equipment. But this unconscious is not simply a negative that sustains the positivity of music through its opposition as the noise that defines it. The difference is not established by a distinction concerning an instrument's operativity or inoperativity, whether or not it is broken, or the competence of the user, whether it can be played or not played. Rather, the machines and instruments, the systems of symbolisation that practically produce music, also produce a whole field of potential utility denoted by the terms misuse, abuse, or even anti-use. Furthermore, the perverse technique that can unlock the secret voice from the unconscious of the music machines proceeds directly from the *amusia* that lies at the extimate heart of Akita's own audio unconscious. However, here the subject of the unconscious is not so easily defined in the shifting distinction between noise and music because this distinction has been rendered tautologous and tautened, bent into a bow: a Merzbow. "Merz" from Kurt Schwitters, summoning the montage of the drive, that takes aim at the unheard and unlistenable in sound, the un-sound.

The goal of early Merzbow was to move entirely beyond the question of form and the limits denoted by aesthetic pleasure. The affect of

Merzbow is not generated through the pleasurable appreciation of good form or through the *jouissance* gained through its transgression in instances of musical dissonance. Although it is pitched beyond the threshold of comfort, this affect has nothing to do with the suffering of *jouissance* that is caused by noise in the form of musical dissonance, or excess of volume, or unfamiliarity, or otherness. Merzbow's sound is not, therefore, a question of taste, the perception of noise as opposed to music. Neither noise nor music, Merbow produce *amusic* where the term *a*musia does not denote a condition of insufficiency, lack, or deficiency but, on the contrary, denotes an affirmation of the noise that is immanent to music, noise that is the same as music but is in pursuit of its principle of pure formlessness. Like absolute unlistenability, pure formlessness is impossible, but provides the sovereign principle of ungovernable excess that drives Merzbow's *a*music. The *a*music of Merzbow is generated out of Akita's amusical perception and his unconscious dialogue with the virtual sounds of perverted audio machines, human and non-human. Neither background nor remainder, noise as unmasterable excess is noise as fulminating life, a general process of expenditure that provides the locus of change, contestation, perversion, and politics of any milieu. In so far as music, as a particular organisation of noise, is a model of social order, Merzbow's amusic denotes both the heterogeneity of noise through which political formations establish order and exercise power, and its inassimilable excess.

The litter of the un-listener

Born in Tokyo in 1956, Masami Akita and his work is an effect of the clash between east and west, experimental and pop culture in the 1960s. "When I was 12 or 13", he recalled, "Tokyo was showered by the new rock movement" (Woodward, 1999, p. 10). He listened to The Rolling Stones, The Doors, Cream, and

> as kids of that age did, I also listened with interest to The Beatles. During that period they were releasing strange stuff like George Harrison's *Wonderwall* and *Electronic Sounds* and John and Yoko's *Unfinished Music No. 1 – Two Virgins*. This was all . . . very influential in the 1960s. (p. 10)

While it might have been "beyond the ken" of everyone in Britain, mercilessly criticised, attacked, and banned (Lewisohn, 2004, p. 283), kids in Japan were into John and Yoko's *Two Virgins*. This might have had something to do with the fact that in Japan, unlike in Britain, Ono's new relationship with John Lennon was "rapturously received across the whole of society" (Cope, 2007, p. 65).

This society, or at least its culture, was, according to Julian Cope, changed forever with the arrival of The Beatles on their tour of Japan in the summer of 1966. The arrival of The Beatles rekindled the interest in western rock and pop that had been initially ignited by the presence of the American military in the 1950s but which had waned, along with rock and roll itself with the drafting of Elvis into the army, followed by Jerry Lee Lewis and Richie Valens, the deaths of Buddy Holly, the Big Bopper, Eddie Cochran, and Little Richard becoming a born again Christian. At the same time, Japanese experimental music emerged with a force and originality to rival anything in the circle of John Cage in New York. The famous Jikken-Koubou experimental workshop, that combined early electronic sounds with Buddhist gagaku percussive rituals, was established in 1951, followed by the influence of *musique concrete*, introduced by Toshiro Mayuzumi, who was studying in Paris and working in Pierre Schaeffer's recording studio Club D'Essaie in early 1952 (for a brief resumé of Japanese experimental music in the 1950s and 1960s and its relation to popular music, see Cope, 2007, p. 41–71). In 1954, Toshi Ichiyanagi, a young musician interested in the *avant-garde*, went to New York with his wife, Yoko Ono, to study with John Cage, in the process becoming one of his star pupils. Pupil turned to "peer and representative" when he triumphantly returned to Tokyo in 1961 to give a hugely successful recital that secured, with the seal of John Cage, his homeland's enthusiastic endorsement of *avant-garde* music. The relative acceptability of experimental music in Japan, in comparison with Britain and America, where its status is extremely marginal, is perhaps one reason why it has had a greater influence on the culture generally and pop and rock music in particular.

For Masami Akita, interest in European progressive music, King Crimson, Van Der Graf Generator, Ashra Temple, Can, was combined with enthusiasm for Ankoku Butoh (Butoh Dance), moving to the conceptual "free" music of Derek Bailey and Han Bennink in response to the arrival of punk rock. By the early 1980s, however, Akita had apparently grown bored with improvised music—indeed, had grown bored with music, in a conventional sense, completely. This discontent grew out of improvisation. After experimenting with a piece of music that evolved using only feedback, Akita "resolved to abandon conventional instrumentation and compositional guidelines", however experimental (Woodward, 1999, pp. 10–11).

Named, of course, after the German Dadaist artist Kurt Schwitter's *Merzbau* project, which constructed a series of houses that gradually became overrun by an accumulation of found objects that were assembled, contorted, and transformed into a virtually uninhabitable art environment, Merzbow produces a similarly unliveable ambient environment. Its *a*music "consists of the debris of music, of sound: pulses, feedback, hisses, whirs, blasts, distortions, pure tones, shrieks, machine noise—all played extremely loud" (Hegarty, 2005, p. 5). The aural collage produces a virtually unlistenable ambient music, an uninhabitable sonic environment. The notion of producing an unlistenable, unmasterable music became part of the discipline of its creation and technique. This was not noise in a dialectical relation with sense and form; on the contrary, "this music is noise all the way down" (Hegarty, 2005, p. 5). While it is not simply random, "there are rhythms to be found, frequencies to be followed", there are no recognisably musical sounds overlaid with distortion or effect, no pulse, patterns, bars or beats, no sense, no automaton of the signifier. Of course, a certain familiarity can be produced through repeated playing of the same pieces. "Perhaps the 'experienced listener' can manage whole albums, concerts" (Hegarty, 2007, p. 5), but Merzbow responds through the sheer excess of its output, hundreds and hundreds of CDs, records, and cassettes, frequently issued in 50-CD box sets. It is, apparently, impossible to compile a definitive Merzbow discography.

The impossibility of the notion of the unlistenable defines a highly disciplined ascesis of sonic production that is attuned to the febrile limits of aural tolerance. The initial desire to make unlistenable albums and forge an inassimilable and unfinished oeuvre (the notion of "unfinished music" deriving, of course, from Yoko Ono) has become modified in a double movement exploring the paradox of the notion of noise as, for example, pollution and waste. While Merzbow has been at the forefront of a wave of nosie artists, the vanguard not only of a genre, but even an internationally renowned aspect of Japanese national culture, Japanese society itself has become increasingly noisy. "I think people have become more tolerant to Noise in general", states Akita (Woodward, 1999, p. 40). This just feeds a desire for more noise: "I believe once we get used to it, there is always a desire to get more. No matter how noisy it is, we soon get used to it, whether we like it or not" (p. 40). Japanese noise music, from the late 1990s, found itself caught in the same logic of contemporary consumption, the continual demand for more, for something louder, faster, more intense, continuous also with the ubiquitous techno-racket pouring out of videogame arcades, clubs, workplaces, and every imaginable electronic gadget, "the soundtrack for the busy technological life of the metropolis" (Morley, 2003, p. 150). But Merzbow is not simply a symptom of the noise of contemporary society generally, an attempt to be the excess of excess.

Nevertheless, from the late 1990s, the question for Akita seemed to be the one posed by excess and its relation to post-industrial consumer society. The cause and symptom of this society is waste, the junk that also provided the means for Merzbow's amusic, particularly the tsunami of worthless, redundant machinery and obsolescent electronic equipment, both analogue and digital, that instantly gives way to the latest upgrade. Finding inspiration initially in Kurt Schwitter's way of making art, "found junk used for sound", such junk long ago ceased to be sought. The sea of junk stretches to the horizon of economic growth and its collapse in the unsustainable world beyond it. Merzbow assembles a paradoxical noise machine that wages a war against noise, its will-to-silence opening up an ecological dimension that, in its development in the early years of the twenty-first century, found expression in a passionate interest in animal welfare. The ecological dimension resides not just in Merzbow's recycling of junk, but also in its combative, non-relation to the society of waste. So, while Merzbow can be seen as the excess of the excess of "the exuberant wastage of autonomist culture" (Stoekl, 2007, p. 137), the amusic emerges from the very dissonance between the two. This absence of relation is positively thematised by Akita in perverse eroticism, that is to say, in the erotic ritual that defines the relative positions of Merzbow's amusic and its un-listener.

Littoral

The ritual deployment and redeployment of excess is a feature of traditional Japanese culture, according to Kasushige Shingu, who notes that the "Japanese have invented multiple practices of enjoyment, such as the waka and haiku, in which the equivocal relation of the letter to the signifier is utilized to the utmost" (Shingu, 2005, p. 57). The letter is the excess, waste, or litter of the signifier with which the Japanese poet–artist both realises and effaces him or herself in the singular characters of his or her writing. Speaking of the Japanese in a piece entitled "Lituraterre" that he wrote after returning from Japan in 1971, Lacan perceived the trait of singularity through the art of calligraphy—"where the singular of the hand crushes the universal" (Lacan, 1987, p. 5). For Lacan, the calligraphic stroke of the pen was exemplary of what he called the "littoral" that comprises "the singular trait and of what effaces it" (p. 5). It is possible to refind in the unfolding cacophony of Merzbow's noise-music Lacan's notion of the littoral, where noise is to music what the letter is to the signifier. The littoral is the line that marks the conjunction "between center and absence, between knowledge and jouissance" (p. 5). That is to say, Merzbow's noise-music is littoral in so far as it designates exactly the border between noise and music, body and image, sex and *savoir-faire*, where the latter achieves the excess that animates its own erasure.

In between knowledge and *jouissance* is the singular know-how of Akita the noise artist, from whom the littoral constitutes a sound that characterises itself as not being emitted from the *semblant* or from form or meaning. This is also evident in the naming of individual pieces or albums that are not tied to videos, performances, themes, or events. Akita affirms, "When I use words, say album titles, they are not chosen to convey any meanings. They are merely selected to mean nothing". At the same time, frequently they evoke the line of the littoral that separates knowledge/*jouissance* through the generation of nonsensical neologisms such as venerology, noisembryo, pornoise, and so on. Merzbow is the expression and erasure of the noise that inhabits it.

Merzbow is detached from the noise that its noise wishes to strike out in a precipitous line of becoming-silent in trance, or white out. Akita's noise is most commonly characterised as a kind of "ecstatic trance music", music to which it is impossible to listen but through which one becomes overwhelmed and erased. As Paul Hegarty writes, Merzbow's "Noise music becomes ambience not as you learn how to listen, or when you accept its refusal to settle, but when you are no longer in a position to accept or deny" (Hegarty, 2005, p. 5). Katharine Norman concurs: Merzbow's "noise obliterates the senses: it over-writes them gradually until there is only whiteness" (Norman, 2004, p. 168). From this observation, two points could be made with regard to the political efficacy of noise. First, as the noise of noise, the excess of Japanese society's excess, Merzbow does not provide some kind of metalanguage, an exterior position from which society might be known, understood, and critiqued. Rather, the noise through which all music is fabricated is the dissonant material force through which music changes, and, thus, the social systems for which it is the formal expression. Merzbow's noise-music traces a precipitous line of affect—or joy—that, in contradistinction to usual forms of subjectification and spaces of disciplinarity, enables and facilitates different modes of anorganic technological existence and communication.

CHAPTER FOURTEEN

The braindance of the hikikomori

Ordinary autism

If the abstract image of the purely self-interested, pleasure-driven proto-subject of neoliberalism is a "paranoid . . . human being sitting alone in a room" (Mirowski, in Curtis, 2007), then its actual realisation is the hikikomori. First coined by the Japanese psychologist Tamaki Saikō, who claims there are over a million such individuals in his country, the term hikikomori usually refers to a boy or girl in a room, son or daughter of a middle-class Japanese family, who has withdrawn indefinitely to his or her bedroom, or, indeed, any space whatever equipped with networked computers, sunk in a kind of autistic *jouissance* outside of any conventional form of social contact. Proto-typical "cyborgs", atrophied larvae of post-human subjectivity generated and enabled by the proliferation of online entertainments, particularly video games and pornography, the hikikomori remain the concrete realisation of the neoliberal subject increasingly defined by the deepening silo of maximised asocial pleasure. Immaterially and indefinably, at work and at play, modifying software, killing aliens, or masturbating, hikikomori have even been known to amass for-tunes playing online poker and trading securities. They even make innovative electronica. As Richard D. James, the "Mozart" of "intelligent dance music", otherwise known as Aphex Twin, writes,

> there's something magical about having all your equipment in the same room as your bed, and you just get out of bed and like do a track and go back to sleep and then get up and do some more and do tracks in your pants and stuff. (James, in Young, 2005, p. 75)

On the one hand, then, hikikomori are exceptional; on the other hand, they simply give a "pathological" image to the normal state of affairs of everyone in so far as our lives and bodies are divided and organised by a multiplicity of screens and networks in which our most significant activity—in fact the entirety of online activity—is the production of data. Three areas intersect with the ambiguous nodal point of the hikikomori that illustrate a particular modality of neoliberal individuation—computer games, management discourse, and so-called intelligent techno and music video—that provide an opportunity to speculate on the psyche not just of speaking beings, but of networked, textual ones as well. If music, as this book has suggested, has its own unconscious effects, what about other systems of symbolisation—code, numbers, patterns?

As Laurent (2012c, p. 129) has suggested, the era of generalised psychosis that marked the last third of the twentieth century (which we suggested might be an effect of the structural imperative imposed by neoliberal governance to act as if one were psychotic) is giving way, in the twenty-first century, to a form of ordinary autism. It could also be suggested that this is a further effect of the acceleration of neoliberalism through networked computers and the online economy that has reinforced the conditions of autistic *jouissance* and facilitated and enhanced certain traits associated with its non-verbal regulation in software systems. In 2001, the new technology journal *Wired* noticed a "significant surge in the number of kids diagnosed with autism throughout California" (Silbermann, 2001, p. 1), noting how this mysterious three-fold increase resulted in mutually beneficial effects in Silicon valley both for the children of autism themselves and the software companies that increasingly employed them when they reached maturity. Silbermann writes, "the autistic fascinations with technology, ordered systems, visual modes of thinking, and subversive creativity have plenty of outlets", noting how very many of these children "become obsessed with VCRs, *Pokémon*, and computer games, working the joysticks until blisters appear on their fingers" (Silbermann, 2001, p. 3). At the same time, like so many people "alone together" (Turkle, 2010) with their smartphones connected online but distant in person, "even when playing alongside someone their own age . . . autistic kids tend to play separately" (Silbermann, 2001, p. 3). Silbermann also notes that in California, in "the diagnostic lexicon, this kind of relentless behavior is called 'perseveration'" (p. 6), a neologism conjuring notions of persistence, severing, or separation and a popular idea of perverse enjoyment. Over ten years later, the commercial exploitation (or profit) of autism has increased exponentially, so that it is no longer just in Silicon Valley or in the USA generally that these skills and pleasures are employed. As Rhodes notes, "IT companies in the UK and beyond are actively recruiting an autistic workforce for its highly technical and concentration skills" (Rhodes, 2012). Rhodes quotes Temple Grandin, an author and professor at Colorado State University, herself autistic, "who believes that without 'the gifts of autism' there would probably be no Nasa or IT industry" (Rhodes, 2012).

The interesting—or disturbing—thing about this recruitment strategy is the way in which it re-calibrates a psychic structure or form of subjectivity into a set of "transferable skills" supposedly embedded in a genetic predisposition. "One thing nearly everyone in the field agrees on [autism is the result of] genetic predisposition" (Silbermann, 2001, p. 2). Consequently, the calls for pharmaceutical companies to develop chemical "tools for neural retraining" (Silbermann, 2001, p. 4) have the commercially attractive potential for enhancing the autistic traits supposed to be responsible for these skills as much as reducing them.

The purely notional, abstract figure of the neoliberal subject of interests grounded in game theory has been neurally "fleshed out" in the subject of autism, becoming the figure of optimal functioning and performance in the now essential relation between people and computers, an idea apparently supported by science and neuroscience. Moreover, it is, no doubt, the latter that, in its determination to replace the "manifest image" of the human being with a scientifically reduced neuro-computational alternative (see, for example, Churchland & Churchland, 1998; Metzinger, 2003, 2009) that promises to enhance its efficiency and capacity for *jouissance*. The potential imagined for cognitive neuroscience has been added to the imperatives informed by cybernetics and information theory that changed the world after the Second World War. Perhaps, soon, even financial crises can be avoided with the elimination of irrational human impulses (currently understood in terms of greed, fear, and panic) that are based on the manifest image of human motives and behaviour based in language. Or, rather, these moods can be more capably managed and ordered through software systems integrated within the conceptual framework of completed neuroscience, such that economic competitiveness can become much more powerful as social sciences dissolve and are colonised and replaced by physical sciences generally. The post-linguistic turn in cognitive science is consistent with the attempt to bypass, across a spectrum of disciplines, political, institutional, and socio-economic practices, systems of symbolic mediation and representation in "an unlimited operational project" in which everything becomes immanent and transparent (see Baudrillard, 2005, p. 15). The promise appeals both to the desire for increased economic performance and efficiency as brains directly interact with each other via screens and scanners but at a pre-conscious level, obviating the need for awkward, socially mediated (that is to say, speech) interactions. The foreclosure from language and the symbols of traditional "paternal" authority that this entails ultimately implies a change or even an eradication of subjectivity that might seem to be entirely undesirable were it not for the compensations of quasi-autistic *jouissance*.

In the meantime, social science has provided a name for this figure that derives not from Silicon Valley in California, but Japan. The phenomenon of the hikikomori, first coined by psychologist Tamaki Saikō was given novelistic expression by Tatsuhiko Takimoto, a self-confessed hikikomori who hoped to exploit his condition by jumping "on the tide of the times" and making "a ton of money" (Takimoto, 2007, p. 231). Since the novel *Welcome to the NHK* quickly became both a manga serial and an anime series (Takimoto & Oiwa, 2006), it is likely that he has succeeded. Reflecting on his pathology throughout the process of writing the book proved to be painful, however, as it details the main character's descent into a "lolicon" obsession with online pornography through his attempt to develop "the greatest *hentai* game ever", an erotic interactive computer game. The central premise of *Welcome to the NHK* is a paranoid fantasy in which the Japanese Broadcasting Corporation, the Nippon Housou Kyoukai, is a front for a sinister conspiracy called the Nippon Hikikomori

Kyoukai. The NHK mass-produce anime otaku, "thereby essentially creating hikikomori on a large scale" (Takimoto, 2007, p. 16). The goal is to produce hikikomori on a mass scale, the ideal consumers of Japanese popular culture, through the seductions of manga, anime, and hentai. But just because this conspiracy theory is the self-serving delusion of a paranoid hikikomori, it does not mean it is not true. There is, then, more to it than just making tons of money; the production of neoliberal subjectivity, through the seductive appeal of simulated, CG (computer generated) transgression is also, Takimoto suggests, a means of governance. Welcome to the NHK.

Games

The conditions for filling in, as if into an empty silo, the content of autistic *jouissance* to the form of the neoliberal subject, the purely rational subject of game theory, were established broadly from the early 1990s through the development of real-time animated combat games such as Doom, Quake, Marathon, and Avara. These games are generally played by people in their bedrooms against both computer-controlled and human-controlled virtual opponents, the human controllers located in similar rooms anywhere in the world. Everyone is the same, and everyone is hostile. "For players, the main game scene displays an image of self, an other, an alien (by definition, a hostile other), and a 'closed-world' setting" (Mackenzie, 2002, p. 155).

As Mackenzie notes, in his chapter "Losing time at the Playstation: real time and the 'whatever' body", interactive games have been one of the most prominent and important forms used in the promotion and marketing of home computers since the 1980s. However, he also acknowledges that these games "stereotypically" appeal to "a fairly unpromising kind of individual" who interfaces with closed worlds "purged of differences and mostly involving narratives that emphasize extermination of differences rather than affirmative engagement with them" (p. 147). While acknowledging that the notional subject of many of these games is coded with an assumed "gender-specific interest" that renders it very unpromising indeed with regard to social inclusivity, Mackenzie, in his analysis, wishes to probe further to a more profound layer of pre-individual, pre-differentiated singularity unfiltered by "dominant codings" (p. 153). He adopts Agamben's notion of the "whatever" that designates human nature as devoid of essence and full of an infinite potential to be "whatever". A human being and a human body have endless possibilities, continuous resourcefulness so long as they are involved in a properly historical process of emergence that is not pre-programmed or pre-determined. Such a process necessarily involves a movement from potential to actual, common to proper, and it is in the manner of emergence or engendering that becomes the focus for an ethos, according to Agamben (Mackenzie, 2002, p. 53). In his chapter, Mackenzie locates a version of this "whatever" being, in play at the games console, in the mediating position between body and image. Both human and machine, the "informatic whatever" become the reference of an ethos through which can be managed, presumably, more promising modes of individuation within circuits of information.

Mackenzie finds such a promise in the temporality associated with a form of play whose desacralisation can be seen as an event that inaugurates change and, therefore, history. This form of play that is open to unexpected and unanticipated events is differentiated both from the temporal structure of sacred ritual, from which it is nevertheless derived, and the classical economic structure where time is money. While acknowledging the economic appropriation of play in the commodification of toys and the making and marketing of computer games, the real problem with computer games ought to lie in the fact that all interactivity is actually pre-programmed. Mackenzie's idea of losing time at the Playstation is not, then, that game-playing is an unproductive waste of effort—it certainly is productive, since, at the very least, it can be regarded as a kind of training. But it may involve a loss of time in so far as all occurrences in computer games are pre-determined. In this sense, time at the Playstation would be lost because nothing happens and there is actually no play at all. Happily, this is not the case, argues Mackenzie. Time at the Playstation is not lost; it is gained. Time is gained and a profit made not just because play can be utilised as a form of training, but this training is enhanced significantly when play is genuine in the interactivity between body and image, and in the "incalculability of delays stemming from the anticipatory element of any gesture", especially when one is involved in playing a competitive game with others.

For his example, Mackenzie selects Avara, one of the real-time animated combat games from the 1990s. As a scenario, it is a CG animation of the abstract world of the game theories that informed neoliberal economics, its players the necessarily paranoid subjects facing opponents that are the mirror images of themselves, "totally implacable, totally hostile and bent on their destruction" (Miroslaw, in Curtis, 2007). In giving his impressive technical analysis of the game, however, Mackenzie is coy about relating his experience as a player, perhaps not wishing to characterise himself as one of the stereotypically "unpromising" individuals associated with these games:

> A much younger friend of mine is always urging me to play computer games. Agreeing to try this game with him, something struck me as he quickly won a succession of games. He was not only anticipating most of my movements, and my gestures, he was also anticipating and manipulating in certain ways the delays introduced by the network we were playing on. (Mackenzie, 2002, p. 166)

The much younger friend's skill in apprehending the computer game's "latency tolerance", as it is called, allows him to win game after game in a way that he would not if he were simply anticipating Mackenzie's movements. The key opponent here that the boy must anticipate and manipulate is not Mackenzie, but the networked machine itself; Mackenzie's movements in this respect are secondary, they are just the necessary condition of the boy's combat with the network. While Mackenzie's quasi-parental or companionable presence is no doubt pleasurable and reassuring, the boy's play is essentially solitary. As Silbermann notes of the youngsters in Silicon Valley, "even when playing alongside someone their own age . . . [they] tend to play separately" (2001, p. 3). For Mackenzie, moreover, this machined play also materialises a "whatever" body. And it is precisely this materialisation that provides Mackenzie's conclusion with the object of his ethical concern and promise. "Understanding this materialization as the 'whatever' body entails the step of apprehending the linkages between bodies and images in the game as the incipient ethos of an informatic whatever" (Mackenzie, 2002, p. 169). This is not a sentence that gives itself readily to the understanding. It is not clear how Mackenzie is appropriating Agamben's notion of "ethos" in relation to the specific computer game example. Agamben defines ethos as "the sphere that recognizes neither guilt nor responsibility; it is . . . the doctrine of happy life" (Agamben, 1999, p. 24). Perhaps, given the specific example, the incipient ethos of Avara's informatic whatever is simply the manner or modality in which happiness or *jouissance* is a warm joystick. However, I am sure that this is not Mackenzie's intention, since, even if such an ethos were implicit in Mackenzie's chapter, it is not supported by the general ethical tendency in the rest of his work, as far as I am aware. On the contrary, I take the sentence to mean that the materialisation of an "informatic whatever" in the particular manner of interactive play provides the potential for the emergence of forms of individuation, but in order for those individuals to be promising rather than unpromising, such interactivity between bodies, machines, and images must be available, if not subject to some kind of ethical management that is, nevertheless, presumably supported and rewarded by the *jouissance* to be gained by interaction with informatic machines. This is both in the sense of the types of images (positive or negative) that might be linked together and in the manner of (non)sociality produced by their interaction (Mackenzie, 2002, p. 154); essentially, solitary *jouissance* mediated by machines has less ethical risk than between beings who interact through speech and each other's bodies.

The idea of an ethical sphere exterior to law, particularly one in which guilt and responsibility are subsumed by the happy life of a machinic assemblage has many attractions. The discourse of ethics has become highly prominent in contemporary social science in its reflexive alliance with neoliberal economics. Where law is impeached as "patriarchal", suspended in times of emergency or displaced in favour of interests, "ethics" is mobilised in its place as a mechanism of regulation and control.

Management discourse

The social science approach evident in Mackenzie's chapter recognises that computer games like Avara are not "just games". They are important factors in the socialisation and individuation of subjects. This is why it is important that Mackenzie's game with his much younger friend should not be interpreted as an "oedipal" conflict, an atavistic, unpromising example of generational and social antagonism that the "third way" politics of the 1990s sought to abolish. Following Ulrich Beck and Anthony Giddens, the most influential social scientists sought to produce conditions of "reflexive modernization", where the adversarial model of politics, of us versus them, does not apply any more. They affirm that we have entered a new era in which politics needs to be envisaged in a completely different way. Radical politics should concern "life" issues and be generative. (Laclau & Mouffe, 2001, p. xv)

So, while the "informatic whatever" materialised through the interactivity with networked machines demonstrated by the child's skill in manipulating latency, tolerance is essential if new forms of informatic life are to be generated and its risks assessed and managed.

Mackenzie is, of course, far from alone in recognising that development and growth cannot be simply pre-programmed, but need to be enhanced through the offices of play; he is also aware that this demands an "ethos". Ethics, guidelines, rules, regulations, codes of conduct, and so on exist primarily in institutions, companies, and corporations keen to subject their employees to special conditions exterior to, or in a supplementary relation with, law. It is the modality of power analysed extensively by Michel Foucault. Consistent with the game ethos (performance, targets, league tables) that has sought to generate and reproduce the subject of game theory in every domain of work and leisure, the idea of a "play ethic" has, in the 1990s and 2000s, reconfigured the notion of work in managerial discourse. According to Pat Kane, "play forms have become legitimate and effective in improving business performance" (Kane, 2004) through opening up "the infinite possibilities arising from full engagement of heart, body and soul" of the worker. (Kane, 2004). Just as the "adaptive corporation" must be open to the event and change if it is not to be wiped out by the "future shock" of constant innovation, according to Toffler (2005), so the worker's capability cannot be regarded as finite, as pre-programmed or delimited by trade, skill, or tradition. The incipient ethos of the "whatever" worker materialised by neoliberal managerialism concerns the constant self-assessment, audit, and appraisal of oneself and one's potential. Regimes of retraining, reskilling and reorientation await the worker, in line with the governing concept and ethos of "life-long learning".

A derecognition of finitude relative to a notion of "infinite human resourcefulness" has been noted by management critics in which human life and its potential, which is opened up in play, has "become the key *locus* of governance in managerialism" (Costea et al., 2007, pp. 246–247). The "whatever" that for Agamben names the infinite potential of human nature becomes, in corporate culture, subject to continual audit, the measure that assumes and seeks to sustain measureless excess.

> Even though it cannot solve the very problem it sets out for itself, the "audit society" has become a binding normative framework for contemporary work. It has become a hegemony facing us with perpetual exhortations to overcome our current limits. (Costea et al., 2007, p. 258)

But it is not just the infinity of human potential (for evil as well as productivity) that becomes individuated as the subject of limitless audit. Perpetual audit also materialises the informatic whatever in the interactive play of the corporate human–machine assemblage that must continually exceed its potential for economic growth. Costea and colleagues argue that management discourse has broached "new horizons of expectation regarding the constitution of what counts as 'work' in relation to 'subjectivity'" (p. 249). As they also show, managerial practice has so closely correlated a subject's needs and interests with performance targets as to have generated a new form of hybrid, corporate proto-subject, or subjectile, that I have called the me-me. Game theory reduces the subject of neoliberalism to a me-me, a being defined and individuated purely by self-interests that are exactly calibrated to the interests of others; in managerial discourse, these are the interests of other employees of the company and the company itself in relation to its competitors. These interests have no essence or limit; they are infinitely flexible. In a perversion of Agamben, following Mackenzie, it could be suggested that "whatever" interests are both singular and common, particular and universal, and that the passage from one to the other becomes visible in the enhanced performance opened up by the interactive play between me-mes in the circuits of information that generate them.

Given the narrow and limitless intensity of this form of corporate subjectification, it is no wonder that many people wish to withdraw from university (where it is particularly intense), work, and society. In Japan, they become known as hikikomori, but the phenomenon is, of course, prevalent throughout the west. The problem with such a withdrawal is that, more often than not, it involves a deeper embedding into highly monitored circuits of information. The apparently withdrawn zone of bedroom online existence is actually the vanguard of corporate existence, where consuming bandwidth is also always productive, wealth-generating for the service providers, and so on. The Japanese have developed a glossary of terms to describe this phenomenon, its culture, and related pathologies from the straight-forward "SOHO", which stands for Small Office, Home Office, some-one who is self-employed working from home in information technology, to the otaku, or entertainments media obsessive. Hikiko-mori are also almost always otaku. Binding otaku to particular obses-sions, whether it consists of various forms and characters from computer games, anime, hentai, and manga, is the force of *"moe"* (pronounced mo-eh). This describes the degree of affect or fetish power emitted by animated characters and symbols.

Braindance

While the bedrooms of most otaku chime and pulse to the sounds of anime pop and game electronica, the form of music that corresponds, in its mode of production, to the experience of the hikikomori is the ambient work of Richard D. James, also known as Aphex Twin. Works such as the critically acclaimed *Selected Ambient Works Vol. 2* (1994) were produced from a bedroom studio in a state of "semi-reverie". This double CD of "chilly soundscapes" evokes a world that knows no day or night, produced in the sleepy sleeplessness of perpetual bedroom existence known to adolescents and students the world over. Working live to tape, his studio equipment within arm's reach, scattered around his bedroom, "sleep deprivation and marijuana lent *Selected Ambient Works Vol. 2* the quality of spectral music" (Prendergast, 2003, p. 420). Speaking of *SAWII*, James recalls, "that was all done lucid dreaming. This was me basically going asleep, dreaming up a track . . . in an imaginary studio with imaginary equip-ment and then waking myself up and re-creating that track" (Prendergast, 2003, p. 420).

More than the rave-recovery "chill out" genre invented by KLF and The Orb, James revitalised Brian Eno's "original notion of Ambient as peripheral, evocative sound" (Shaughnessy, in Young, 2005, p. 74). Moreover, he did it by literally recreating the environment of its initial inspiration where, confined to his sick bed, barely audible harp music combined with rain to generate for Eno a listening experience in which music was "a place, a feeling" (Eno, 1995, p. 295). Critics have noted, however, that while *SAW II*'s use of "enormously long reverberation" and "forests of digital delay" produce a mood that is apparently calm and reflective, "repeated listening reveals a fundamental instability: tones waver and wobble, recording levels nudge into the red of distortion, rhythmic traces never quite assert themselves" (Shaughnessy, in Young, 2005, p. 74). The expression of an "informatic whatever" that is materialised between an ensemble of electronics and a receptive, yet semi-conscious, brain, James's ambient music is not fundamentally relaxed and reflective, it is tense and dissonant, even as that dissonance is echoed into infinity by the enormous delay and reverberation.

Richard D. James emerged as AFX and Aphex Twin (among many other aliases) in the late 1980s at the height of the techno, house, and rave era. Gaining experience as a DJ in various clubs in the south of England, his collection *Selected Ambient Work 1985–1992* nevertheless tracks a movement of withdrawal from Ibiza-style dance music to more cerebral forms of electronica released on Warp and his own Rephlex label. No doubt derived from the Warp compilation *Artificial Intelligence* (1992) that featured Aphex Twin, Autechre, Richie Hawtin, among others, the phrase "intelligent techno" or "intelligent dance music" named and established a new post-rave form of experimental electronic music that frequently owes as much to Stockhausen, Philip Glass, Ligeti, Xenakis, and Reich as to Juan Atkins, Frankie Knuckles, acid house, or jungle. The phrase "intelligent dance music" has been attributed to Alan Parry, who set up an IDM mailing list in 1993. However, in Britain, where the idea of intelligence is treated with suspicion generally, it has become a derogatory term, marking the withdrawal of techno from the "dancefloor to the armchair" or, indeed, the bedroom. Simon Reynolds, in his chronicle of "generation ecstasy" (1999), is highly critical of the "post-rave experimental fringe". Although resembling the contemporary high-speed polyrhythms of "jungle" and "drum and bass", intelligent techno is, for Reynolds, dance music without the dance:

> the mini-genre of jungle by non-junglists for non-junglists—AFX, Plug, Witchman, Squarepusher . . . is sometimes jocularly referred to as drill and bass, because the breakbeats are so sped up they sound like Woody Woodpecker on PCP. Because these producers don't belong to the drum and bass community, they are free to take the idiomatic features of jungle—fucked up breakbeats, mutant bass,

sampladelic collage—and exacerbate them way beyond any use-value to DJ or dancer. (Reynolds, 1999, p. 382)

For Reynolds, the value of dance music is directly correlated to its utility. If it clears the dance floor, a piece of music is worthless. Its form and development is modified by its use, its aim the continual heightening of bodily as well as aural pleasure. As such, dance music is always a collective mode of enunciation, the expression of a community or subculture rather than a specific individual. As soon as it withdraws from the site of this collective enunciation, then, the fate of the post-rave experimental fringe can only be to render dance music undanceable.

Aphex Twin rejects the phrase "intelligent techno" that seems to implicitly suggest that every other form of techno is dumb. Nevertheless, his term "braindance", which it rivals, is happy to stress the cerebral and cerebrally stimulating–disturbing aspect of the music. *Braindance* (2001) became the title of a compilation album featuring artists linked to the Rephlex label that was founded by James and Grant-Wilson Claridge. The notion of braindance implies a certain scientific materialism unusual in dance music, which is traditionally more interested in quasi-metaphysical notions of "soul" or "spirit" that are linked to an ecstasy of the body. Common pop musical appeals to "body" and "soul" generally bypass the brain, at least where it is understood conventionally as an organ of thought rather than feeling. The notion of braindance displaces that opposition, however, opening up the cranium to the pulse of electronica in the same way that the bedroom of the hikikomori is linked to the audio-visual virtual world of online entertainments. Braindance is consistent with the old house trope, borrowed from the cyberpunk of William Gibson, of "jacking in" to cyberspace. Braindance establishes, through multiple rhythms, tones, and timbres, electronic continuity between neural circuits and circuits of digital information. There is, then, a different relation to a collective or an assemblage than strictly on the dance floor, one that is in common with the online world of work and play that takes place primarily though interaction with a screen or headset. Braindance music unravels, neuron by neuron, silcon chip by silicon chip, the audio unconscious of the drive towards complete interactivity within a human–machine system. The autistic brain connected to its rim of *jouissance*, neuronally dancing to the pulse and rhythm of electrical stimulation, promises to take subjectivity, emotion, feeling, and the thought that follows in its wake, into the extrinsic networks of information.

James has been accused of a kind of solipsism, or creative hedonism, with regard to his music, as if it concerned no one but himself, as if he were a direct heir to Yoko Ono, for whom all art of any significance is solely about the artist. Shaughnessy argues that the "overriding point" of James' work is that "all of this music is about himself" (Young, 2005, p. 78), citing the multiple anagrams of his own name, various aliases, and personal associations that he uses for song titles, assuming that all the music must be made to refer back to himself. Prendergast further suggests that James is indifferent to his audience and is interested in "only making music for himself" (Prendergast, 2003, p. 420), to the point of releasing just enough music to keep himself solvent and make more music, erasing as much as he produces. The music is produced entirely for his own satisfactions, but in an active rather than passive way. and in relation to machines that take the place of fellow musicians or a theatre audience that provide, as we saw with David Byrne, the conditions for the fabrication of a persona and an armature of sound that enabled a mode of social interaction through performance that was much more successful than through the awkward intimacy of conversation. For Richard James, the theatre has contracted to the bedroom and the "Other" constituted by a bank of computers and music software. "His real passion [is] the creative act itself, the very moment when his mind connected to the equipment and produced sound" (Prendergast, 2003, p. 420). The musical interface between brain and equipment, taking place below the threshold of conscious perception, materialises the informatic whatever that generates infinite resourcefulness and a "creative ease" that has led to him being likened to Mozart (Prendergast, 2003, p. 418).

But if Richard James, the bedroom Mozart, is solely interested in himself, that notion of self is subject to same "sampladelic" logic as techno: it is set free from any point of origin or essence. The name is "de-composed", in the phrase of Drew Hemment, in a process familiar to electronic music, in which music is decompartmentalised into fragments, samples, and "musemes", then remixed according to a principle of general iterability in which they can become almost unrecognisable. "In de-composition, difference-in-repetition displaces an economy of imitation and re-presentation" and becomes instead a "reworking . . . a nomadism where the musical fragment changes along with the territory that it traverses" (Hemment, 2006, p. 89). Looped-together and repeated fragments become audible or sonorous in a different way, new refrains that transform the terrains that they demarcate in brains and bodies, collective and individual.

Evident, perhaps, in the music, but certainly in the artwork, graphics, and especially the videos made with Chris Cunningham, is a replicant form of self unleashed to exceed its limits, "mutate and spread virally across the musical landscape" (Young, 2005, p. 78). The anagrams do not, therefore, refer back to a single name or origin, but are the linguistic equivalent of an endless fractal mutation. This is especially the case with the CDs that followed *Selected Ambient Works II*: *Donkey Rhubarb* (1995), *I Care Because You Do* (1995), *Come To Daddy* and *Windowlicker* (1999). The cover of *I Care Because You Do* depicts a digitally modified image of James' bearded face sporting his characteristic sinister grin, as if he were Richard Branson's evil double and apotheosis. In the accompanying artwork and window displays, this face is multiplied in various sizes, while the cover of *Donkey Rhubarb* details the grin that is again repeated thirty times. Like these images, the title of the album *I Care Because You Do* evokes the me-me structure in which the notion of "care" is fractured to infinity in an endless series of self-reflecting interests: I care because you care that I care because you care that I care because you care . . .

This form of self-replication is repeated to spectacular effect in the famous videos for *Come to Daddy* and *Windowlicker*, by Chris Cunningham. In the former, another example of fear of music, or music of fear, a "horror–jungle piece", James' face is multiplied and morphed on to midget children; in the latter, it becomes the ubiquitous face of US corporate dance music and sexual excess. The video parodies a Miami-style rap video that begins with a long sequence in which the uncompromising courtship of two young women by a pair of stereotypically foul-mouthed boys from the 'hood demonstrates the brutal inefficiency of language and the absence of a sexual relation. The foul-mouthed courtship is literally pushed aside as the boys' ride is bumped out of the way by James in the guise of a pimp multi-millionaire tycoon arriving in an apparently infinitely extendable limousine (thirty-eight windows long), wearing a white suit and wafting a white parasol bearing the morphed "AT" of the "Aphex Twin" corporate logo. Language is displaced by a wordless sequence of music and dance. Immediately,

James becomes the focus of the young women's avid attention. Consistent with music video male fantasy, more bikini-clad women are discovered on the Miami seafront dancing to the master's tune. But this masturbatory hip-hop reverie lasts only a moment as all the women are revealed to be James himself, complete with sinister grin and straggly red beard. Evidently the absence of a sexual relation has been overcome: they have become One. The finale, in which James' head, with its digitally enhanced ugliness and evil morphed on to the virtually naked bodies of glamour models, becomes, as Mulholland writes, "genuinely terrifying, and by the end of the promo all notions of money, fame, physical attractiveness, sexual identity and American excess had been surgically exposed for the empty charade that they are" (Mulholland, 2002, p. 422).

The braindance of the "windowlicker", a term in colloquial English that denotes someone mentally handicapped or psychically disturbed, is conveyed through the amusical arrhythmia of the machined beats. At the same time, the title's reference is also presumed to be a translation of *faire du lèche-vitrine*, in a tribute to his French partner at the time, meaning "window shopper". In a crude and no doubt offensive way, then, "Windowlicker" conjoins psychosis and consumer capitalism. The correlation suggests that this is the fevered erotic dance of a brain "interacting" with a screen, a "window" on to a pornucopia of electronic sounds and images. The latter is, of course, evoked in Cunningham's video, where the ubiquity of James' face suggests the reflection of the windowlicker in the screen that overlays the images of micro-bikini-clad models. It is the braindance of the porn-obsessed hikikomori, but also, by extension, of the whole bio-electrical erogenous zone that is online consumer capitalism.

But, further, from a psychoanalytic perspective, we can not only clearly see, in the foreclosure from a principle of prohibition (the name-of-the-father), the return of the spectre of *père jouissance* in the form of the brain-dancing master of the primal horde, but also that the primal horde is itself a series of clones of the father of enjoyment, that the father/phallic principle has become subject to bio-computational reproduction and gender mutation. As Aphex Twin's electronic music splurges towards its machined climax and whimper, below slo-mo images of champagne ejaculation, we are presented with the ambivalent sound-image of the realisation of scientific *jouissance*: the order of joy in all its monstrous poly-pluripotency (see Wilson, 2008).

CHAPTER FIFTEEN

The three delusions

Throughout this book, three artists, if that is the right word, have been prominently featured whose practice has, in different ways, amplified the *a*musical discontents of contemporary culture. Through the specific modality of joy immanent to their practice, a modality that crackles in the dissonant frisson of *a*musia, Brian Eno, Yoko Ono, and Masami Akita both disclose and, in some ways, compensate for the maladies of western society exacerbated by the strategies of neoliberal governance. As I have argued in *The Order of Joy* (2008), the latter specifically concerns the reappropriation of symbolic authority in the form of instrumental directives and imperatives in the conjugation of war and commerce. In this book, I have focused on the (proto-)subject that has been produced both as an effect and agent of this policy: the me-me of game theory, upon whose interests international relations, economics, and biology in both its genetic and digital forms are based. The wholesale production of this minimal subject and its supply of autistic *jouissance* has enabled the conditions for the emergence of something like a generalised psychosis that is rapidly mutating to the point where a version of autism is becoming the normal, that is to say, most operative, state of the subject in contemporary capitalism accelerated by digital information systems.

As I also argue in *The Order of Joy*, war, new modes of symbolisation, and commerce correspond, in their relation to each other, to real-
Symbolic-Imaginary (rSI) in Lacan's topology of the Borromean knot.
I want to try to demonstrate how, in different ways, the practices of
Eno, Ono, and Akita operate as a fourth term that ties together the
rings of the knot through the supplementation of the three delusions
of discourse that testify to a certain failure and loosening of the ties
that bind rSI in the Borromean knot. The delusion of ignorance, for
example, results from the subtraction of the Imaginary (S◇r – I); the
delusion of love, the real (I◇S – r); the delusion of hatred, the
symbolic (I◇r – S) (see Weslaty, 2000, p. 59). The modality of joy
immanent to the specific practices of Eno, Ono and Akita supplement
each delusion through the activation of the missing term in the affect,
both common and singular, that produces the subject of *a*musia in the
locus of the audio unconscious.

The delusion of ignorance

' "Everything for the other" says the obsessive, and that is what he
does, for being in the perpetual whirlwind [*vertige*] of destroying the
other, he can never do enough to ensure that the other continues to
exist' (Lacan, 1960–1961, p. 241). After he left Roxy Music, Brian Eno
made his reputation as an innovative producer transforming and revi-
talising the work and careers of other artists. Most notable, perhaps,
were the profound changes he oversaw in David Bowie and, through
Bowie, Iggy Pop in the 1970s in recording sessions in Berlin. Albums
such as *Lust for Life* (1977) or *The Idiot* (1977), on the one hand, and
Bowie's *Low* (1977), *"Heroes"* (1977) and *Lodger* (1979), on the other,
bear little relation to previous work done by Pop and Bowie but
propelled both their careers in new directions. Indeed, while Eno's
profound influence and ghostly presence is generally accepted to be
all over these albums, he was not even the officially credited producer,
that being Tony Visconti. Yet, Bowie's albums in particular are
regarded as "an ambient/electronic adventure inspired by Bowie's
working friendship with Brian Eno" (Mulholland, 2006, p. 9).

Similarly, in his commentary on the Talking Heads' album, *Fear of
Music*, Jonathan Lethem describes Eno as a "Trojan Horse" (2012,
p. 11) who, in his work on their third album, "conquered" "the original

band's integrity" (p. 11), adding many new effects, musicians, and styles to produce an entirely new sound. *Fear of Music* was just the beginning—or, for Lethem—"the last" recognisable Talking Heads record. By the time of *Remain in Light* and *Speaking in Tongues*, Eno was producing a completely different, post-rock band whose minimal back beat had been replaced by the polyrhythms of multiple African drums. It was a long way from the CBGBs in New York.

Throughout his career, Eno, the "Trojan Horse", has moved behind the scenes, from band to band, destroying them only to renew and keep them alive, effacing himself in the role of producer for and of the other, while at the same time establishing a huge, mysterious reputation. Eno's work exceeds that of a conventional record producer, as indeed it exceeds or, rather, transforms the conventional role of artist or composer. It is even as if it has also been his desire to neutralise or annihilate himself, as one thing or other, working tirelessly in order to continually renew himself. Eno stands at the juncture where artist and worker become transformed into a completely different creature of econopoietic management, a machine that regenerates even as it exhausts itself in a constant round of creative consultancy. During the same year as he produced The Microsoft Sound, Eno was commissioned to write a diary detailing his hectic production, design, and charity work that was subsequently published as *A Year with Swollen Appendices* (1995). The liberation of art from work that it details in his interest in new mechanical processes of creativity might seem like freedom, but sometimes it still feels like hard labour. Indeed, the opening pages of the book give ample testament to the mountain of bureaucracy that accompanies each of his creative endeavours (Eno, 1995, pp. xi–xii)

While we can see in Eno's hectic activity and apparent self-efface-ment relative to his work with other bands, the signs of an obsessive structure, it is not simply the case here that, as Bruce Fink suggests, "the obsessive takes the object for himself and refuses to recognise the Other's existence, much less the Other's desire . . . the obsessive seeks to neutralize or annihilate the Other" (Fink, 1999, p. 119). For Eno, "I" is also an other that is neutralised relative to the object—generative music or art—that replaces the artist as the producer and even as site of enunciation, thereby sustaining the "unspeakableness" of its demand. Furthermore, that site is filled in by the processes of computer generation that overwrite the real. It is the annihilation of voice and the production of music as pure digital symbol that results in what Pat Kane, referring to The Microsoft Sound, calls a "bloodless, precise . . . scary and inhuman" noise (Kane, 1995).

Throughout his career making art and music objects and machines, Eno has emphasised process rather than product. The sounds unfold in a space emptied of art whose value could be grounded in the intrinsic qualities of an object or in the skill and labour of an artist. Similarly, as he has emphasised many times, Eno's ambient music is not there to be listened to or appreciated; it is not meant to be interesting. It becomes a barely perceptible part of the environment that is felt but not thought about. Following in the tradition of John Cage, for whom the task of art was to imitate nature in its manner of operation, Eno's avant-garde principles have become central to both high-end and mainstream productive processes, feeding into and enabling the correlation of art, commerce, and bio-technology. As such, these generative systems that "evolve" art, music, and audio-visual experiences in machinic assemblages provide an effective environment for co-evolutionary processes of becoming that operate below the threshold of thought, sustaining ignorance in processes that are non-reflective, unaware of themselves. Generative systems like Spore materialise "generatively" on the basis of simple genetic principles and are now ubiquitous in games and activities based on multi-user domains, computer animation, and environments. As Eno predicted on their emergence in the 1990s, these virtual environments (now become social media) had already become the paradigm of cultural, social, and economic interaction, replacing popular music. In art, science, and business processes of artificial creation, where selection is dependent on fitness and function in the context of a bio-economic ecosystem, these processes become the basis of emergence, transmission, and transformation, placing economic, leisure, and creative activities on the same plane.

Eno's multi-screen sound and light installation, *Constellation (77 Million Paintings)* (2007) with its performance–presentation of the beauty of a turbulent art–nature of continual and indefinite change, mutability, and expenditure is consistent with these mainstream "CG" processes. The installation is generated by a computer programmed to create 77 million unrepeatable aural and audio experiences. Reporting on the installation, Rachel Campbell-Johnston writes, "appearing on a pattern of screens, the images transmute to the accompaniment of an entrancing electronic tune. The sounds cluster and recluster in strange unearthly songs" (Campbell-Johnston, 2007, p. 14). She quotes Eno staring at one of the images and saying, "What absolutely intrigues me . . . is that I've never seen this before and I'm never going to see it again. Each image is unique . . . and each moment in the music is unique" (Campbell-Johnston, 2007, p. 14). Even at the fastest speed available to the software, it would apparently take 9,000 years to view the entire show.

Eno's software programme allows a finite number of audio-visual elements to yield a practically unlimited diversity of combinations that are, at the same time, perfectly equivalent and exchangeable. The automata of the symbolic (algorithms, numerical systems, digital biology) erases the letter and overwrites the real in the sense of generating a digital ground in which nothing repeats but everything is in a constant churn of creation and destruction, life and death. But there is no life or death, no trauma or trace of an irruption of the real. As such, this art is the perfect sign of a techno-science that is divested not just of all semblance of meaning, but all utility. Its scientific death drive has foreclosed the imaginary dimension in which death might become meaningful for a subject. There is no subject, no musician, no artist, no listener or viewer, just an undead process of emergence and expenditure programmed to last 9,000 years. Neither marble nor the gilded monuments of princes shall outlive it. And yet, it has Brian Eno's signature. In his interview with Rachel Campbell-Johnson captured on YouTube, Eno comments on the remarkable posterity of his work by suggesting that "When I look at this I see things that I didn't predict because I can't possibly have seen 77 million combinations, and I probably never will do". Again, Eno highlights his delight that the uniqueness and originality of the artwork lies with the machine, not with him. It is the machine that "speaks" without knowing anything about it, that "addresses", interminably and idiotically, an audience of which it is completely unaware. Eno's satisfaction in witnessing his installation is qualified only by that mysterious "probably" that hints that something in Brian Eno is not entirely convinced that he is not going to live for a further 9,000 years and witness the complete the entire 77 million combinations.

In his adumbration of clinical categories in psychoanalysis, Bruce Fink notes that the obsessive "lives for posterity and not for today . . . [he] lives posthumously, sacrificing everything (all satisfaction in the here and now) for the sake of his name – having his name live on" (Fink, 1999, p. 129). Eno's generative art and music functions in a similar way to the name that lives on, but also displaces and substitutes in its machined originality his own voice and the singularity of its demand to the Other concerning its existence, the very reason to make art. In this sense, it is improper to read Brian Eno's 77 *Million Paintings* as the audio and visual symptom, or even sinthome, of his own particular mode of *jouissance* other than to suggest that it is designed to keep everyone in the dark about it. Eno is, after all, a cultural entrepreneur rather than an artist. It is not the specific *jouissance* of the body that generates the music and the image, but a software programme that, in an application such as Bloom, can be marketed and sold to the owners of smartphones so that they can interact with the programme and create their own Enomusic. Eno is essentially the brand name (that haunts the actual brand names of specific products) of an assemblage involving other software engineers, programmes, and designers. Nevertheless, inherent to the programme and its particular organisation of noise, a structure of desire is clearly perceptible that is related to an imaginary utopia of social order based on biotechnology and theories of evolution, economic churn, and equilibrium that also inform neoliberalism. Nevertheless, there remains in the work a ghostly subjective dimension precisely to the degree that it is haunted by his name. While the role of the artist-as-creator is effaced, his name haunts the undead process of computer generation. The effacement of the artist's own voice, therefore, is predicated on a ghoulish narcissism that gives imaginary consistency to the work of the machines, interactive or not. The name of the ghost supports the symbolic and stops the work becoming completely operational in its scientific (mathematic, algorithmic) reformatting of the real through its hyperbolic doubling of the order of simulation.

The delusion of love

"In the hysteric's fantasy . . . separation is overcome as the subject constitutes herself, not in relation to the erotic object she herself has 'lost' but as the object the other is missing" (Fink, 1999, p. 120). When Yoko Ono was introduced to John Lennon by John Dunbar at the Indica Gallery in 1966, she apparently had no idea who he was and neither had she paid any attention to The Beatles other than to note quizzically to herself that a "Ringo" is a Japanese apple. In the *avant-garde* world of the 1950s and 1960s, it seems, popular music was disregarded as a serious form. It would not have taken her long to discover that, to a large extent, John Lennon shared her views on this. He had by now come to hate being a Beatle and his and the other Beatles' artistic yearnings that were nurtured by the German art students Astrid Kirchherr and Klaus Voormann in Hamburg at the start of the 1960s were pressing in productive ways on their new studio-based output. The death in Hamburg of Lennon's highly talented best friend, Stuart Sutcliffe, who left The Beatles to concentrate on his career as a painter but died of a brain tumour in 1962, is symbolic of this loss. As Ono herself recalled, "I felt I knew Stuart because hardly a day went by that John didn't speak about him" (Ono, 2012, p. 1). As artist and mentor, Ono would replace both Sutcliffe and Paul McCartney as Lennon's creative partner, but initially, it seems, through joining The Beatles recording sessions and offering her own input, she also seems to have been keen to offer her ideas in order to supplement what she and her new partner clearly felt was lacking in their work. As we have seen, this gift of love was not well received by the other members of the group and was greeted with intense xenophobic hatred by many, if not the majority, of their British fans, being routinely blamed for the break-up of the group that followed closely the break-up of Lennon's marriage to his first wife. As we have seen, her voice in particular became a focus for, in Lacanian terms, moral desire, summoning the law in the form of the arrest for the possession of cannabis that marked the end of the evident conspiracy of indulgence practised by Press and Police hitherto.

In her engagement with war, Yoko Ono's main strategy, in conjunction with her husband, was to introduce the resources of art into some of the most ubiquitous and reviled forms of popular commercial culture, notably billboard advertising and the Christmas pop song. The Christmas pop single is one of the most unbearable forms of music, both formally and, of course, in its interminable repetition throughout the festive period. Every year, in Britain at least, for a whole month, over-familiar ditties from Bing Crosby to Cliff Richard, Nat King Cole to Slade, Johnny Mathis to George Michael torture the British public through their ubiquity and endless replaying on every popular music radio channel, retail outlet, and Christmas party. John

Lennon and Yoko Ono's "Happy Xmas (War Is Over)" entered this dubious canon in 1971. In the general banality of its liberal sentiments, addressing itself to a world of old and young, rich and poor, weak and strong, black and white, and so on, it is unremarkable and more or less equivalent to any other Christmas song. The difference between this song and most of the others, however, lies with the parenthetical supplement, "War Is Over". The Christmas song proffers a Christmas gift, the equivocal nature of which is signalled in its own bracketed condition "(If You Want It)".

Finding herself infamous, Yoko Ono sought to exploit her notoriety and newly found wealth by taking the war directly to the mediascape. More or less concurrent with the Plastic Ono Band project (its inaugural appearance was at the Toronto Rock'n'Roll Revival in October 1969), Ono staged with her husband various worldwide media events advertising peace. The "Bed-in for Peace" event in Amsterdam (March 1969) was followed by another Bed-In in Montreal (May, 1969) and, in December of the same year, the couple launched their "WAR IS OVER! (If You Want It)" billboard and poster campaign. Ono began her advertising art in 1965 with the *IsReal Gallery* project that advertised for sale a number of purely imaginary art works from an exhibition that did not take place in a non-existent gallery. Playful and paradoxical, Ono's advertising events take up the imperative form of advertising in a way that is not simply subversive. For Kevin Concannon, "these works in many ways prefigure the trajectory of Conceptual Art's development through the 1960s and 1970s" (Munroe & Hendricks, 2000, p. 177), but they are also contemporary with the move advertising itself made in the 1960s into a form of conceptual thinking that had its end point, in the 1980s and 1990s, in the marketing of pure concepts rather than products. As Deleuze and Guattari wryly remark, "marketing has preserved the idea of a certain relationship between the concept and the event" (Deleuze & Guattari, 1994, p. 10).

Munroe argues that while Ono was one of the pioneers of conceptual art in the 1960s, her approach differs significantly from Sol LeWitt, Joseph Kosuth, Hans Haacke, and others officially canonised as the originators of conceptual art. While the latter employed language, nonsense, participation, and minimalism to "critique the art system and the definition of art itself", Ono's use of similar techniques does not engage in a critique or form of negation (Munroe &

Hendricks, 2000, p. 25). Rather, they "posit the mirror as a primary form of the imaginary ... going beyond genres and categories to include all art and thought" (Miyakawa Atsushi, cited in Munroe & Hendricks, 2000, p. 25). Like the Freudian unconscious, they know no negation, but are, like all her works, affirmative events, "the closest word for [which] may be a 'wish'" ("To the Wesleyan People", 1966; in Munroe & Hendricks, 2000, pp. 288–289). They "in-struct" as they construct imaginary and fictional, yet incomplete, spaces or events that assume "fiction as fiction, that is, as fabricated truth" ("The word of a fabricator", 1962, in Munroe & Hendricks, 2000, p. 26).

This concept of "instructure" informs both the Instruction Pieces and the Unfinished works that require the involvement of participants, imaginary or real, virtual or actual, in order to be "completed", although the ways in which the works and pieces can be completed can be as variable as the participants themselves. As such, like the ambivalent space of the mirror, the event can be unpleasurable as much as pleasurable, distressing as much as reassuring, the fabrication disclosing (self-)hatred as much as love. The writing piece "On Instructure" refers to "something that emerged from instruction and yet not quite emerged—not quite structured never quite structured ... like an unfinished church with a sky ceiling". With regard to her advertising art, one might suggest that the architectural form of instructure resembles not a church, but a shopping mall open to the sky, which markets an approximately infinite universe of useless and conceptual objects, as with her "Ono's Sales List" (1965). A soundtape of snow falling at dawn priced at twenty-five cents per inch, a crying machine retailing at $3,000, circle and hole events at $150 each, and underwear to make you high at about $10 to $35 were just a few of the many products offered.

Much larger in scale, the "WAR IS OVER! (If You Want It)" project involved a multi-media advertising campaign including billboards posted in different languages in twelve major cities around the world, posters, newspaper advertisements, radio spots, and postcards. Reputed to have cost $72,000, the campaign constituted a huge and highly equivocal gift to the anti-war movement. One might even say it was a form of potlatch, given the self-promotion necessarily implied in the gesture and the adverse publicity it generated. Was this about the war or about John-and-Yoko? Although not a direct imperative, like Coca-Cola's "Enjoy", with which it is directly contemporary, or Nike's "Just

Do It" of the 1990s, "War is Over! (If You Want It)" operates in exactly the same way. It is a *mot d'ordre*, an order-word, in the phrase of Deleuze and Guattari, that instructs not by giving information but by ordering or commanding obedience.

> We call *order-words*, not a particular category of explicit statements (for example, in the imperative), but the relation of every word or statement to implicit presuppositions, in other words, to speech acts that are, and can only be, accomplished in the statement. (Deleuze & Guattari, 1988, p. 79

These statements, through their clear link, direct or indirect, to presuppositions, assumptions, and assumed obligations, not only compel the bodies that they address, but transform and mobilise them.

John and Yoko's message does not, however, describe or promise a passage from war to peace, even if it may take the form of a wish for such a passage. Rather, it produces an experience and self-consciousness of war through the antagonism it generates. "WAR IS OVER! (If You Want It)" actually means "WAR IS FOR EVER! (And You Have No Choice)". Happy Christmas, John and Yoko. They say it every year: on every popular music radio channel, every retail outlet, every Christmas party, the conjunction between antagonism and commerce, war and advertising is announced, placing the festive cheer and universal love of Christmas on the path of ex-sistence. In the same way that many people find Ono's famous instruction poems—"Watch the sun until it becomes square"—as annoying as they do charming, "WAR IS OVER! (If You Want It)" cannot help but produce hostility precisely through demanding the impossible. A small collection of instruction poems is one thing. But an impossible demand, framed in the form of a Christmas present commanding world peace, screaming silently but insistently across the world in huge billboards and across the mass media, cannot fail to produce antagonism. For David Ross, director of the San Francisco Museum of Modern Art and a member of the curatorial staff of Lennon and Ono's "This is Not Here" exhibition (also staged in 1971), Ono's events are examples of how she has "managed to use the simple concept of love as a universal social construction as the content for her own aesthetic and philosophical stance. This is not here, it is everywhere and eternal" (in Munroe & Hendricks, 2000, p. 57). These references to love as both a "social construction" and "everywhere and eternal" once again indicate quite clearly that the discourse of love is marked by an essential delusion. In their conjunction of art, commerce, and the gift, Ono's marketing events employ this discourse informed by the delusion of love in the name of peace. What these events actualise and foreground, however, is quite the opposite. "Bag Peace", "Hair Peace", "Give Peace a Chance", "WAR IS OVER! (If You Want It)": through the formal effect of commercial repetition (irrespective of any profit-motive) these statements produce pure dissonance.

According to The Beatles' biographer Bob Spitz, "Yoko's appearance in the studio functioned as a declaration of war" (Spitz, 2007, p. 777). This seems excessive, but, at the very end of her own authorised documentary of Lennon's life and legacy, *Imagine* (Solti, 1988), Ono's reflections on her relations with her dead husband are short, simple, and revealing. She lists a series of roles, apparently in an ascending order of significance. "He was my husband, he was my lover, he was my friend. He was my partner. And . . . (pause) . . . he was an old soldier that fought with me (brief smile)."

The delusion of hate

While Masami Akita, like many composers of sound-music and electronica, does much of his recording in his bedroom surrounded by "computers, some instruments and audio equipment" (Akita, in Batty, 2006), the music that Akita makes and listens to is not the anime pop favoured by most hikikomori. On the contrary, it is informed by a hatred of such music. This is evident in one of Akita's most famous statements, that "there is no difference between noise and music in my work. If noise means uncomfortable sound, then pop music is noise to me" (Akita, cited in Norman, 2004, p. 168). This reversal of noise-perception between pop and Merzbow's *a*music seems to keep the latter captured within imaginary opposition. Merzbow's recordings are, therefore, not raised to the power of music as a distinct symbolic form, but remain at the level of the noise-fetish. Constructed out of the aural junk and detritus of Japanese society, Akita's art would seem, in its fetishistic disavowal of a clear symbolic distinction between music and noise, to involve a purely imaginary relation to the real without symbolic mediation (I◊r − S).

Yet, in the singular know-how of Akita, the lost objects of Japanese society further lose all distinction in a general process of loss and expenditure. Merzbow's dissonance is "littoral" in the sense that his *a*music is inseparable from the Japanese noise that its noise wishes to strike out in a precipitous line. "Sometimes I would like to kill the much too noisy Japanese by my own Noise. The effects of Japanese culture are too much noise everywhere. I want to make silence by my Noise" (Akita, 2008, p. 61; cited in Cox & Warner, 2004). In its creative violence, Merzbow's *a*music becomes elevated to the dignity of the Thing in Lacanian terms. Or, to paraphrase Heidegger, the noisiness of Merzbow's noise does not at all lie in the sound of which it consists, but in the silence that holds (Heidegger, 1971, p. 169).[15] Merzbow's noise-Thing functions as the purely aural signifier of a fatal desire to kill the too noisy Japanese of which it is its own singular expression. Merzbow's *a*music becomes a pure signifier that would bear and testify to the death of Japanese culture and the herald of some Other Thing that would arise from the ashes.

As such, it would be easy to suggest that the trauma of dissonance that is repeated in Merzbow's *a*musical unconscious is the profound noise of the big bangs that flattened Tokyo, Hiroshima, Nagasaki, and much else of Japan in 1945. The overwhelming defeat enacted by these big bangs also heralded the subsequent rapid rise in Americanisation and consumer culture that caused a profound mutation in post-war Japanese culture. On the other hand, it is the sound of that which remains untouched by the nuclear devastation much as one of Graham Harman's favourite examples, the essence of the cotton thread that is not exhausted by the fire that consumes it. Tokyo, and, indeed, Japan, has known catastrophe before and rebuilt using western influences. The razing of cities in 1945 was itself just another repetition of more "natural" disasters. Speaking of his interest in architecture in an interview in 1999, Akita cited the earthquake of 1918 that required Tokyo to be completely rebuilt.

> In the old downtown area which dated from Edo period, they had no architects, so they redid the Western idea. The buildings in that area are not by architects but just by ordinary carpenters who interpreted western references. (Obrist & Bauer, 1999)

In the same interview, Akita iterates his hatred of the Japanese music industry even as he denies the influence of traditional Japanese musical forms, such as Gagaku, to which Merzbow has been compared. On the contrary, Akita affirms his own dependence on western musical influences in the development of the singular noise with which he opposes the noise of contemporary Japanese society. It is never, therefore, with Akita, a question of opposing the west and western influence with traditional Japanese culture—except, perhaps, that element which embraces its own obliteration. Whole cities and societies obliterated only to be reborn from nothing, or, rather, from debris, refuse, and the waste of violent expenditure. Immanent and unconscious, therefore, to the "obliterating white out" that is caused by the ferocious ecstasy of Merzbow (Norman, 2004, p. 168) is the silence of the death drive inhabiting a "creationist sublimation" that Lacan finds at the heart of Freud's notion of the "nirvana principle" (Lacan, 1992, p. 213). That is to say, that the audio unconscious immanent to Merzbow's *a*music seeks obliteration in order to provoke a desire to begin again from the rubble, detritus, the senseless junk that remains, out of which the future may be discerned.

The hum

The phenomenon of the hum, first noted a few decades ago, and reported across the world, consists of a low-pitched drone, the source of which, indefinably outside and inside, both domestic and alien, is unidentifiable. It is so persistent that it has caused suicide, and the Low Frequency Noise Sufferer's Association suggests that "the problem is on the increase . . . it receives two or three new cases every week". According to the BBC, however, these people "are generally over 50 and are mostly female".

> It's worst at night. It's hard to get off to sleep because I hear this throbbing sound in the background and you know what it's like when you can't get to sleep and you're tossing and turning and you get more and more agitated about it . . . People assume you must be hearing things, but I'm not crackers . . . this is not in my head. It's just as though there's something in your house and you want to switch it off and you can't. It's there all the time. (Katie Jacques, BBC News, 19 April 2009)

It would appear that the world is becoming a David Lynch film. Certainly, the hum resonates with a point Slavoj Žižek makes at the end of his extended essay on *Lost Highway* (Lynch, 1997). For Žižek, "Lynch's entire work" is "an endeavour to bring the spectator 'to the point of hearing inaudible noises'" (Žižek, 2000, p. 44), most notably the mythical noise, another ultra-low frequency hum, that the first viewers of Lynch's *Eraserhead* (1978) believed caused them feelings of "unease, even nausea" (p. 44). Such noises are condensed, as always for psychoanalysis, on the voice of the Other that is inaudible because it is located in the site of "the fundamental fantasy", the comic horror of the mother's unspeakable enjoyment, a *jouissance* in which the auditors can participate in so far as they experience it, in the form of the hum, without knowing anything about it (Lacan, 1999, p. 74). We can agree, then, with Katie Jacques that she is not "crackers"; rather, the world has indeed become Lynchean and testifies to the reality of cinema.

In 1982, appropriately enough in the Lynchean state of California, Friedrich Kittler concludes his essay "Dracula's legacy" on Lacan, technicity, and the welding of desire to the despotic law of the "infernal machine"; he writes that from now on we are no longer simply subjects of the signifier, but of "gadgets and instruments of mechanical discourse processing" (Kittler, 1997, pp. 83–84). The penultimate sentence of the essay, he ends with a personal observation, writing his last sentence before looking away from the screen: "I turn off the hum of the office machine, lift my eyes and see in the fog over the bay, the Golden Gate Bridge, our hyper-realistic future" (Kittler, 1997, pp. 83–84). The hum, here, is the *jouissance* of the machine, enjoying itself at our expense, the machine's quiet hum of satisfaction at the *jouissance* expended in the attempt to keep up with the demands and endless upgrades of everyday technocapitalism; the *jouissance* lubricating and accelerating the machine to its moment of so-called "singularity", the point from which it becomes entirely autonomous from the finitude of human desire.

Whatever it is, the hum is evidence that the human psychic apparatus is becoming attuned to the drone of a new ambience. For Dr Baguley of the Acoustics Laboratory, Salford University, it is an effect of an over-sensitisation of the auditory apparatus that amplifies an otherwise innocuous sound to monstrous proportions. He says,

> The initial "signal" may vary from person to person, but the outcome is the same. It becomes a vicious cycle . . . The more people focus on the noise, the more anxious and fearful they get, the more the body responds by amplifying the sound, and that causes even more upset and distress. (BBC News, 19 April 2009)

A certain noise becomes all-encompassing, ultimately filling the whole universe for that particular someone, obliterating all other sounds and images. No longer the celestial music of the spheres, then, or a scream passing through nature; rather, an ambient anorganic hum continuous with the reverberating acceleration of a disintegrating universe, the desertification and disappearance of all matter; this is indeed real, occurring all the time and audible with the correctly attuned (mechanical) perceptual apparatus.

If the hum is a delusion, it is the very delusion of form itself, and its perception. That is to say, the hum gives minimal form to the infinite resonance of one's own distress and radical meaninglessness that is continuous with the formlessness of the chaotic abyss: all the discontents of the world, both interior and exterior, comical and horrifying, here and there, utterly singular and yet held in common, signify "in the manner of a vibration that always gives the same sound" (Barthes, 1982, p. 125).

1. Arguably, it sounds even more musical in German: "Propylpräparat, Propylen . . . Propionsäure . . . Trimethylamin . . ." (Freud, 1942, p. 112).
2. Spielberg would be supported in this idea by Karl-Heinz Stockhausen, for whom "music [is] the language of more highly developed beings. . . . Music – even the most sophisticated music – will be the universal language one day when we are more developed" (Stockhausen, 1989, p. 18).
3. The author and editors of the series *Psychoanalysis and Popular Culture*, Caroline Bainbridge and Candida Yates, would like to point out that we do not regard fantasies of violence against women as a cause for levity, even when they are being used as a crass foil to point at the absurdities of romance. I would like to thank the editors for allowing me to retain the example on the understanding that it is important for psychoanalysis to confront the dark side of things and listen to all acts of speech, even the most offensive.
4. In a chapter on musical dreams, Sacks describes dreaming of some deeply disturbing and unpleasant music that continued in his head even after he awoke. He was hearing songs in German, a language he did not speak, that "seemed full of melancholy and a sort of horror". Calling a colleague to whom he hummed some of the songs, he was informed that they were Mahler's *Kindertotenlieder*, songs on the death of children. Sacks

and his friend put the appearance of these songs down to the fact that he had, the day previously, resigned from the children's ward at the hospital where he was working and burned a book of essays he had just written (Sacks, 2007, p. 280).

5. Indeed, her view is shared by some people with a highly developed sense of musical taste. In a heated debate in the letters page of *The Times* concerning the introduction of jazz and world music on Radio 3, the BBC's classical music channel, a correspondent wrote, "I have always enjoyed the jazz and world music content. The problem for me ... is opera and operatic singing ... I get great pleasure from most forms of music, but not from maniacal screaming. Give us music, Radio 3, and we will return" (7 May 2008, p. 20).

6. For an interesting conceptual character illustrating the psychopathology of this nevertheless essentially machinic function, see the character Laney in William Gibson's novel *Idoru* (1996). Laney is a "netrunner", or data researcher, who "had a peculiar knack with data-collection architectures, and a medically documented concentration-deficit that meant he could toggle, under certain conditions, into a state of pathological hyperfocus" enabling him to fish through patterns of information and find "nodal points" in "vast floes of undifferentiated data" (p. 25).

7. Lacan gives the specific example of a West Indian man who "found himself one day in possession of a woman who announced to him that she was going to have a baby. It wasn't known whether it was his or not, but nevertheless within several days his first hallucinations declared themselves" (Lacan, 1993, p. 306).

8. In his autobiographical statement, Nash seems to support this view himself:

> At the present time I seem to be thinking rationally again in the style that is characteristic of scientists. However this is not entirely a matter of joy ... One aspect of this is that rationality of thought imposes a limit on a person's concept of his relation to the cosmos. For example, a non-Zoroastrian could think of Zarathustra as simply a madman who led millions of naïve followers to adopt a cult of ritual fire worship. But without his "madness" Zarathustra would necessarily have been only another of the millions or billions of human individuals who have lived and then been forgotten. (Nash, in Nasar & Kuhn, 2002, p. 10)

9. The number twenty-three has quite a significant cultural existence, from William Burroughs to two recent feature films: Joel Schumacher's *The*

Number 23 (2007) and Hans-Christian Schmid's *23* (1998). See also Robert Anton Wilson and Robert Shea's novels *The Illuminatus! Trilogy* (Dell, 1974).

10. While it is known that Schreber was a musician, nothing much to my knowledge has been made of this fact. And yet, in his *Memoir*, Schreber locates piano-playing as the activity through which he negotiates his relationship with his ignorant and scornful God, pacifies and controls the divine rays so that he can overcome their opposition to him emptying his bowels, thereby enabling him to experience the soul-voluptuousness that he needs to cultivate in order to serve God (Schreber, 2000, pp. 275–276).

11. A few pages earlier, Sylvia Nasar records another example of Nash's jocular use of music to torment his colleagues and friends:

> Lloyd [Shapely, friend and rival] liked to sleep late and was often asleep at two o'clock in the afternoon . . . [Nash and acolytes] dropped hot candle wax on him . . . played 45rpm records of Lloyd's favorite Chinese music without the little insert so that it oscillated all over the place [making an] excruciating noise. (Nasar, 2001, p. 101)

12. This is the central premise of Darren Aronofsky's film *Pi* (1998), in which a young mathematical genius (suffering episodes of movie-psychosis), working under the assumption that "mathematics is the language of nature", seeks out the numerical patterns that will enable him to predict the working of the New York stock market only to discover that this pattern is the same as that sought by Hasidic Jews, who believe it to be the number through which God speaks, communicating through code to his chosen people.

13. The trauma in America that Lennon's "The Beatles are bigger than Jesus" statement caused is curious. The fact that the anger directed at the statement always assumes it is some kind of boast rather than a reflective comment on the relative decline of established religion does nothing but reinforce Lennon's point. Never is it argued that Christianity and The Beatles are such heterogeneous objects that comparisons are absurd. On the contrary, the assumption of a system of equivalence in which Jesus and The Beatles are rival attractions is not in doubt. This strange mutation of religion in America is evident in the assumption that Jesus Christ exists in a hit parade of world popularity irrespective of whether or not he is sliding down the charts relative to Elvis and The Beatles. This is to say that, in America, religion is just part of show business. Everything must take place within an aesthetic–economic order that defines the

threshold of existence. Outside of its hall of images, nothing is visible, nothing has economic life, and, therefore, no life at all. The ubiquity of this aesthetic–economic order provides the condition in which Chapman can confuse himself with Lennon, or God, or Holden Caulfield, or all the other ideal images, but, more crucially, can locate there the question of his existence, that is, confuse the image reservoir that supports his ideal ego with his Ego-Ideal.

14. Ono's own website is almost exclusively an online store selling books, CDs, and other merchandise of the Ono–Lennon legacy.

15. Heidegger says that "the Thing's thingness does not lie at all in the material of which it consists, but in the void that holds" (Heidegger, 1971, p. 169).

REFERENCES

Agamben, G. (1993). *Stanzas: Word and Phantasm in Western Culture.* Stanford, CA: Stanford University Press.

Agamben, G. (1999). *The Man without Content.* Stanford, CA: Stanford University Press.

Akita, M. (2008). The beauty of noise. In: C. Cox & D. Warner (Eds.), *Audio Culture: Readings in Modern Music* (pp. 59–64). London: Continuum.

Alvarez, C. (1987). *Memories of Che,* J. Fried (Trans.). Secaucus, NJ: L. Stuart.

Ansermet, F., & Magistretti, P. (2007). *Biology of Freedom: Neural Plasticity, Experience and the Unconscious.* New York: the Other Press.

Anzieu, D. (1974). L'envelope sonore de soi. *Revue française de psychanalyse,* 37(1): 161–179.

Baker, S. (2009). *They've Got Your Number . . . Data, Digits and Destiny – How the Numerati are Changing our Lives.* London: Vintage.

Barthes, R. (1978). *A Lover's Discourse.* New York: Hill and Wang.

Barthes, R. (1982). The metaphor of the eye. In: G. Bataille (Ed.), *Story of the Eye* (pp. 119–127). Harmondsworth: Penguin.

Bataille, G. (1986). *Erotism: Death and Sensuality.* San Francisco: City Lights.

Batty, R. (2006). 'Animal instincts' in *Musique Machine* (2006–04–05) www. musiquemachine.com/articles/articles_template.php?id=73

Baudrillard, J. (2005). *The Intelligence of Evil or the Lucidity Pact*. London: Berg.

Benjamin, W. (1999). *Illuminations*. London: Pimlico.

Bogue, R. (2003). *Deleuze on Music, Painting and the Arts*. London: Routledge.

Botting, F. (1999). *Sex, Machines and Navels*. Manchester: Manchester University Press.

Bowie, A. (1990). *Aesthetics and Subjectivity: from Kant to Nietzsche*. Manchester: Manchester University Press.

Boyle, F. (2010). *My Shit Life So Far*. London: Harper Collins.

Byrne, D. (2012). *How Music Works*. London: Canongate.

Campbell-Johnston, R. (2007). 77 million reasons to love Brian Eno. *The Times* (*Times2*), Tuesday 23 January, p. 14.

Churchland, P. M., & Churchland, P. S. (1998). *On the Contrary: Critical Essays 1987–1997*. Cambridge, MA: MIT Press.

Clayson, A., with Jungr, B., & Johnson, R. (2004). *Woman: The Incredible Life of Yoko Ono*. Surrey: Chrome Dreams.

Coker, C. C. (2004). *The Future of War*. Oxford: Blackwell.

Cope, J. (2007). *Japrocksampler*. London: Bloomsbury.

Costea, B., Crump, N., & Amiridis, K. (2007). Managerialism and infinite human resourcefulness: a commentary on the therapeutic habitus, "Derecognition of finitude" and the modern sense of self. *Journal for Cultural Research*, 11(3): 245–264.

Cox, C., & Warner, D. (Eds.) (2004). *Audio Culture: Readings in Modern Music*. London: Continuum.

Curtis, A. (2007). *The Trap: What Happened to Our Dream of Freedom?* BBC, 11 March 2007.

Cusick, S. G. (2006). Music as torture/Music as weapon. *Revista Transcultural de Música*/Transcultural Music Review #10. Accessed at: www.sibetrans.com/trans/trans10/cusick_eng.htm

Davies, H. (1981). *The Beatles: The Authorised Biography*. London: Granta.

Deleuze, G. (1989). *The Logic of Sense*. London: Athlone Press.

Deleuze, G. (1990). *The Logic of Sense*. London: Athlone Press.

Deleuze, G. (1997). *Difference and Repetition*, P. Patton (Trans.). London: Continuum.

Deleuze, G. (1998). *Essays Critical and Clinical*, D. W. Smith & M. A. Greco (Trans.). London: Verso Press.

Deleuze, G., & Guattari, F. (1988). *A Thousand Plateaus: Capitalism and Schizophrenia* II. London: Athlone Press.

Deleuze, G., & Guattari, F. (1994). *What is Philosophy?* London: Verso.

De Lisle, T. (2004). Hallelujah: 70 Things about Leonard Cohen at 70. *Guardian*. Accessed at: www.leonardcohenfiles.com.

Demme, J. (1984). *Stop Making Sense*. Talking Heads, Arnold Stiefel.

Dennis, J. (2005). *Guardian*, 8 December. Accessed at: arts.guardian.co.uk/comment/story/0,16472,1662680,00.html

Derrida, J. (2002). *Acts of Religion*, G. Anidjar (Ed.). London: Routledge.

Diamond, S. (2012). Why we love music – and Freud despised it. *Psychology Today*, 10 November 2012. Accessed at: http://www.psychologytoday.com/blog/evil-deeds/201211/why-we-love-music-and-freud-despised-it

Dolar, M. (2006). *A Voice and Nothing More*. Cambridge, MA: MIT Press.

Edwards, H. (2004). Yoko *Crawdaddy* (29 August 1971) 34–35. Cited in Yes 234.

Ellis, B. E. (1989). *American Psycho*. Harmondsworth: Penguin.

Ellmann, R. (1981). *James Joyce*. Oxford: Oxford University Press.

Elms, R. (2005) Not-so Fab Four. Accessed at: www.bbc.co.uk/london/content/articles/2005/10/12/robert_elms_beatles_feature.shtml

Eno, B. (1995). *A Year with Swollen Appendices*. London: Faber and Faber.

Eno, B., & Kelly, K. (1995). Gossip is philosophy: an interview with Brian Eno. *Wired*, 3 May: 1–14.

Farah, M. J. (2004). *Visual Agnosia*. Cambridge, MA: MIT Press.

Fink, B. (1999). *A Clinical Introduction to Lacanian Psychoanalysis*. Cambridge, MA: Harvard University Press.

Fink, B. (2004). *Against Understanding: Commentary and Critique in a Lacanian Key*. London: Routledge.

Fink, B. (2007). *Fundamentals of Psychoanalytic Technique: A Lacanian Approach for Practitioners*. New York: W. W. Norton & Co.

Foucault, M. (1970). *The Order of Things*. London: Tavistock.

Foucault, M. (1987). Maurice Blanchot: the thought from outside. In: *Foucault/Blanchot*. New York: Zone Books.

Foucault, M. (1988). *Politics, Philosophy, Culture: Interviews and Other Writings 1977–1984*, L. D. Kritzman (Ed.). London: Routledge.

Foucault, M. (2008). *The Birth of Biopolitics. Lectures at the Collège de France 1978–1979*. London: Palgrave.

French, K. (1999). *Apocalypse Now: A Bloomsbury Movie Guide*. London: Bloomsbury.

Freud, S. (1900a). *The Interpretation of Dreams. S. E., 4–5*: 1–315. London: Hogarth.

Freud, S. (1914b). *The Moses of Michelangelo. S. E., 13*: 211–240. London: Hogarth.

Freud, S. (1920g). *Beyond the Pleasure Principle. S. E., 18*: 7–66. London: Hogarth.

Freud, S. (1930a). *Civilization and Its Discontents. S. E., 21*: 59–145. London: Hogarth.

Freud, S. (1932a). The acquisition of and control of fire. *S. E., 22*: 183–194. London: Hogarth.

Freud, S. (1939a). *Moses and Monotheism. S. E., 23*: 3–137. London: Hogarth.

Freud, S. (1942). *Gesammelte Werke Die Traumdeutung Über den Traum.* Frankfurt am Main: Fischer.

Freud, S. (1963). *Sexuality and the Psychology of Love.* New York: Collier.

Freud, S. (1990). *Art and Literature.* Harmondsworth: Penguin.

Gay, P. (1988). *Freud: A Life for Our Time.* London: Dent.

Gibson, W. (1996). *Idoru.* London: Viking Press.

Goodall, H. (2001). *Big Bangs: The Story of Five Discoveries That Changed Musical History.* London: Vintage.

Guattari, F. (1995). *Chaosophy.* New York: Semiotext(e).

Guéguen, P.-G. (2013). Who is mad and who is not? On differential diagnosis in psychoanalysis. In: *Culture/Clinic* 1 (pp. 66–85). Minneapolis, MN: University of Minnesota Press.

Guevara, E. (1961). *Guerilla Warfare.* www.evokeforever.groupsite.com

Hegarty, P. (2005). Full with noise: theory and Japanese noise music. Accessed at: www.art-omma.org

Hegarty, P. (2007). *Noise/Music: A History.* London: Continuum.

Heidegger, M. (1971). *Poetry, Language, Thought.* London: Harper & Row.

Hemment, D. (2006). Affect and individuation. In: I. Buchanan & M. Swiboda (Eds.), *Deleuze and Music* (pp. 76–94). Edinburgh: Edinburgh University Press.

Higashida, N. (2013). *The Reason I Jump*, K. A. Yoshida & D. Mitchell (Trans.) with an Introduction by D. Mitchell. London: Sceptre.

Howard, R. (2001). *A Beautiful Mind* (Film). Universal Studios and Dreamworks.

Janov, A. (1970). *The Primal Scream.* London: Garstone Press.

Johnston, A., & Malabou, C. (2013). *Self and Emotional Life: Philosophy, Psychoanalysis and Neuroscience.* New York: Columbia Press.

Jones, J. (1992). *Let Me Take You Down: Inside the Mind of Mark David Chapman.* London: Virgin.

Joyce, J. (1982). *Ulysses.* Harmondsworth: Penguin.

Joyce, J. (2000). *Finnegans Wake.* Harmondsworth: Penguin.

Kane, P. (1995). Jingle the other one. *The Guardian*, 20 October 1995. http://music.hyperreal.org/artists/brian_eno/interviews/guard95b.html

Kane, P. (2004). *The Play Ethic: A Manifesto for a Different Way of Living*. London: Macmillan.

Kelly, K. (1998). *New Rules for the New Economy: Ten Ways the Network Economy is Changing Everything*. London: Fourth Estate.

Kemp, M. (1992). She who laughs last: Yoko Ono reconsidered. *Option, Music Alternatives*, (July–August), p. 78.

Kittler, F. (1997). *Literature, Media, Information Systems*, introduced by J. Johnston (Ed.). London: G&B Arts.

Kristeva, J. (1984). *Revolution in Poetic Language*. New York: Columbia University Press.

Kuhn, H. W., & Nasar, S. (2002). *The Essential John Nash*. Princeton, NJ: Princeton University Press.

Lacan, J. (1932). *De la psychose paranoïaque dans ses rapports avec la personnalité*. Paris: Librairie le François.

Lacan, J. (1960–1961). *The Seminar of Jacques Lacan Book VIII: Transference*, C. Gallagher (Trans.) from unedited transcripts.

Lacan, J. (1976). *Four Fundamental Concepts of Psychoanalysis*, A. Sheridan (Trans.). Harmondsworth: Penguin.

Lacan, J. (1986). *The Four Fundamental Concepts of Psychoanalysis*, J.-A. Miller (Ed.). Harmondsworth: Penguin.

Lacan, J. (1987). Lituraterre, J. W. Stone (Trans.). *Ornicar?*, 41: 5–13.

Lacan, J. (1988). *The Seminar of Jacques Lacan: Book II: The Ego in Freud's Theory and in the Technique of Psychoanalysis*, J. Forrester (Trans.). Cambridge: Cambridge University Press.

Lacan, J. (1992). *The Ethics of Psychoanalysis: Seminar VII*, D. Porter (Trans.). London: Routledge.

Lacan, J. (1993). *The Psychoses: The Seminar of Jacques Lacan. Book III 1955–56*, J.-A. Miller (Ed.), R. Grigg (Trans.). London: Routledge.

Lacan, J. (1999). *Encore: Seminar XX*, B. Fink (Trans.). New York: Norton.

Lacan, J. (2005). *Le séminaire XXIII: Le sinthome*, J.-A. Miller (Ed.). Paris: Éditions du Seuil.

Lacan, J. (2006). *Écrits*, B. Fink (Trans.). New York: Norton.

Laclau, E., & Mouffe C. (2001). *Hegemony and Socialist Strategy*. London: Verso.

Lacoue-Labarthe, P. (1990). *Heidegger, Art and Politics*. Oxford: Blackwell.

Lanier, J. (2010). *You Are Not a Gadget*. Harmondsworth: Penguin.

Lanier, J. (2013). *Who Owns the Future?* London: Allen Lane.

Laurent, E. (2012a). Autism and psychosis. In: P. Naveau & N. Wulfing (Eds.), *Psychoanalytical Notebooks (25): Autism* (pp. 11–26). London: London Society of the New Lacanian School.

Laurent, E. (2012b). Spectres of autism. In: P. Naveau & N. Wulfing (Eds.), *Psychoanalytical Notebooks* (25): *Autism* (pp. 50–64). London: London Society of the New Lacanian School.

Laurent, E. (2012c). Autism: epidemic or the ordinary state of the subject? In: P. Naveau & M. Wulfing (Eds.), *Psychoanalytical Notebooks* (25): *Autism* (pp. 125–129). London: London Society of the New Lacanian School.

Lethem, J. (2012). *Fear of Music*. London: Continuum.

Levitin, D. J. (2006). *This Is Your Brain on Music*. London: Dutton.

Lewisohn, M. (1988). *The Complete Beatles Recording Sessions*. London: Hamlyn.

Lewisohn, M. (2004). *The Complete Beatles Chronicle*. London: Chancellor Press.

Lynch, D. (1997). *Lost Highway* (film).

MacDonald, I. (2005). *Revolution in the Head: The Beatles' Records and the Sixties*. London: Pimlico.

Mackenzie, B. (2002). *Transductions: Bodies and Machines at Speed*. London: Continuum.

Malabou, C. (2000). *Plasticité*. Paris: L. Scheer.

Maleval, J.-C. (2009). *L'autiste et sa voix*. Paris: Seuil.

Maleval, J.-C. (2012). Why the hypothesis of an autistic structure? In: P. Naveau & N. Wulfing *Psychoanalytical Notebooks* (25) *Autism* (pp. 27–49). London: London Society of the New Lacanian School.

McAllister, B. (1971). Review on sleeve note of Yoko Ono's album, *Plastic Ono Band*.

Metzinger, T. (2003). *Being No One: The Self-Model Theory of Subjectivity*. Cambridge. MA: MIT Press.

Metzinger, T. (2009). *The Ego Tunnel: The Science of the Mind and the Myth of the Self*. New York: Basic Books.

Miller, J. (1993). *The Passion of Michel Foucault*. New York: Harper Collins.

Miller, J.-A. (2007). Jacques Lacan and voice. In: V. Voruz & B. Wolf (Eds.), *The Later Lacan*. (pp. 137–146). New York: SUNY Press.

Miller, J.-A. (2009). Ordinary psychosis revisited. In: N. Wülfing (Ed.), *Ordinary Psychosis. Psychoanalytic Notebooks* (19). London: London Society of the New Lacanian School.

Miller, J.-A. (2013a). Psychoanalysis, its place among the sciences. In: N. Wülfing (Ed.), *Science and the Real. Psychoanalytical Notebooks* (27). London: London Society of the New Lacanian School.

Miller, J.-A. (2013b). Everyone is mad. In: *Culture/Clinic* (pp. 17–42). Minneapolis, MN: University of Minnesota Press.

Morley, P. (2003). *Words and Music*. London: Bloomsbury.

Mulholland, G. (2002). *This is Uncool: The 500 Greatest Singles Since Punk and Disco*. London: Cassell Illustrated.

Mulholland, G. (2006). *Fear of Music: The 261 Greatest Albums since Punk and Disco*. London: Orion.

Munroe, A., with Hendricks, J. (2000). *Yes Yoko Ono*. New York: Harry Abrams.

Murphy, A. (2011). The importance of music . . . autism, aspergers. *Apergers & the Alien*, online blog. Accessed at http://aspergersthealien. blogspot.co.uk/2011/05/importance-of-musicautism-aspergers.html

Nasar, S. (2001). *A Beautiful Mind: The Life of Mathematical Genius and Nobel Laureate John Nash*. New York: Touchstone.

Nash, J. F. Jr (1994). John F. Nash – Biographical. *Nobelprize.org*. http://www.nobelprize.org/nobel_prizes/economic-sciences/laureates/1994/nash-bio.html

Nash, J. F. (2006). Interview with John Nash. Accessed at: www.pbs.org/wgbh/amex/nash/sfeature/sf_nash_01.htm

Norman, K. (2004). *Sounding Art: Eight Excursions into Electronic Music*. London: Ashgate.

Obrist, H. U., & Bauer, U. M. (1999). Interview with Merzbow. *Nettime*, 22 August. Accessed at: www.nettime.org/Lists-Archives/nettime-l-9908/msg00083.html

Ono, Y. (2000). *Grapefruit*. New York: Simon & Schuster.

Ono, Y. (2007). Beth Ditto meets Yoko Ono. *Observer Music Monthly, 50*: 37–41.

Ono, Y. (2012). *Music Week: The Business of Music* 15 February, p. 1.

Patel, A. D. (2008). *Music, Language and the Brain*. Oxford: Oxford University Press.

Piddington, A. (2006). *The Killing of John Lennon*. Universal Pictures.

Pieslak, J. (2009). *Sound Targets: American Soldiers and Music in the Iraq War*. Bloomington, IN: Indiana University Press.

Pinker, S. (1997). *How the Mind Works*. New York: W. W. Norton.

Poundstone, W. (1992). *Prisoner's Dilemma: John von Neumann, Game Theory, and the Puzzle of the Bomb*. New York: Doubleday

Prendergast, M. (2003). *The Ambient Century: from Mahler to Moby . . . The Evolution of Electronic Sound in the Electronic Age*. London: Bloomsbury.

Régnault, F. (2012). Music and psychoanalysis. *The Symptom, 11*. Accessed at: www.lacan.com/symptom11

Reich, S. (2000). Early tape pieces: interview with Jason Gross. *Perfect Sound Forever*. Online Magazine, http://www.furious.com/perfect/ohm/reich2.html

Reich, S. (2002). *Writings on Music 1965–2000*. Oxford: Oxford University Press.

Reynolds, S. (1998). Introduction and prologue. In: *Energy Flash: A Journey Through Rave Music and Dance Culture*. London: Macmillan.

Reynolds, S. (1999). *Generation Ecstasy: Into the World of Techno and Rave Culture*. New York: Routledge.

Rhodes, G. (2012). Autism: how computers can help. *Guardian*, 26 February.

Robertson, R. (1999). Introduction, Sigmund Freud. *The Interpretation of Dreams*. Oxford: Oxford University Press.

Rosolato, G. (1974). La voix: entre corps et langage. *Revue française de psychanalyse, 37*(1): 75–94.

Ross, A. (2008). *The Rest Is Noise: Listening to the Twentieth Century*. New York: Harper Collins.

Roudinesco, E. (1997). *Jacques Lacan*. Cambridge: Polity Press.

Russolo, L. (1913). *The Art of Noises*. London: Pendragon Press, 1986.

Sacks, O. (2007). *Musicophilia: Tales of Music and the Brain*. London: Picador.

Samels, M. (2002). *A Brilliant Madness*. WGBH Education Foundation. Transcript accessed at www.pbs.org/wgbh/amex/nash/filmmore/pt.html

Sass, L. A. (1992). *Madness and Modernism*. New York: Basic Books.

Schreber, D. P. (2000). *Memoirs of My Nervous Illness*, I. Macalpine & R. A. Hunter (Eds. & Trans.). New York: New York Review of Books.

Schwarz, D. (1997). *Listening Subjects: Music, Psychoanalysis, Culture*. Durham, NC: Duke University Press.

Shingu, K. (2005). Freud, Lacan and Japan. www.discourseunit.com/matrix/shingu_mpm_paper.doc

Silbermann, S. (2001). The geek syndrome. *Wired, 9*(12).

Silverman, K. (1988). *The Acoustic Mirror*. Bloomington, IN: Indiana Press.

Smith, A. (1976). *An Inquiry into the Nature and Causes of the Wealth of Nations*, R. H. Campbell & A. S. Skinner (Eds.). Oxford: The Clarendon Press.

Soler, C. (2014). *Lacan—The Unconscious Reinvented*. London: Karnac.

Solti, A. (1988). *John Lennon: Imagine*. DVD.

Sonic Flux (2007). www.walkerart.org/pa/sonicflux/ono/

Spitz, B. (2007). *The Beatles*. New York: Aurum Press.

Stockhausen, K.-H. (1989). *Towards a Cosmic Music*, T. Nevil (Trans.). Longmead: Element Books.

Stoekl, A. (2007). *Bataille's Peak: Energy, Religion and Postsustainability*. Minneapolis, MN: University of Minnesota Press.

Takimoto, T. (2007). *Welcome to the NHK*. Los Angeles: Tokyopop.

Takimoto, T., & Oiwa, K. (2006). *Welcome to the NHK* 01. Los Angeles: Tokyopop.

Talking Heads (1977). *Talking Heads 77*. Sire Records.

Talking Heads (1979). *Fear of Music*. Sire Records.

Talking Heads (1980). *Remain in Light*. Sire Records.

Talking Heads (1983). *Speaking in Tongues*. Sire Records.

Talking Heads (1992). *Sand in the Vaseline*. Popular Favourites. Sire, EMI Records.

Thompson, M., & Biddle, I. (2013). *Sound Music Affect: Theorizing Sonic Experience*. London: Bloomsbury.

Toffler, A. (1985). *The Adaptive Corporation*. Aldershot: Gower.

Toop, D. (2004). Growth and complexity. In: *Haunted Weather: Music, Silence and Memory*. London: Serpent's Tail.

Toop, D. (2010). *Sinister Resonance*. London: Continuum.

Turkle, S. (2010). *Alone Together*. New York: Basic Books.

Virno, P. (2004). Ten theses on the multitude and post-Fordist capitalism. In: *A Grammar of the Multitude: For an Analysis of Contemporary Forms of Life*. New York: Semiotext(e).

Voruz, V. (2012). *L'autiste et sa voix* by Jean-Claude Maleval. In: P. Naveau & N. Wülfing (Eds.), *Psychoanalytical Notebooks* (25) *Autism* (pp. 207–210). London: London Society of the New Lacanian School.

Weslaty, H. (2000). Jacques Lacan in love, hatred and ignorance. *Anamorphosis*, 3: 55–83.

West, G. (1964). Pythians Ode XII: to Midas of Agragas. In: *The Odes of Pindar in English*. Oxford: Clarendon Press.

Whittle, M. (2007). Primal scream: sounds from the big bang. Accessed at: http://astsun.astro.virginia.edu/~dmw8f/index.php

Williams, R. M. (1981). *Hank Williams*. Alexandria: Time-Life.

Wilson, S. (2008). *The Order of Joy: Beyond the Cultural Politics of Enjoyment*. New York: SUNY Press.

Wilson, S. (2010). The braindance of the hikikomori: towards a return to speculative psychoanalysis. *Paragraph*, 33(3): 392–409.

Wilson, S. (2012). Amusia, noise and the drive: towards a theory of the audio unconscious. In: M. Goddard & B. Halligan (Eds.), *Reverberations* (pp. 26–39). London: Continuum.

Wilson, S. (2013). Violence and love: in which Yoko Ono encourages Slavoj Zizek to 'Give Peace a Chance'. In: S. Goodman & G. Matthews (Eds.), *Violence and the Limits of Representation*. London: Palgrave.

Woodward, B. (1999). *Merzbook: The Pleasuredome of Noise*. Melbourne: Extreme.

Young, R. (1996). Presents for future use. *The Wire*, 147.

Young, R. (2005). *Warp: Labels Unlimited*. London: Black Dog.
Žižek, S. (2000). *The Art of the Ridiculous Sublime: On David Lynch's* Lost Highway. Seattle: University of Washington Press.

INDEX

For Product Safety Concerns and Information please contact our EU
representative GPSR@taylorandfrancis.com
Taylor & Francis Verlag GmbH, Kaufingerstraße 24, 80331 München, Germany

www.ingramcontent.com/pod-product-compliance
Lightning Source LLC
Chambersburg PA
CBHW050343270326
41926CB00016B/3596